First World War
and Army of Occupation
War Diary
France, Belgium and Germany

3 INDIAN (LAHORE) DIVISION
Divisional Troops
Royal Army Medical Corps
7 British Field Ambulance
11 August 1914 - 31 December 1915

WO95/3920/1

The Naval & Military Press Ltd
www.nmarchive.com
Published in association with The National Archives

Published by

The Naval & Military Press Ltd

Unit 10 Ridgewood Industrial Park,

Uckfield, East Sussex,

TN22 5QE England

Tel: +44 (0) 1825 749494

www.naval-military-press.com

www.nmarchive.com

This diary has been reprinted in facsimile from the original. Any imperfections are inevitably reproduced and the quality may fall short of modern type and cartographic standards.

© Crown Copyright
Images reproduced by permission of The National Archives, London, England, 2015.

Contents

Document type	Place/Title	Date From	Date To
Heading	WO95/3920/1		
Heading	BEF 3 Ind Lahore Division Troops No 7 British Field Ambulance 1914 Aug-1915 Dec To Mesopotamia		
War Diary	Lahore Cantonment	11/08/1914	15/08/1914
War Diary	En Route To Karachi	16/08/1914	16/08/1914
War Diary	Karachi	17/08/1914	28/08/1914
War Diary	Kiamari on Board H.T. Castalia	29/08/1914	29/08/1914
War Diary	H T Castalia	30/08/1914	05/09/1914
War Diary	Aden	06/09/1914	06/09/1914
War Diary	H T Castalia	07/09/1914	13/09/1914
War Diary	H T Castalia Suez	14/09/1914	14/09/1914
War Diary	H T Castalia Suez Port Said	15/09/1914	15/09/1914
War Diary	H T Castalia	16/09/1914	16/09/1914
War Diary	H T Castalia Alexandria	17/09/1914	19/09/1914
War Diary	H T Castalia	19/09/1914	25/09/1914
War Diary	Marseilles	26/09/1914	26/09/1914
War Diary	Champagne De L'eveque	27/09/1914	30/09/1914
War Diary	Champagne De L'eveque Marseilles	01/10/1914	01/10/1914
War Diary	In Train Ek Route to Orleans	02/10/1914	03/10/1914
War Diary	Camp Cercotte Orleans	04/10/1914	17/10/1914
War Diary	En Route In Train	18/10/1914	19/10/1914
War Diary	Hallines	20/10/1914	21/10/1914
War Diary	Vallan Capelle Bailleul	22/10/1914	22/10/1914
War Diary	Bailleul Estares	23/10/1914	23/10/1914
War Diary	Estaires Lacassan	24/10/1914	24/10/1914
War Diary	La Cassan	25/10/1914	26/10/1914
War Diary	La Gorgue	27/10/1914	27/10/1914
War Diary	Viellechapelle	27/10/1914	30/10/1914
War Diary	Lagorgue	30/10/1914	31/10/1914
Miscellaneous	Appendix I	09/10/1914	09/10/1914
Miscellaneous	Units are to be ready to entrain at two hours notice order of March. Appendix II	14/10/1914	14/10/1914
Miscellaneous	Order of movement on the 17th. Appendix III	06/10/1914	06/10/1914
Operation(al) Order(s)	Operation Order No 1 by Colonel B.B. Grayfoot I.M.S. A.D.M.S. Lahore	22/10/1914	22/10/1914
Miscellaneous	Order by Lieut Colonel L. Way R.A.M.C. O.C. No.7 B.F.A. Bailleul. Appendix 5	22/10/1914	22/10/1914
Operation(al) Order(s)	Operation Order No 2 by Col Grayfoot A.D.M.S. Lahore	23/10/1914	23/10/1914
Miscellaneous	Appendix 7	23/10/1914	23/10/1914
Miscellaneous	Ref Maps. St Omer & Arras 1/80,000. Appendix 8	26/10/1914	26/10/1914
Miscellaneous	No.4 F.A. Order by Lieut Colonel L. Way R.A.M.C. O.C. No.7 B.F.A. La Lacon. Appendix 9	26/10/1914	26/10/1914
Miscellaneous	A Form. Messages And Signals. Appendix 10		
Miscellaneous	A Form, Messages And Signals	30/10/1914	30/10/1914
Miscellaneous	No.5 F.A. Order by Lieut Colonel L. Way R.A.M.C. O.C. No.7 B.F.A. La Gorgue. Appendix 11	30/10/1914	30/10/1914
Miscellaneous	A Form. Messages And Signals. Appendix 12	31/10/1914	31/10/1914
Miscellaneous	No.6 F.A. Order by Lieut Colonel L. Way R.A.M.C. O.C. No.7 B.F.A. La Gorgue. Appendix 13	31/10/1914	31/10/1914

Heading	War Diary of No 7 British Field Ambulance From 1-11-14 To 30/11/14 29 To 40 Volume I		
War Diary	Lagorgue	01/11/1914	16/11/1914
War Diary	Lagorgue Locon	17/11/1914	17/11/1914
War Diary	Locon	18/11/1914	22/11/1914
War Diary	La Cassan	23/11/1914	30/11/1914
Miscellaneous	No.6 F.A. Order by Lt Colonel L. Way R.A.M.C. O.C. No.7 B.F.A. La Gorgue. Appendix 15	03/11/1914	03/11/1914
Miscellaneous	Memorandum. Appendix 14	03/11/1914	03/11/1914
Miscellaneous	To The O.C. No 7 B.F.A		
Miscellaneous	Memorandum. Appendix 16	04/11/1914	04/11/1914
Miscellaneous	No.7 F.A. Order by Lieut Colonel L. Way R.A.M.C. O.C. No.7 B.F.A. La Gorgue. Appendix 17	04/11/1914	04/11/1914
Miscellaneous	A Form. Messages And Signals. Appendix 18	05/11/1914	05/11/1914
Miscellaneous	No.7 F.A. Order by Lieut Colonel L. Way R.A.M.C. O.C. No.7 B.F.A. La Gorgue. Appendix 19	05/11/1914	05/11/1914
Miscellaneous	Memorandum. Appendix 20	06/11/1914	06/11/1914
Miscellaneous	No.7 F.A. Order by Lieut Colonel L. Way R.A.M.C. O.C. No.7 B.F.A. La Gorgue. Appendix 21	06/11/1914	06/11/1914
Miscellaneous	A Form. Messages And Signals. Appendix 22	04/11/1914	04/11/1914
Miscellaneous	No.7 F.A. Order by Lieut Colonel L. Way R.A.M.C. O.C. No.7 B.F.A. La Gorgue. Appendix 23	07/11/1914	07/11/1914
Miscellaneous	A Form. Messages And Signals. Appendix 24	23/11/1914	23/11/1914
Miscellaneous	No.11 F.A. Order by Lieut Colonel L. Way R.A.M.C. O.C. No.7 B.F.A. La Cassan. Appendix 25	23/11/1914	23/11/1914
Miscellaneous	A Form. Messages And Signals. Appendix 26		
Miscellaneous	No.12 F.A. Order by Lt. Colonel L. Way R.A.M.C. O.C. No.7 B.F.A. La Cassan. Appendix 27	24/11/1914	24/11/1914
Miscellaneous	A Form Messages And Signals.		
Miscellaneous	No.13 F.A. Order by Lt. Colonel L. Way R.A.M.C. O.C. No.7 B.F.A. La Cassan. Appendix 29	25/11/1914	25/11/1914
Miscellaneous	A Form Messages And Signals.		
Miscellaneous	No.14 F.A. Order by Lt. Colonel L. Way R.A.M.C. O.C. No.7 B.F.A. La Cassan. Appendix 31	26/11/1914	26/11/1914
Miscellaneous	A Form Messages And Signals.		
Miscellaneous	No.15 F.A. Order by Lt. Colonel L. Way R.A.M.C. O.C. No.7 B.F.A. La Cassan. Appendix 33	27/11/1914	27/11/1914
Miscellaneous	A Form Messages And Signals.		
Miscellaneous	No.16 F.A. Order by Lt. Colonel L. Way R.A.M.C. O.C. No.7 B.F.A. La Cassan. Appendix 35	28/11/1914	28/11/1914
Miscellaneous	A Form. Messages And Signals. Appendix 36		
Miscellaneous	No.17 F.A. Order by Lt. Colonel L. Way R.A.M.C. O.C. No.7 B.F.A. La Cassan. Appendix 37	29/11/1914	29/11/1914
Miscellaneous	No.18 F.A. Order by Lt. Colonel L. Way R.A.M.C. O.C. No.7 B.F.A. La Cassan. Appendix 39	30/11/1914	30/11/1914
Miscellaneous	A Form. Messages And Signals. Appendix 38		
Heading	War Diary of No 7 British Field Ambulance From 1-12-14 To 31-12-14 Volume I Pp 41 To 50		
War Diary	La Cassan	01/12/1914	03/12/1914
War Diary	La Cassan Zelobe	04/12/1914	04/12/1914
War Diary	Zelobe	05/12/1914	11/12/1914
War Diary	Bethune	11/12/1914	24/12/1914
War Diary	Bethune Auchel	24/12/1914	24/12/1914
War Diary	Auchel	24/12/1914	31/12/1914
Miscellaneous	A Form Messages And Signals.		

Miscellaneous	No.19 F.A. Order by Lt. Colonel L. Way R.A.M.C. O.C. No.7 B.F.A. La Cassan. Appendix 41	01/12/1914	01/12/1914
Miscellaneous	A Form Messages And Signals.		
Miscellaneous	No.20 F.A. Order by Lt. Colonel L. Way R.A.M.C. O.C. No.7 B.F.A. La Cassan. Appendix 43	02/12/1914	02/12/1914
Miscellaneous	A Form Messages And Signals.		
Miscellaneous	No.22 F.A. Order by Lt. Colonel L. Way R.A.M.C. O.C. No.7 B.F.A. La Cassan. Appendix 45	03/12/1914	03/12/1914
Miscellaneous	A Form Messages And Signals.		
Miscellaneous	No.23 F.A. Order by Lt. Colonel L. Way R.A.M.C. O.C. No.7 B.F.A. Bethune. Appendix 47	15/12/1914	15/12/1914
Miscellaneous	A Form. Messages And Signals. Appendix 48		
Miscellaneous	No.24 F.A. Order by Lt. Colonel L. Way R.A.M.C. O.C. No.7 B.F.A. Bethune. Appendix 49	20/12/1914	20/12/1914
Miscellaneous	A Form Messages And Signals.		
Miscellaneous	No.25 F.A. Order by Lt. Colonel L. Way R.A.M.C. O.C. No.7 B.F.A. Bethune. Appendix 51	21/12/1914	21/12/1914
Heading	War Diary of No 7 British Field Ambulance Lahore Division From 1st January 1915 To 31st January 1915		
War Diary	Auchel	01/01/1915	15/01/1915
War Diary	Zelobe	16/01/1915	24/01/1915
War Diary	Vendin	24/01/1915	25/01/1915
War Diary	Auchel	25/01/1915	31/01/1915
Operation(al) Order(s)	Operation Order No 61 by Major-General H.D'U Keary, C.B., D.S.O. Commanding Lahore Division	21/01/1915	21/01/1915
Miscellaneous	March Table		
Miscellaneous	Operation Order No 39 by Lieut Colonel L. Way R.A.M.C. S.M.O. Lahore Battalion	21/01/1915	21/01/1915
Miscellaneous	Appendix 12 From S.M.O. Lahore Dept Zelobes.	22/01/1915	22/01/1915
Miscellaneous	A Form. Messages And Signals. Appendix 13		
Miscellaneous	A Form Messages And Signals.		
Miscellaneous	Headquarter, Sirhind Brigade. Appendix 16	27/01/1915	27/01/1915
Miscellaneous	Appendix 17	27/01/1915	27/01/1915
Miscellaneous	Appendix 18	31/01/1915	31/01/1915
Operation(al) Order(s)	Operation Order No 10 by Lt Colonel A.H. Dennys Commanding Sirhind Brigade	31/01/1915	31/01/1915
Miscellaneous	O.C. No.7 B.F.A. Appendix 1	11/01/1915	11/01/1915
Miscellaneous	A Form Messages And Signals.		
Miscellaneous	A Form, Messages And Signals		
Miscellaneous	A Form Messages And Signals.		
Miscellaneous	From S.M.O. Sirhind and Jullundur Bdes. Appendix 4	16/01/1915	16/01/1915
Miscellaneous	From S.M.O. Sirhind & Jullundur Bde. Appendix 5	16/01/1915	16/01/1915
Miscellaneous	From S.M.O. Lahore Detachment. Appendix 6	18/01/1915	18/01/1915
Miscellaneous	From S.M.O. Lahore Detachment. Appendix 7	18/01/1915	18/01/1915
Miscellaneous	From S.M.O. Jullundur & Sirhind Brigade. Appendix 8	19/01/1915	19/01/1915
Miscellaneous	From O.C. No. 7 B.F.A. Appendix 9	19/01/1915	19/01/1915
Miscellaneous	March Table		
Heading	War Diary With Appendices No 7 British Field Ambulance From 1st February 1915 To 28th February 1915		
War Diary	Auchel	01/02/1915	01/02/1915
War Diary	Rues Des Vaches	01/02/1915	02/02/1915
War Diary	Calonne Sur La Lys	03/02/1915	09/02/1915
War Diary	Vielle Chapelle	09/02/1915	24/02/1915
War Diary	Robecq	24/02/1915	26/02/1915
War Diary	Calonne Sur Le Lys	27/02/1915	28/02/1915

Operation(al) Order(s)	Operation Order No 10 by Brigadier General W.C. Walker V.C. C.B. Commanding Sirhind Bde	07/02/1915	07/02/1915
Miscellaneous	March Table		
Miscellaneous	Messages And Signals.		
Heading	War Diary of No 7 British Field Ambulance Lahore Division From 1st March 1915 To 31st March 1915		
War Diary	Calonne Sur La Lys	01/03/1915	09/03/1915
War Diary	Robecq L'Etinette La Cix Marmuse Road Bethnne Map 1-40000, Square R.136	10/02/1915	10/02/1915
War Diary	L'Epinette Square R 136	11/03/1915	30/03/1915
War Diary	Vielle Chapelle	31/03/1915	31/03/1915
Operation(al) Order(s)	Operation Order No 17 by Brig General E.P. Strickland C.M.G. D.S.O. Commanding Jullundur Bde	01/03/1915	01/03/1915
Miscellaneous	A Form. Messages And Signals. Appx 2		
Miscellaneous	A Form Messages And Signals.		
Miscellaneous	No 7 BFA		
Miscellaneous	A Form Messages And Signals.		
Miscellaneous	To, Capt. O Riordan R.A.M.C. Appx VI	11/03/1915	11/03/1915
Miscellaneous	A Form Messages And Signals.		
Miscellaneous	To, Capt. C.D.K. Seaver R.A.M.C. Appx IX Vol III	13/03/1915	13/03/1915
Heading	War Diary With Appendices Of No 7 British Field Ambulance Lahore Division From 1st April 1915 To 30th April 1915		
War Diary	Vielle Chapelle	01/04/1915	12/04/1915
War Diary	Re Robecq	13/04/1915	24/04/1915
War Diary	Mt Descat	25/04/1915	25/04/1915
War Diary	Westoutre	25/04/1915	26/04/1915
War Diary	Ouderdom	26/04/1915	30/04/1915
Miscellaneous	To, The O.C. No. 7 B.F.A. Appx I	08/04/1915	08/04/1915
Miscellaneous	A Form Messages And Signals.		
Miscellaneous	O.C. No. 7 B.F.A. Appx IV	12/04/1915	12/04/1915
Miscellaneous	To, The O.C. No. 7 B.F.A. Appx V	12/04/1915	12/04/1915
Miscellaneous	A Form Messages And Signals.		
Miscellaneous	O.C. No. 7 B.F.A. Appendix XII	20/04/1915	20/04/1915
Miscellaneous	A Form Messages And Signals.	01/05/1915	01/05/1915
Miscellaneous	A Form Messages And Signals.		
Heading	War Diary With Appendices No 7 British Field Ambulance From 1st May 1915 To 31st May 1915		
War Diary	Ouderdom	01/05/1915	03/05/1915
War Diary	Line Of March	04/05/1915	04/05/1915
War Diary	Fletre	04/05/1915	04/05/1915
War Diary	Paradis	05/05/1915	06/05/1915
War Diary	L'Epinette	06/05/1915	30/05/1915
War Diary	La Gorgue	31/05/1915	31/05/1915
Miscellaneous	A Form Messages And Signals.		
Operation(al) Order(s)	Operation Order No 56 by Br General W.C. Walker V.C. C.B. Commanding Sirhind Brigade	03/05/1915	03/05/1915
Miscellaneous	A Form Messages And Signals.		
Miscellaneous	App XII Vol V		
Miscellaneous	A Form Messages And Signals.		
Heading	War Diary of No 7 British Field Ambulance Lahore Division From 1st June 1915 To 30th June 1915		
War Diary	La Gorgue	01/06/1915	30/06/1915
Miscellaneous	A Form Messages And Signals.		
Miscellaneous	To, Lieut C.L. Spackman R.A.M.C. Appendix III	15/06/1916	15/06/1916
Miscellaneous	Appendix IV	15/06/1915	15/06/1915

Miscellaneous	A Form Messages And Signals.		
Heading	War Diary With Appendices Of No 7 British Field Ambulance Lahore From 1st July 1915 To 31st July 1915		
War Diary	La Gorgue	01/07/1915	31/07/1915
Miscellaneous	A Form Messages And Signals.		
Miscellaneous	Appendix 3		
Miscellaneous	A Form Messages And Signals.		
Miscellaneous	O.C. No. 7 B.F.A. Appendix V		
Miscellaneous	A Form Messages And Signals.		
Heading	War Diary With Appendices Of No 7 British Field Ambulance From 1st August 1915 To 31st August 1915		
War Diary	La Gorgue	01/08/1915	14/08/1915
War Diary	L'Epinette	14/08/1915	31/08/1915
Miscellaneous	A Form Messages And Signals.		
Map	Aid Posts Of Lahore Division (Northern Section)		
Miscellaneous	A Form Messages And Signals.		
Miscellaneous	A Form. Messages And Signals. Appx VI		
Heading	War Diary of No 7 British Field Ambulance From 1st September 1915 To 30th September 1915		
War Diary	L'Epinette	01/09/1915	30/09/1915
Miscellaneous	A Form Messages And Signals.	03/09/1915	03/09/1915
Operation(al) Order(s)	Medical Operation Orders No 48 By Colonel B.B. Grayfoot I.M.S. A.D.M.S. Lahore Division	23/09/1915	23/09/1915
Miscellaneous	Field Ambulance Order No.1 Appendix III	24/09/1915	24/09/1915
Miscellaneous	A Form Messages And Signals.		
Operation(al) Order(s)	Field Ambulance Order No 2 by Capt. I.J. Mitchell R.A.M.C. OC No 7 B.F. Ambulance	28/09/1915	28/09/1915
Heading	War Diary With Appendices Of No 7 British Field Ambulance Lahore Division From 1st October 1915 To 31st October 1915		
War Diary	L'Epinette	01/10/1915	19/10/1915
War Diary	La Gorgue	19/10/1915	31/10/1915
Miscellaneous	B Form Messages And Signals.		
Miscellaneous	Position of AID Posts on Spot Map. Appendix 4	19/10/1915	19/10/1915
Miscellaneous	A Form Messages And Signals.		
Miscellaneous	B Form. Messages And Signals. Appendix VI		
Miscellaneous	Position of AID Posts on Spot Map. Appendix 7	23/10/1915	23/10/1915
Miscellaneous	A Form. Messages And Signals. Appendix VIII		
Miscellaneous	Position of AID Posts on Spot Map. Appendix 9	29/10/1915	29/10/1915
Map	Spot Map Of Aid Posts		
Heading	War Diary With Appendices Of No 7 British Field Ambulance From 1st November 1915 To 30th November 1915		
War Diary	La Gorgue	01/11/1915	08/11/1915
War Diary	Ham O.27.C.3.5. Ref 1-40000 France Map Sheet 36 A	08/11/1915	08/11/1915
War Diary	Ham	09/11/1915	18/11/1915
War Diary	Enguinegatte M Y D	18/11/1915	18/11/1915
War Diary	Enguinegatte	19/11/1915	29/11/1915
War Diary	Matringham	29/11/1915	30/11/1915
Miscellaneous	A Form. Messages And Signals. Appendix I		
Map	Appendix II		
Miscellaneous	A Form. Messages And Signals. Appendix 3		
Miscellaneous	Officer Commanding, No. 7 B.F.A. Appendix IV	17/11/1915	17/11/1915
Operation(al) Order(s)	Ferozepore Brigade Operation Order No 61	17/11/1915	17/11/1915
Miscellaneous	A Form. Messages And Signals. Appendix II		

Operation(al) Order(s)	Ferozepore Brigade Operation Order No 62	28/11/1915	28/11/1915
Miscellaneous	March Table		
Heading	War Diary of No 7 B.F. Ambulance From 1st Dec. 1915 To 31st Dec. 1915 (Volume)		
Heading	War Diary December 1915		
War Diary	Matringham Amettes	01/12/1915	01/12/1915
War Diary	Amettes	02/12/1915	13/12/1915
War Diary	Lillers To Marseilles	14/12/1915	16/12/1915
War Diary	La Valentine Camp. Marseilles	17/12/1915	18/12/1915
War Diary	S S Chakdina	19/12/1915	31/12/1915
Operation(al) Order(s)	Ferozepore Brigade Operation Order No 63	30/11/1915	30/11/1915
Miscellaneous	March Table		

No 95/3020/1

BEF

3 IND' LAHORE DIVISION TROOPS

No 7 BRITISH FIELD AMBULANCE

1914 AUG — 1915 DEC

To MESOPOTAMIA

LIEUTENANT - COLONEL L. WAY.   VOLUME 1
O.C. NO 7. BRITISH FIELD AMBULANCE

Army Form C. 2118.

WAR DIARY of Lt-Colonel L Way
                    or   O.C. No 7 British Field Ambulance
INTELLIGENCE SUMMARY. From 11-8-14
                                      To 30-9-14

Instructions regarding War Diaries and Intelligence
Summaries are contained in F. S. Regs., Part II,
and the Staff Manual respectively. Title pages
will be prepared in manuscript.

(Erase heading not required.)

Hour, Date, Place.	Summary of Events and Information.	Remarks and references to Appendices
9 a.m. 11-8-14 LAHORE CANTONMENT	Reported my arrival to A.D.M.S. 3rd (Lahore) Division. Went to the Mobilization Store and arranged to Mobilize No 7 British Field Ambulance.	Unmobilized Field Ambulance O.C. No 7 B.F.A.
5 p.m.	Reported progress to A.D.M.S. Mobilization progressing favourably.	
9 a.m. to 5 p.m. 12-8-14 LAHORE CANTONMENT	Continued mobilization. Reported following ambulances & personnel to A.D.M.S. Hospital Stretcher bearer grade 1; Ward servants 9; Cook 1; Water carrier 1; Ward Sweeper 1; Dhobies 3; Army Bearers Corps 133. Mobilization continuing daily. Reported progress to A.D.M.S. Weather fairly cool – fine.	LW

Army Form C. 2118.

WAR DIARY
or
INTELLIGENCE SUMMARY.   No 7 B. F. A

(Erase heading not required.)

Instructions regarding War Diaries and Intelligence Summaries are contained in F. S. Regs., Part II, and the Staff Manual respectively. Title pages will be prepared in manuscript.

Hour, Date, Place.	Summary of Events and Information.	Remarks and references to Appendices
9 a.m. to 5 p.m. 13-8-14 LAHORE CANTONMENT.	Mobilization continued. Deficient of Hospital Storekeeper 1; Ward Servants 3; Army Bearer Corps 133. Referred purchase to A.D.M.S. Matters getting letter-paper.	L.W.
9 a.m. to 6 p.m. 14-8-14 LAHORE CANTONMENT.	Mobilization continued and completed. Deficient of Officers (near sons) to change to 2 D.M.S. Indents to join later. Indents to D.M.S. passed the Unit. 132 A.B.C. privates. Went Railway requirements formed the 10 privates. Syces, Dhobies, Palkies & punkah. Wards - Deficient of Hospital Storekeeper 1; Ward Servants 3. Wrote to obtain tents for the Army Bearer Corps & some of the Army Hospital Corps. Camphor shoes by men listed. Mobilization complete. Units into 28 E. Punjabi Barracks. Reported to A.D.M.S.	Officers Lt-Colonel L. Way Ravine (in Command) Major B. C. Bartlereau Capt. ? J. Intelett " D.H.S. Mc Arthur Lieut A.G. Biggeon " Sub Surgeons 1st Class H.V. Dewey 9th AD 3rd " P.C. Calvert " " G. H. Lawrence " " G. R. Blake " E. Cullen

3.

Army Form C. 2118.

WAR DIARY
or
INTELLIGENCE SUMMARY. No 7 B.F.A.

(Erase heading not required.)

Instructions regarding War Diaries and Intelligence Summaries are contained in F. S. Regs., Part II, and the Staff Manual respectively. Title pages will be prepared in manuscript.

Hour, Date, Place.	Summary of Events and Information.	Remarks and references to Appendices
9 a.m. to 5 p.m. 14-8-14 LAHORE CANTONMENT	Orders from A.D.M.S. to entrain for KARACHI. Tomorrow morning at 9.30 a.m. Weather fine but hot.	3/Col. Asst. Surgeon G.A. Pinto - C.A. Emile KP Quay LN.
9 a.m. 16-8-14 LAHORE CANTONMENT	Marched to Drumtri Stores, West Station, and entrained the unit. MAJOR B.S. BARTLETT, R.A.M.C. reported himself to duty in orders A.D.M.S. Still deficient of Hospital Storekeeper, and Ward Servants. 3.	
10.30 a.m.	Started to KARACHI at 10.30 a.m. The following Units were on the train. No 6/B F.A. Nos 111, 112 + 113 9.F.A. No provision made for ice on the train. Weather very hot and sultry.	LN.
16-8-14 En route to KARACHI	In the train all day Weather very hot and sultry.	LN.

Army Form C. 2118.

WAR DIARY
or
INTELLIGENCE SUMMARY. No 7 B. F.A.

(Erase heading not required.)

Instructions regarding War Diaries and Intelligence Summaries are contained in F. S. Regs., Part II, and the Staff Manual respectively. Title pages will be prepared in manuscript.

Hour, Date, Place.	Summary of Events and Information.	Remarks and references to Appendices
9. a. m. 17-8-14 KARACHI	Arrived at KARACHI and went into the Rest Camp. Officers & B. Tents and hammocks in 160 lb cots. Good Sanitary camp with good water supply. High wind warning – very dusty – weather cool.	
11. a. m.	Reported my arrival in person to the A.D.M.S. KARACHI Brigade.	LN
18-8-14 KARACHI.	Detailed the personnel and equipment to the sections. A.H.C. & A.B.C. instructed in company drill. Water windy/cool	LN
19-8-14 KARACHI.	Quinine gr V daily issued as a prophylactic to all ranks by order of A.D.M.S KARACHI Brigade owing to prevalence of anopheles mosquitos. Weather cloudy/humid and cool	LN
20-8-14 KARACHI.	Drew Rs 3129 on a statem[ent] for hospital equipment. Indented rolls of lint sent to the A.D.M.S. 3rd (Lahore) Division with notes for same – Two A.B.C. men transferred to hospital to have their teeth repaired.	LN

Gulab Singh & Sons, Calcutta—No. 22 Army C.—5-8-14—1,07,000. D. M. S.

Army Form C. 2118.

WAR DIARY
or
INTELLIGENCE SUMMARY. No 7 B.F.A.

(Erase heading not required.)

Hour, Date, Place.	Summary of Events and Information.	Remarks and references to Appendices
21-8-14 KARACHI.	A.H.C. + A.B.C. put through Company drill. Weather fine + cloudy with a cool breeze. LW	
22-8-14 KARACHI	Personnel of Benow Division detailed with instructors A.H.C. + A.B.C. The A.B.C. are not all provided with rifles which are a reported on - not obtainable. Drill as above — Weather as above. LW	
23-8-14 (Sunday) KARACHI	Detailed two ward servants + one dresser Pte S.S. GLASGOW by order of A.D.M.S. of War Division. Detailed 3rd Class Aselt Surgeon G.V. OAKLEY P.S.L.D. to relieve on such Assistant-Surgeon on S.S. AMBALA by order of A.D.M.S. 3rd War Division. By order of A.D.M.S. 3rd War Division the two orders attached to the Units were returned to LAHORE CANTONMENT. Made and fatigue) stedding orders of the Units. Weather as above. LW	
24-8-14 KARACHI	By order of A.D.M.S. 3rd War Division Captain T. MITCHELL R.A.M.C. detailed for indent with the D.M.S. GLASGOW to Hospital Ship... LW	

WAR DIARY

or

INTELLIGENCE SUMMARY. No 7 B.F.A.

(Erase heading not required.)

Army Form C. 2118.

Instructions regarding War Diaries and Intelligence Summaries are contained in F. S. Regs., Part II, and the Staff Manual respectively. Title pages will be prepared in manuscript.

Hour, Date, Place.	Summary of Events and Information.	Remarks and references to Appendices
25-8-14 KARACHI	3rd Class Asst Surgeon G.H. BLAKER I.S.M.D reported his arrival from KASAULI to relist 3rd Class Asst Surgeon G.V. OAKLEY I.S.M.D who was ordered to Rs270 on a return of his command to the British Division and Mesopotamia. The latest guide KARACHI sent copies of presents to sepoys & sowars of the Field Artillery. Sgt acknowledged in Lt-Col. WHAITE RA. as above. O.C. No 8 B.F.A. Drill as above. Weather as above.	LN.
26-8-14 KARACHI 2 p.m.	7 men A.B.C. were moved from QUETTA in view of the two transferred to the Hospital. Demands issued to prepare 5 Field Medicines. Orders received for embarking Staff to have hutments readied to embark to-morrow. Drills as above. Weather as above.	LN.
4 p.m. 27-8-14 KARACHI	Orders for embarkation cancelled. Have transferred Gunner I.A.B.C. was transferred to Hospital for Venereal. Weather as above.	LN.

Army Form C. 2118.

WAR DIARY
or
INTELLIGENCE SUMMARY. No 7 B.F.A.

(Erase heading not required.)

Hour, Date, Place.	Summary of Events and Information.	Remarks and references to Appendices
9.30 a.m. 28-8-14	Orders received two Embarkation Officers to embark Battery on S.S. CASTALIA - H.T. No 7. Arrived Unit at 12.30 p.m. train started at 2.30 p.m.	
KARACHI 3 p.m.	Arrived KIAMARI DOCKS	
5 p.m.	Detained	
7.30 p.m.	Started to place equipment & baggage on board last mule on board, found arrangements with lighters very scanty the mules had been embarked at hope of light which meant they were unable to chance to all fastenings for which there were 8 draft mules for No 2 mules.	
8 a.m.	70 tons over Coolies for the mule town transfer were wanted.	
7 p.m.	Received Schedule & Route for the use of the train up the line for the night.	
	For Embarkation Some Regimental & Ordnance — Some Regimental.	
	Sub copies of Embarkation relations to Embarking.	
	Officers — Secret Document No 2078 & 1500 — B	
	KIAMARI 27 August 1914 Received from Embarkation Officer 60 tons water ashore.	
29-8-14 KIAMARI on board H.T. CASTALIA	Received Draught dressed. Completed - Capt Hutchinson RAMC Asst Surgeon DEWEY - LAWRENCE and PINTO. Unit complete with exception of one ABC Range Finder & Takoma. Ship sailed at 1.30 p.m. LW	

Army Form C. 2118.

WAR DIARY
or
INTELLIGENCE SUMMARY. No 7 B.F.A

(Erase heading not required.)

Instructions regarding War Diaries and Intelligence Summaries are contained in F. S. Regs., Part II, and the Staff Manual respectively. Title pages will be prepared in manuscript.

Hour, Date, Place.	Summary of Events and Information.	Remarks and references to Appendices
30-8-14 H.T. CASTALIA	The following were on board No 7 & BTA 111-112 & 1 Section 113 J.F.A. - 32nd Div. Signalling Coy + Newport detail. Attempts were made daily to provide deck physical training in accordance with weather. Run 157 knots - Sea rather heavy. Light breeze S.W. + Northerly sea. Sighted Newfoundland - convoyed by H.M.S. ——. LN. NORTHBROOK.	
31-8-14 H.T. CASTALIA.	Resumed D.7.A exercise. - Run 173 knots. Weather above. LN.	
1-9-14 H.T. CASTALIA.	Resumed D. Unit exercises. - Run 161 knots. Weather above + calm. LN	
2-9-14 H.T. CASTALIA.	Personnel employed in classes in Field Medical Organization & Officers Call. Run to 10 ft front Surveying started Earth - Run 168 knots - Weather above + cold. LN	
3-9-14 H.T. CASTALIA	Personnel exercised as above and instructed in use of life belts. Sailed through Straits of Orcledio. A.H.C.+ M.B.C. in afternoon - officials Gulf Stream. Details, O.C. + Hut Inspect, Weather calm. Run 172 knots LN.	

Army Form C. 2118.

WAR DIARY
or
INTELLIGENCE SUMMARY. No 7 B.F.A.

(Erase heading not required.)

Instructions regarding War Diaries and Intelligence Summaries are contained in F. S. Regs., Part II, and the Staff Manual respectively. Title pages will be prepared in manuscript.

Hour, Date, Place.	Summary of Events and Information.	Remarks and references to Appendices
4-9-14 H.T. CASTALIA	Exercise & lectures as above. Officers + N.C.O's inoculated for Enteric – Weather uniform – Run 181 knots	LW
5-9-14 H.T. CASTALIA	lectures as above – Weather hotter. Run 212. Practice H.M.S. CHATHAM joined the Convoy	LW
6-9-14 (Sunday) ADEN	Arrived at 8 p.m. – Weather fair + warmer. Run 209 knots	LW
7-9-14 8 p.m. H.T. CASTALIA	Left for PORT SAID – Weather warmer & fine. No one allowed to land at ADEN.	LW
8-9-14 8 a.m. H.T. CASTALIA	Passed PERIM – Run 136 knots – Head wind – much warmer. Lectures re-commenced.	LW
9-9-14 H.T. CASTALIA	Work executed as above – Quinine given on a prophylactic measure to troops. Run 239 knots. Head wind. Weather moderate cool – Captain ALEXANDER S.T. Corps lectured on loose cases + management of Pursers Ashousably.	LW
10-9-14 H.T. CASTALIA	Lectures re-commenced as above. Run 217 knots. Weather cool. Head wind.	LW

Army Form C. 2118.

WAR DIARY
or
INTELLIGENCE SUMMARY. No 7 B.F.A.
(Erase heading not required.)

Instructions regarding War Diaries and Intelligence Summaries are contained in F. S. Regs., Part II, and the Staff Manual respectively. Title pages will be prepared in manuscript.

Hour, Date, Place.	Summary of Events and Information.	Remarks and references to Appendices
11-9-14 H.T. CASTALIA	The Commander of the Ship "Captain Mitchell" was found dead in his cabin this morning — Reported by Medical Officer of Ship to have died of heart failure. Aged 68 — Had been failing for some days getting confused. Funeral took place at 10 a.m. — British troops paraded — Cavalries for the ship's crew told by Commandant — feeling quiet at usual. Run 202 knots — Temperature 86° — Weather cooler with a strong head wind.	
12-9-14 H.T. CASTALIA	Exercises and tables as above — Run 222 knots. Weather cool & fine with a head wind. Lauth 82° W.	
13-9-14 (Sunday) H.T. CASTALIA	Divine Service at 11 a.m. for the Troops. From ships of the Convoy firstly the escort H.M.S. — CHATHAM went on ahead at 8 a.m. to SUEZ to announce our arrival & getting through the Canal. Run 218 knots W. Weather as above.	
14-9-14 H.T. CASTALIA SUEZ.	Arrival at SUEZ at 8.30 in last night — 32 nd Dunct arrival. Signal Cos landed here today — Two British Field Anhirphai — All these ordered to proceed to CAIRO tonight this Ship also landed to proceed to ALEXANDRIA. Weather cool and fine — Run 82 miles W.	

//

WAR DIARY
or
INTELLIGENCE SUMMARY. No 7 B.F.A.

(Erase heading not required.)

Army Form C. 2118.

Instructions regarding War Diaries and Intelligence Summaries are contained in F. S. Regs., Part II, and the Staff Manual respectively. Title pages will be prepared in manuscript.

Hour, Date, Place.	Summary of Events and Information.	Remarks and references to Appendices
15-9-14 H.T. CASTALIA SUEZ 9 a.m. PORT SAID 8 p.m.	Left for PORT SAID at 9 a.m. and entered the SUEZ CANAL. Arrived at PORT SAID at 8 p.m. Started coaling ship at 9 p.m. and finished at 3.30 a.m. 16/9/14 — Weather fine and warm. LW	
16-9-14 H.T. CASTALIA 9 p.m.	Left PORT SAID 6 a.m. for ALEXANDRIA. Lectures and exercises of sorts — Run 88 knots to ... Weather fine + cool with a head wind. Arrived at ALEXANDRIA	
17-9-14 H.T. CASTALIA ALEXANDRIA	Came in to the Docks at 9 a.m. — Orders received not to sail tomorrow morning. Weather fine + cool.	LW
18-9-14 H.T. CASTALIA ALEXANDRIA	Still in the Docks — Not leaving till tomorrow evening. Yesterday orders countermanded. 1 p.m. — The 32nd Sig.l. Company arrived from CAIRO and started embarking on the ship. Neither time to complete — A.D.M.S. 3rd Wars LW Division arrived from CAIRO taken to embark on H.T. GLASGOW.	
19-9-14 H.T. CASTALIA ALEXANDRIA	Left ALEXANDRIA harbour at 11 a.m. + waited outside to assemble of Convoy — Convoy consisting of 16 ships + H.M.S. WEYMOUTH sailed at 2 p.m.	LW

Army Form C. 2118.

WAR DIARY
or
INTELLIGENCE SUMMARY.   No 7 B.E.A.

(Erase heading not required.)

Instructions regarding War Diaries and Intelligence Summaries are contained in F. S. Regs., Part II, and the Staff Manual respectively. Title pages will be prepared in manuscript.

Hour, Date, Place.	Summary of Events and Information.	Remarks and references to Appendices
19-9-14 H.T. CASTALIA	In MARSEILLES. At 6 p.m. met by Convoy of 7 ships escorted by H.M.S. INDOMITABLE. An interview was obtained with the Convoying Officer & the Unit transport up before the Commanding Officer. 1) the ship's charged with the (1) Being absent without leave from the ship; (2) Being drunk; and were awarded 3 days No 1 Field Punishment. 9124 Pte N TRAYNOR 1st WEST RIDING REGIMENT 18757 Pte J. MOORE 1st WEST RIDING REGIMENT. Weather fine and warm.	
20-9-14 (Sunday) H.T. CASTALIA	Divine Service at 11 a.m. = Regn 198 knots with a head wind. Run. Weather fine and warm. 198 knots.	
21-9-14 H.T. CASTALIA 2 p.m.	Kit inspection & Unit held at 9 a.m. and after deficiencies noted & articles taken from which will be made good on arrival at MARSEILLES. Assistant Surgeon received to or treatment of wound received in the field at the dressing station of Field Ambulance. Practical demonstration of the attestation of the 1st Field Dressing to Christians of the Unit who worked at 2 Nos 4 to Stretcher Squads. H.M.S. INDOMITABLE left the Convoy at 3 a.m. to the DARDANELLES. (see receipt)	

Gulab Singh, & Sons, Calcutta—No. 22   Army C.—5-8-14—1,07,000.

Army Form C. 2118.

/3

WAR DIARY

or

INTELLIGENCE SUMMARY. No 7 B. F.A.

(Erase heading not required.)

Instructions regarding War Diaries and Intelligence Summaries are contained in F. S. Regs., Part II, and the Staff Manual respectively. Title pages will be prepared in manuscript.

Hour, Date, Place.	Summary of Events and Information.	Remarks and references to Appendices
21-9-14 H.T. CASTALIA	MARCONGRAM from Senior Naval Officer MALTA — Run 218 knots — Weather fine & calm.	L.W.
22-9-14 2p.m H.T. CASTALIA. 4 p.m	Lectures continued as above to future Interpreters and Christians A.B.C. 13 Newfoundland with Sentinels and escorted by H.M.S. MINERVA received en route to EGYPT. H.M.S. WEYMOUTH events were exchanged with the Convoy to EGYPT and H.M.S. MINERVA remained as Weather cloudy, telegraph heavy with a few slight showers. Run 216 knots.	L.W.
23-9-14 12 noon H.T. CASTALIA.	Passed lighthouse two miles of MALTA — H.M.S. MINERVA went into the harbour of VALETTA — Lectures continued as above — Weather overcast & clear with intervals of sunshine. Issued orders for Disembarking all ranks to wear service clothing — Run 185 knots.	L.W.
24-9-14 H.T. CASTALIA.	H.M.S. MINERVA rejoined the Convoy during the night — 12.30 p.m. lecture to Interpreters Care and management of transport animals by CAPTAIN ALEXANDER, S/T CORPS — Demonstration later by Christians A.B.C. — Weather fine & cool — Run 220	D.N.
25-9-14 10.30 am H.T. CASTALIA	Vessel reported after 6 p.m. by interpreter 10 dogs & 7 horses died and were thrown dead & unfit for service. Weather continued fine & warm. Run 237 knots. All 12 north 200 miles from MARSEILLES.	L.W.

WAR DIARY or INTELLIGENCE SUMMARY. No 7 B.F.A.

Army Form C. 2118.

Hour, Date, Place.	Summary of Events and Information.	Remarks and references to Appendices
26-9-14 MARSEILLES	8 a.m. Arrived at MARSEILLES — Whole Unit disembarked by 4 p.m — 10 a.m. Ordered by A.D.M.S. 3rd War Division to proceed to Field Amb. CAMPAGNE DE'VEQUE to relieve sick of British troops & the arrival of line of communication units — 7 p.m. had 16 admitted ready to take in sick — 8 p.m. these such admitted to Hospital — 10 a.m. MAJOR SHAE R.A.M.C. joined Unit as Surgical Specialist by order of A.D.M.S. 3rd WAR DIVISION, and LIEUT T.A.G. BIGGAM R.A.M.C. was transferred to No 4 CAMPAGNE IN BRITISH FIELD AMBULANCE — CAMPAGNE DE'VEQUE consisting of 4 large rooms taken for use of Hospital — Property County of No 7 B.F.A. Pitched for a Field SOUTH of the House. Water from Cabin—hole in compound drawn with alum to purify — bath with chlorine were stored in stretcher baths for drinking purposes — trench system of latrines used — 2 refuse pits were cleaned with disinfectants — Refuse to be incinerated. Weather fine. Camp cook. 5 men A, B C + 1 Public B. health sufferl Sick to No 111 I.F. A. INFANTRY the 2 p.m. SERGEANT NAILLE 141st FRENCH HN G... the Unit at Interpreter.	

Army Form C. 2118.

WAR DIARY
or
INTELLIGENCE SUMMARY. No 7 B.F.A.

(Erase heading not required.)

Instructions regarding War Diaries and Intelligence Summaries are contained in F. S. Regs., Part II, and the Staff Manual respectively. Title pages will be prepared in manuscript.

Hour, Date, Place.	Summary of Events and Information.	Remarks and references to Appendices
27-9-14 (Sunday) CHAMPAGNE DE L'EVÊQUE	16 Patients admitted to Hospital — 10 returned calls now in hospital said to be contacted at CAIRO. 3 said to be at KARACHI — 1 said to have FEROZEPORE and 1 influenza — Weather fine — fly cool at night — Standing orders made known out the Camp.	
28-9-14. 10 a.m. CHAMPAGNE DE L'EVÊQUE	A.D.M.S. 3rd WAR DIVISION inspected Hospital. Usual drills + parades carried out during the day — 18 cases including 1 Officer admitted to Hospital — 12 cases of relieved now in Hospital — contracted at CAIR[O] and 1 at ALEXANDRIA — 7 P.M. Inspected BASE COMMANDANT over sick to No 34 B.F.A. on the 30th instant. Nursing Orderly No 1659 Pte O'SULLIVAN was awarded 10 days Field Punishment No 2 at Sessa without leave + Drunk in the Docks, so the 26th instant — Weather fine + dry throughout.	
29-9-14 CHAMPAGNE DE L'EVÊQUE	4 cases admitted to Hospital today — 2 cases discharged from Hospital — Nursing Orderly No 1659 Pte O'SULLIVAN of MANCHESTER REGT was returned to his requisite Corps and he was relieved by No 970 Pte MALONEY of the same regiment — Drill as before — Weather fine + dry throughout.	

Army Form C. 2118.

WAR DIARY
or
INTELLIGENCE SUMMARY. No 7 B.F.A.

(Erase heading not required.)

Instructions regarding War Diaries and Intelligence Summaries are contained in F. S. Regs., Part II, and the Staff Manual respectively. Title pages will be prepared in manuscript.

Hour, Date, Place.	Summary of Events and Information.	Remarks and references to Appendices
30-9-14 CHAMPAGNE DE L'EVÊQUE	40 admissions to Hospital today — Total in Hospital 70 cases — 18 cases evacuated with supply train journeying to Beau-Bois; 3 MANCHESTER and 10 1st CONNAUGHT RANGERS — 6 cases of Venereal admitted (men contracted in INDIA at EGYPT) Total Venereal in Hospital 18 cases. Venereal instructions. No 7 B.F.A. told today.	
5 p.m.	Orders received to entrain until tomorrow after.	
10.30 a.m.	at D'ARENC Station.	
6 p.m.	Handed over patients in Hospital to No 19 B.F.A. belonging to 7th Nov Division together with + Warren Field Instruments and all surplus kit not removed today.	W.M. Holland Major O.C. No 7. B.F.A.

LIEUT-COLONEL L. WAY VOLUME I FROM 1-10-14
R.A.M.C. TO 31-10-14.
O.C. / No. 7 BRITISH FIELD AMBULANCE

Army Form C. 2118.

WAR DIARY
or
INTELLIGENCE SUMMARY. No. 7 BRITISH FIELD AMBULANCE

(Erase heading not required.)

Instructions regarding War Diaries and Intelligence Summaries are contained in F. S. Regs., Part II, and the Staff Manual respectively. Title pages will be prepared in manuscript.

[Stamp: No 3 Section A. G's Office at Base I. E. Force Passed to Gen'l S. Sect'n on 12.11.14]

Hour, Date, Place.	Summary of Events and Information.	Remarks and references to Appendices
1-10-14 8.30 a.m. CHAMPAGNE DE L'EVEQUE MARSEILLES	Unit paraded at 8.30 a.m. and marched to D'ARAMC Military Station MARSEILLES to entrain. Entrained station at 10.30 a.m. No. 111 INDIAN FIELD AMBULANCE (commanded by LIEUT-COLONEL FROST IMS) and 1 SECTION VETERINARY FIELD HOSPITAL commanded by CAPTAIN STEELE A.V.C. entrained in the same train - LIEUT COLONEL FROST Commandant of train. Accommodation very cramped for Officers; men fitted with impedimenta; horses (draught) in horseboxes, for WOILY COY (Mens Vans), Ponies and mules for cart (wagons), Spare trucks in that train for carts. Train routed to ORLEANS.	
2-5 p.m.	At 2.5 p.m. - Detailed a guard of 1 NCO and 6 men to travel on engine, two other N.C.O.s of the train with full instructions; the Summons were (1) IND'N COM'D, (2) O.C. INDIAN FIELD AMBULANCE - Detailed an orderly officer to the train Regt. Gd. duty. Passed an orderly in case of sickness. Weather fine and warm.	
2-10-14 9 train enroute to ORLEANS.	Arrived at TOULOUSE at 10.35 a.m. and halted for 3½ hrs for cooking; detrained at 1.40 p.m. President for men were wade and good and water provided. The FRENCH authorities taking a personal interest [illegible] were present on a duty about lunch with the Officers. General [illegible] and others called on Prefect's men as [illegible] shewing a courteous and helpful to all. Weather fine and cool. L.W.	

17

WAR DIARY

or

INTELLIGENCE SUMMARY. No 7 B.E.A.

Army Form C. 2118.

(Erase heading not required.)

Instructions regarding War Diaries and Intelligence Summaries are contained in F. S. Regs., Part II, and the Staff Manual respectively. Title pages will be prepared in manuscript.

Hour, Date, Place.	Summary of Events and Information.	Remarks and references to Appendices
3-10-14 En route to ORLEANS	10.30 a.m. Arrived at ARGENTON at 10.30 a.m. Halted for 1 hour & departed at 11.30. Had a breakdown for 3 hrs in woods about 20 miles by FRENCH authorities. Watered horses. men relieved etc. 7.30 p.m. Arrived at ORLEANS at 7.30 pm and detained at once — Marched to camp & went into camp at SERCOTTE and arrived 11.30 pm went into camp. Weather fine & warm but cold at night. JW	
4-10-14 CAMP CERCOTTE ORLEANS	Reptd. reconnoitred camp site, shown in to the lines by Camp Commandant — Drought water in camp to camp stand — 100 yds East of Camp. Regimental water cart, latrines, burnt in usual manner. Went to Ordnance Dept. to check up & have got about 2 weeks S.E. of the camp — Taken over 6 G.S. Wagons & 2 horsed Ambulances, was promised 4 but only given 2 horsed water carts. No public utensils provided for horses. No canvas 30 yds wattle. Met D.A.D.M.S. MO BILIZATION, was informed they provide for divine only — their own mobile workshops etablishment to provide for hospital. Weather fine warm — cold at night. JW	
5-10-14 CAMP CERCOTTE ORLEANS	Went to A.D.M.S. about the divine for the water carts having been promised. Then shifted on embulance Found the A.B. Coy in greater difficulties without Reported. Indented for warm clothing for whole of the Personnel of Unit. Reqts. returned — left to supply to. But. rest personnel & went to Notre Dame — no attention. Line touch with Sir Wat. A.G. Bale born enlisted up to 30-9-74	

Army Form C. 2118. 18

WAR DIARY
or
INTELLIGENCE SUMMARY. No 7 B.F.A

(Erase heading not required.)

Instructions regarding War Diaries and Intelligence Summaries are contained in F. S. Rgs., Part II, and the Staff Manual respectively. Title pages will be prepared in manuscript.

Hour, Date, Place.	Summary of Events and Information.	Remarks and references to Appendices
6-10-14 9 a.m. CAMP CERCOTTE ORLEANS.	Stables Drill N°1 for A.B.C left at 9 a.m — Drawing Stationery established and Brevre Division fitted at 12 noon — Hearts Subministered to hospital for investigation. Note gun (n.t.) for outlied — talks for absence for completing publies 3 Cpls & M.L.S 2 horses & 9 Augusta wages which to Vetirinary D.d. Hospital.	
12 noon	Issued warm clothing to A.H.C - A.B.C and 15.7 hospital orderlies, (drawers, Drifus and shirts) sent the clothing back to the School of Ordnance. Draft - 3rd Cl ASSISTANT SURGEON C. EMILE admitted to No 8 B.F.A. Suffering from Renal Colic (Not admitted to No 7 B.F.A. not opened for sick)- A.F.A 36 sent A.G. BASE N-4. line and Rachite N.W	
7-10-14 CAMP CERCOTTE ORLEANS.	Drill as above — Personnel taken for a run every morning — Received two horses used for ambulance wagons to replace two lost with Col D. Requisitioned medical ASC Driv + mules Col D — Departure 3rd CLASS ASST LAHORE DIVISION INDIAN CONTINGENT SURGEON EMILE had been admitted to STATIONARY HOSPITAL ORLEANS — written two days night R.N.	

Gulab Singh & Sons. Calcutta—No. 22 Army C.—5-8-14—1,07,000.

Army Form C. 2118.

WAR DIARY
or
INTELLIGENCE SUMMARY. No 7 B.F.A.

(Erase heading not required.)

Instructions regarding War Diaries and Intelligence Summaries are contained in F. S. Regs., Part II, and the Staff Manual respectively. Title pages will be prepared in manuscript.

Hour, Date, Place.	Summary of Events and Information.	Remarks and references to Appendices
8-10-14 9 a.m. CAMP CERCOTTE ORLEANS	Drills as as above — Divisional stores established and ambulance tent fitted at 9 a.m. Acknowledged receipt of transfer of personnel & confidential reports of Asst Surgeons EMILE — CUZEN — ELLOY to A.D.M.S. 3J LAHORE DIV & AREA — Weather fine & sunny, frost at night. JW	
9-10-14 CAMP CERCOTTE ORLEANS	Drills and Parades as above — Sent in strength of Field Ambulance & few Nom Establishment to D.A.D.R.T transport for railway transport — Applied to A.D.M.S. 3J LAHORE DIV for an ASST SURGEON to replace ASST-SURGEON EMILE — Made to Adjutant Horse Transport about for spare Mule Corps asking for spare mules to replace casualties. Weather fine & sunny, cold at night. JW	Strength of Field Ambulance — see attached appendix
10-10-14 4 p.m. CAMP CERCOTTE ORLEANS	Drills and Parades as above — At 4 p.m. received orders to transport to the Unit — IC 5, 9, 8 wagons, carts & mules. Detailed O.C. 2 officers & 1 NCO for our Unit. These Details were detailed from the Unit by A.D.M.S. to Report in accordance with the 9th BHOPAL INFANTRY — Weather fine & sunny at night. JW	

Army Form C. 2118.   26

WAR DIARY
or
INTELLIGENCE SUMMARY.

(Erase heading not required.)

Instructions regarding War Diaries and Intelligence Summaries are contained in F. S. Regs., Part II, and the Staff Manual respectively. Title pages will be prepared in manuscript.

Hour, Date, Place.	Summary of Events and Information.	Remarks and references to Appendices
11-10-14 7 a.m. CAMP CERCOTTE ORLEANS. (Sunday)	10 Officers and 50 men A.B. Corps started for Orleans with us to enquire about trouble by order of A.D.M.S. & to relieve at Widows by amb... A.B. Corps. Received 200 1st field dressings from A.D.M.S and 29 linen Towels for hospital use to tip up. Cooks for experimental company. Field Service envelopes received from O.C No 6 B.F.A Weather changeable — Cpl Pratyat of No 6 B.F.A. Weather [illegible] No hospital available at Ordnance Stores for A.H.C & A.B.Cpls. Drills as usual — 10 a.m. W. Pratap [illegible]	
12-10-14 10 a.m. CAMP CERCOTTE ORLEANS.	Sections — Received from A.D.M.S Amts return and Amts. Stop/transfers seen. 20 tubes of each sent [illegible] indented on the Ordnance Stores for officers changed and [illegible] Shoes for N PENN Y^d DUKE of WELLINGTONS REG^t No 9859 Pte J.W. for Stukers. Awarded 10th punishment No 2 — A.H.C — Weather fine cloudy 3rd GRADE COOK LALLCHAND.	
13-10-14 CAMP CERCOTTE ORLEANS	Drills as usual — Applied for anti-typhoid vaccine for 14 double vaccinations. Drew an advance of 85 francs for transue Chest for men of A.S.C attached to Unit. Gob Shoes for the Frankfort arrived indented for yesterday. Weather cloudy & raining, somewhat mild. W.	

Army Form C. 2118.

WAR DIARY
or
INTELLIGENCE SUMMARY. No 7 B.F.A.

(Erase heading not required.)

Instructions regarding War Diaries and Intelligence Summaries are contained in F.S. Regs., Part II, and the Staff Manual respectively. Title pages will be prepared in manuscript.

Hour, Date, Place.	Summary of Events and Information.	Remarks and references to Appendices
14-10-14 10 a.m. CAMP CERCOTTE ORLEANS	Drills as usual — Attended at No 8 B.F.A at 10 a.m. Received orders from the A.D.M.S. LAHORE DIVISION with regard to positions of F.A.'s on the line of march. All letters and reports from divs. are alternative days pending 2 attached. 9 wiring to enter transfer followers — S.W. wind and weather raining.	Orders w A.D.M.S LAHORE DIVISION attached appendix II
15-10-14 CAMP. CERCOTTE ORLEANS	Unit taken to a route march — Section ordered to the Ordnance Depot for clothing boots to complete equipment of Units — B hundred wind to A.H.C. & A.B.C. Weather foggy and cold.	L.W.
16-10-14 CAMP CERCOTTE ORLEANS 8.45 p.m. 3 p.m.	Drills as usual — Three found at horses sent to HOSPITAL today — three horses suffered from 3 horses received at 5 p.m. in lieu of horses sent sick. Order for entrainment received from A.D.M.S. at 8.45 p.m. Unit to entrain at PORT SEC. STATION ORLEANS at 9.30 p.m. on 17-10-14 — Board of Survey on Ordnance tents & vaccination before leaving taken over by Government. 12 h inspection of Unit—held at 3 p.m. — Weather cold and foggy with a N.W. wind.	Appendix III attached. Order for entrainment L.W.
17-10-14 CAMP CERCOTTE ORLEANS	Preparing for entrainment today — Handed over empties hire to Depot 59th RIFLES — ASST SURGEON G.H. BLAKER (Sub on in advance to take over billets) — Left Camp at 7:15 a.m. turn PORT SEC — R/- NAHON F.R. 05,000 CH INFANTRY reported twenty-one interior _____	

Gulab Singh & Sons, Calcutta—No. 22

Army Form C. 2118.

WAR DIARY
or
INTELLIGENCE SUMMARY. No 7 B.F.A.

(Erase heading not required.)

Instructions regarding War Diaries and Intelligence Summaries are contained in F. S. Regs., Part II, and the Staff Manual respectively. Title pages will be prepared in manuscript.

Hour, Date, Place.	Summary of Events and Information.	Remarks and references to Appendices
17-10-14. CAMP CERCOTTE ORLEANS.	9 Infantry to the Unit temporarily till SERGT MAILLÉ 141st FRENCH INFANTRY, came for duty — Received a letter from the D.M.S. ARMY HQs INDIA notifying us that a sum of Rs.600 had been allotted for the Unit from the IMPERIAL INDIAN RELIEF FUND, the Indian Soldiers Contracts. Wrote to D.M.S. INDIA thanking him for the same. 9.30 p.m. Marched to PORT SEC STATION ORLEANS and entrained at 9.30 p.m. Train started at 11.30 p.m. Night cannot on account of the equipment left the aircraft mule cart which were unloaded owing to absence of brakesmen the left unattended horses though carried up to the area, was drug completely of thousand men (annexed) and one horse hatcher - HEAD QUARTERS 9 DIVISION travelled by Same train. Weather for civilian and matt - good arrangements were made at the departure station for horses and interior.	
18-10-14. EN ROUTE IN TRAIN	En route in train. Weather wet, stormy and cold.	

Army Form C. 2118.

WAR DIARY
or
INTELLIGENCE SUMMARY. No 07 B.F.A

(Erase heading not required.)

Instructions regarding War Diaries and Intelligence Summaries are contained in F. S. Regs., Part II, and the Staff Manual respectively. Title pages will be prepared in manuscript.

Hour, Date, Place.		Summary of Events and Information.	Remarks and references to Appendices.
19-10-14 EN ROUTE IN TRAIN		En route by train. Two long stoppages owing to breakdowns on the railway. Arrived at CALAIS at 4 a.m. and departed about 1 p.m. Arrived at ARGUE at 5:30 p.m. and commenced detraining. Entire Ambulance detrained, waggons loaded and transport marshalled for Divisional transport and ready to move off by 8:30 p.m.	
	8:30 p.m.	to BLANDECQUE and billeted for night. B. Wing Officers and men slept in a field with straw; sufficient food; horses in farm stables. Weather wet & cold.	
20-10-14 HALLINES	10.a.m.	A.D.M.S. arrived and gave me verbal order to march to HALLINES and open Ambulance in Chateau. Marched at 11 a.m. and arrived at	
	11.a.m.	HALLINES. Had hospital ready for receipt of sick at 3 p.m. Received orders for holding A.H.CORPS and A.B.CORPS Wittes in	
	2 p.m.	close to the Chateau. Transport parked near field opposite to the Chateau. Two patients in hospital. Weather fine & cold.	
21-10-14 HALLINES	12 noon	8 patients admitted to hospital. Transfd 10 patients to WIZERN Station & handed over to D.D.M.S. for transfer to clearing Hospital.	
	11.20.a.m.	to VELLANCAPELLE - Bearer Division received orders to close Hospital with Advance Gd of 7th BRIGADE, remainder of unit to be at head	
	11.a.m.	of Ammunition Column. Surgeon General MACPHERSON visited	

Army Form C. 2118.

WAR DIARY or INTELLIGENCE SUMMARY. 7 B.F.A.

(Erase heading not required.)

Hour, Date, Place.	Summary of Events and Information.	Remarks and references to Appendices.
21-10-14 HALLINES	Hostilities at 11 a.m. Forward had attention to the wound 5 horses — orders from A.H. Corps & A.B. Corps — premonition [?] to A.D.M.S. — got permission to disperse S 18 cart to lighten the load on G.S. Wagon. Sent three by rail to BASE COMMANDANT MARSEILLES. 10.30 p.m. Arrived at VALLAN CAPELLE at 10.30 p.m. No arrangements had been made for billeting. I made arrangements [?] to [?] the [?] head to farmers in the field. Weather fine.	J.W.
22-10-14 VALLAN CAPELLE BAILLEUL 7 p.m.	8.30 a.m. Ordered to march to BAILLEUL — Bearer Division marched with Advance Guard. 7th BRIGADE — Arrived at BAILLEUL at 4 p.m. went with to B Wala — 7 p.m. Orders received for A.D.M.S. to send 1 Tent Subdivision with by Bearer Division Commander tomorrow 23rd 6 a.m. to accompany 7th BRIGADE. Issued an orders at 7 p.m. See appendices 2&3. Weather fine.	Appendices 4 & 5. 6 & 7 attached J.W.
23-10-14 BAILLEUL ESTARES	4.00 a.m. Operation orders received from A.D.M.S. 4.30 a.m — issued orders 4.45 a.m. See appendices 6 & 7. — Marched to ESTAIRES with Units less D Section 6 & 7 — to Bearer Division and arrived at ESTAIRES at 5.30 p.m. — billetted for the night. On arrival message received from Capt. MITCHELL commanding D to Bearer Division — that Advance Guard had been fired on in evening at LAVENTIE (shell fire) but no casualties reported. Refused much light to A.D.M.S. Capt. MITCHELL was ordered to remain where he was till further [?] ordered to send further report in the morning. Weather fine [?].	Appendices 6 & 7 J.W.

Army Form C. 2118.

25

WAR DIARY
or
INTELLIGENCE SUMMARY. No 7 B.F.A.

(Erase heading not required.)

Hour, Date, Place.	Summary of Events and Information.	Remarks and references to Appendices.
ESTAIRES. 24-10-14.	Sent 10 carts to BASE COMMANDANT MARSEILLES 12.—160 lbs tents lighter pitch and 4.80 lbs carts to Base Division etc. which reduces the weight of baggage considerably — leaves the Unit most mobile.	
LA CASSAN. 10.30	Received orders to move at to LA CASSAN wire huts/trenches at 4.30 p.m. and we moved into billets. Weather fine — warm.	J.W.
25-10-14 LA CASSAN	Received orders to inspect / or huts, to look for water convent. Sent in details in books. Weather fine — warm. Received 274 lbs socks and 4 builders lanterns.	J.W.
26-10-14 12.50 p.m. LA CASSAN	Indented [Nutters +] Barclaws cups for A.H.S. A.B.C. and Stretchers establishment — 12.50 p.m. received orders from A.D.M.S. to send to Beaver Division to LEDRUMEZ to relieve ½ Beaver Division No 113 I.F.A. See appendix 6 — Sent Capt MITCHELL R.A.M.C. See appendix 9 — Sent 3 Ambulance wagons to LAGORGUE jointly in order of A.D.M.S. See appendix 8 — 9 wagons A.B. Carts reported	Appendices 6, 8 + 9 attached.
7.30 pm	from No 15 CLEARING HOSPITAL — 7.30 p.m. received orders from A.D.M.S. to march to LAGORGUE to-morrow morning. Weather fine.	J.W.

Army Form C. 2118.

WAR DIARY
or
INTELLIGENCE SUMMARY. No 7 B.F.A.

(Erase heading not required.)

Instructions regarding War Diaries and Intelligence Summaries are contained in F. S. Regs., Part II, and the Staff Manual respectively. Title pages will be prepared in manuscript.

Hour, Date, Place.	Summary of Events and Information.	Remarks and references to Appendices.
27-10-14 7.15 a.m. LA GORGUE 9 p.m.	Left LACASSAN at 7.15 a.m. and marched to LAGORGUE and went into billets — 9 p.m. received verbal order from A.D.M.S. to march to VIEILLE CHAPELLE and open tent divisions in building to receive wounded from 9th BHOPAL INFANTRY — 47th SIKHS and SAPPERS and MINERS. I.a.m. arrived in LAGORQUE and	
VIEILLE CHAPELLE 1 a.m.	opened the tent division A. section in a Brewery. The following were attached temporarily to Tent Division previous to Beare Division withdrawal. 10 Bearers + stretchers from 111 I.F.A — 72 Bearers and 18 stretchers from 112 I.F.A. and 20 Bearers and	
28-10-14 2 p.m.	5 stretchers from No 8 B.F.A. — Sent Lieut. MAJOR FRAN-KLIN with 1/2 Bearer Division to ROUGECROIX with 2 ambulance wagons, and MAJOR ODLUM I.M.S III I.F.A. with 1/2 Bearer D. with 2+ two ambulance wagons to PONT LOGI — MAR. SHEET 91 OMER.	
28-10-14 6 a.m. VIEILLE CHAPELLE	Named 67 9th BHOPALS, 47th SIKHS and SAPPERS and MINERS began arriving — 12 British and 104 Indian wounded received up to midnight — 54 cases were evacuated to Clearing Hospital at LAGORGUE. LIEUT COLONEL H.L. ANDERSON 9th BHOPAL INFANTRY was slightly wounded. Reported to have been the above and of spine. A few haymaker grenades unscrewed by A.D.M.S. A large majority of the wounds were gunshot. Weather rainy and cold.	

R.W.

WAR DIARY or INTELLIGENCE SUMMARY.   No 7 B.?.A.

Army Form C. 2118.

(Erase heading not required.)

Instructions regarding War Diaries and Intelligence Summaries are contained in F.S. Regs., Part II, and the Staff Manual respectively. Title pages will be prepared in manuscript.

Hour, Date, Place.	Summary of Events and Information.	Remarks and references to Appendices.
29-10-14 VIEILLE CHAPELLE	44 wounded admitted for the night up to midnight. 29.10 – 30.10 Lt Colonel ANDERSON 9th BHOPAL INFANTRY died at 1.15 p.m. reported to A.G. BASE wounds and A.D.M.S. Reporting of officer 9th BHOPAL OCCUPATIONS Colonel Wilcocks Stafford Baill	
6 p.m.	EUL – Lieut J.E. LAWRIE 1st SEAFORTH HIGHLANDERS admitted with shell wound of head (slight) Reported in mine to A.G. Base and to A.D.M.S. man of SAPPERS and MINERS died from wound at Advance Weather raining and cold. L.W.	
8 p.m.	War from A.D.M.S. to evacuate wounded and move to LAGORGUE (signed)	
30-10-14 VIEILLE CHAPELLE	LIEUT COLONEL ANDERSON 9th BHOPALS was interred in the Church cemetery at 11 a.m. and the Sappers and Miners in the field behind	
12 a.m.	wards of DEVAUX DE GRAND BRASSERIE. Evacuated 42 INDIAN, 4 BRITISH SOLDIERS and 1 OFFICER	
12 a.m.	to Clearing hospital at LAGORGUE – unwounded	
LAGORGUE 4 p.m.	to LA GORGUE. Opened A SECTION for reception of wounded	
5.35 p.m.	in order of A.D.M.S. in the ECOLE LIBRE – relieved order from A.D.M.S. 5.25 p.m. to send up to Braeval Divisional Head LE DRUM 62 and opened offer of advance in reserve of the Field Ambulance at Braeval raining and cold. 4 sick admitted inc Connaught Rangers, HW.	Appendices 10 and 11 attached.

Army Form C. 2118.

WAR DIARY
or
INTELLIGENCE SUMMARY. No 7 B.E.A.

(Erase heading not required.)

Instructions regarding War Diaries and Intelligence Summaries are contained in F. S. Regs., Part II, and the Staff Manual respectively. Title pages will be prepared in manuscript.

Hour, Date, Place.	Summary of Events and Information.	Remarks and references to Appendices.
31–10–14 LA GORGUE	Admitted 10 Officers 9 E BHOPAL INFANTRY NYD FORTH HIGHLANDERS, 9 wounded, 1 wound left arm; 1 wound 1st SEA CONNAUGH RANGERS 93rd BATTY R.F.A. N.Y.D from 4 men evacuated to Clearing Hospital BETHUNE.	Appendices 12 to 13 ante extent
4.2.0.h m	Orders received from ADMS 4.30 p m for Dressers Stretchers and reinforcement for interpreters. Signed copy orders see Officer aires 10 + 13 attached. Reinforcements in Workshops Lorry in LW	

Gulab Singh & Sons, Calcutta—No. 22 Army C—5 8-14—1,07,000.

Appendix. 1
Strength of ambulance as per War Establishment.

British Officers.	5
Assistant Surgeons	8
British rank & file	34
A.H. Corps.	50
A.B. Corps	133
S & T. Establishment	13
Horses draught	28
Mules	8
Riding animals	5
Ambulance Wagons 4 wheeled	6
G.S. Wagon	5
Cook Wagon	1
Water Cart 2	2
A.T. Carts	4
Approximate Baggage	18,000 lbs.

Orleans.
9.10.1914

Hvay Lieut Colonel Rame
O.C. No 7 B.F. Ambulance

Orders by A.D.M.S. LAHORE DIVISION

Appendix II.

Units are to be ready to entrain at two hours notice

Order of March.

1. Advance Guard.

Bearer Division of a Field Ambulance will be detailed daily by the A.D.M.S. to march in rear of Advanced Guard. In rear of leading Infantry Brigade there will be two Ambulance Wagons.

After Heavy Batteries R.G.A. two more ambulance wagons.
After Heavy Battery Ammunition Column remainder of the Field Ambulances.

Order of March of Field Ambulance.

1. Officer Commanding
2. Bearer Division (Bearers 3 abreast with stretchers, remainder of personnel of Bearer Division — 1 Water Cart and 2 A.T. Carts.)
3. Ambulance Wagons.
4. Personnel of 4 Sections with G.S. Wagons, 1 water cart and 2 A.T. Carts.
5. Rear Guard to consist of 1 Warrant Officer & 3 men to pick up anything falling out of wagons etc.

Billeting — Divided into 4 Areas.

Area No 1. Bearer Division with advanced Guard.
Area No 2. Two Field Ambulances.
Area No 4. 2½ Field Ambulances.

Orders for Billeting

Parties will be permanently detailed as below and will march with the Advance Guard.

For 2 British Fd Ambulance Officer 1. Rank & file 2.
 „ 3. Indian   „   „   Officer 1 „   „ 2.

On resuming the March units are to fall in and take up position behind the Heavy Battery Ammunition Column.

Cooking Wagon to be in rear of each Fd ambulance

Supply Wagon will march with Supply Section of the Divisional Supply Train — After handing over Supplies daily to unit, it will rejoin the Divisional Supply Train.

In Action

Site for Tent Division will be selected by A.D.M.S.
O/C. Field Ambulance will select site for Dressing Stations
O/C. must see that Dressing Stations are not opened too soon

<u>Dressing Stations</u> to be organized as follows:-

1. Reception station where wounded will be Sorted
    a). Seriously wounded.
    b). Slightly wounded
2. Both Medical Officers of Bearer Division to be at the Dressing Station
3. The Bearers of Dressing Station will work between Regimental Aid post and Dressing Station – Red Cross boards will be put up by units shewing position of Regtl aid posts
4. Ambulance Wagons of Tent Division are to work between Tent Division and Dressing Station

The O/C. will keep A.D.M.S. continually informed of the situation –

ORLEANS
14-10-14

Lieut Colonel
O C No 7 B F A.

Appendix III

No. 112-Q

Head Quarters Lahore Division.
16th October 1914

From

The A.Q.M.G.
Lahore Division.

Memorandum

The attached statement showing the order of movement on the 17th instant, is forwarded for information and communication to all concerned, immediately.

Sd/- H.D.Price.

Major,
D.A.Q.M.G. Lahore Division.

To

The A.D.M.S. Lahore Division.

No 58/28 d/-16-10-14

Memorandum,

Forwarded for information and necessary action.

Jno Sloan
Maj
for Colonel, I.M.S.,
A.D.M.S. Lahore Division.

To

The Officer Commanding No. 7 British Field Ambulance.
The Officer Commanding No. 111 Indian Field Ambulance.

Appendix III

Order of movement on the 17th

Troops	Time of Entrainment		
	Port Sec.	Murlins	Orleans
1 British Field Ambulance No.7 (L346) Divisional Head Quarters (L 301)	9-30 p.m.	......	......
1 Indian Field Ambulance No.111 (L 347) Divisional Artillery Head Quarters (L 320) 18th Brigade R.F.A. Head Quarters (L 321)	......	......	10 p.m.

Received ??? A.D.M.S. 18.45 p.m.
Amon ????
????
O.C. No.7 B.F.A

CAMP DE ROCOTT
ORLEANS
16/10/79

Appendix 4   BAILLEUL   Copy No 2

Operation Orders No 1
                                22/10/14
Colonel B.B. Grayfoot I.M.S.
        ADMS Lahore

Ref. Map
Belgium OSTEND Sheet 1 1/100,000

1. The 7th Bde. will march from BAILLEUL tomorrow morning on the BAILLEUL – ARMENTIERE road the head of the main body passing the PLACE BAILLEUL at 6 a.m.

2. A mixed field ambulance will accompany the Bde. composed of
   1 Tent Subdivision No 7 B.F.a
   3 Tent Subdivision No 111 I.F.a
   Bearer division to consist of
   ½ B.D. No 7 B.F.a & the B.D. of 111 I.F.a.

   Ambulance Waggons:—
      3 from No 7 B.F.a
      6 from No 111 I.F.a

3. The Tent Subdivision No 7 B.F.a with Bearer Division complement & waggons will proceed to WOLVERGHEM and Open.
   The Tent subdivisions No 111 I.F.a with B. Div. Ambulance Waggons

will proceed to GROOT VIERSTRAAT & open.

4. Officer commanding tent subdivision at both these points will select sites for advanced dressing stations.
5. Ambulance waggons are not to be sent forward from tent subdivision without great caution
6. Supply waggons should be parked at the PLACE & come under the orders of the Bde. Supply Officer
7. One days cooked ration to be taken
8. Reports to ADMS BAILLEUL

By hand
Copy No 1 Daniel
No 2 OC No 7 B+a
No 3 OC No 8/19+a

4.30 pm

BMGregory Ent
Col.
ADMS

Appendix 5 — No 2

Order by LIEUT COLONEL
L WAY RAMC O.C No 7
B.F.A.

BAILLEUL
22-10-14

Ref OSTEND 1 SET. A
SHEET 1 $\frac{1}{100,000}$

Ref. Operation Order No by A.D.M.S.
LAHORE DIVN.

1. D. SECTION TENT SUB
DIVISION will accompany
the 7th INFANTRY BRIGde.
tomorrow the 23/10/14

2. 7be BEARER SUBDIVN.
of B + D SECTIONS will
also accompany the 7th
INFANTRY BRIGde.

3. The head of the 7th INFANTRY BRIGd will pass the PLACE at 6 a.m.

4. Three Ambulance wagons, one G.S. wagon, one watercart and two A.T. carts will accompany the above.

5. Cooked rations will be carried for the personnel.

6. Rations for the 24 10/14 will be taken.

7. One hundred rations for wounded will be carried.

8. The TENT SUBDIVN will open at WULVERGHEM

9. One hundred extra FIRST FIELD DRESSINGS will be taken.

10. The Ambulance wagons will not go to DRESSING STATION till ordered by O.C. TENT SUBDIV^N

11. The above details will march in rear of the AMUNITION COLUMN.

12. Reports to be sent to A.D.M.S at BAILLEUL

　　　　　Wray Lieut-Colonel
　　　　　　　　R.A.M.C
　　　　　O.C. No 7. B.F.A.

After order
The supply wagon will Park in the PLACE at 6 a.m 23rd. BRIGADE SUPPLY will send
Issued to O.C/o SECTIONS by hand at 7 p.m.

Appendix 6.   BAILLEUL 12
              23.10.14

Operation Order No 2
        by
    Col Dryfoot Comdg Lahore

Ref Map:
1/81,000 Cassel 5,000

1. The Division less detach ment given in operation order No 1 will march today to ESTAIRES via VIEUX BERQUIN

2. Starting point cross roads 600 SE of 'E' in BELLE CROIX Fme about 1½ miles S.E of METEREN

3. Main body (in order of march) to pass starting point at 5-45 am

4. Mixed Field Ambulance (under command of Lt. Col WAP) composed of ½ Bearer division N° 7 BFa
   3 tent sub divisions N° 7 BFa
   1 tent sub division N° 111 97a
   with 3 ambulance wagons
   N° 7 BFa will accompany the force

5. The ½ Bearer Division should accompany the Advance Guard

which will be clear of the starting point at 5-30 a.m.

6. Reference 8 of Operation Order No 1 by AJDm/s dated 22.10.14 reports should be sent to ESTAIRES. Otherwise to head of Main body.

7. Order of March
   1 Troop 15th Lancers
   H. Q & Div. Section Signal Coy
   1 Field Coy R.E.
   2 Batts. 8th Inf. Bde
   Div. H. Q.
   1 Company 34th Pioneers
   18th Bde (less 1 battery)
   109th Heavy Batt R.G.A.
   34th Pioneers (less 1 Coy)
   Field Artillery Bde. Amm. Col.
   Heavy Batt. Amm. Col.
   Field Ambulance
          (less ½ B. Div.)
   Train
   Rear Guard

8. O.C. Field Ambulance will report his arrival in ESTAIRES to AJDm/s

9. One Billeting Officer & 1 Assist. Surgeon should march in rear of Advance Guard & report to

A GOC or his representative

NB M[?] y [?] Col
 [?]toms
Copy No 1 retained
No 2 OC No 7 BTC[?]
No 3 OC No 111 BTC[?]
By messenger of No 7 BTC[?]
4-10 am.

Received 4.45 a.m.

Appendix 7

BAILLEUL No 3
23/10/14
Copy No 1

Order by Lt-Colonel L. Way
R.A.M.C. O.C. No 7 B.F.A.
Ref. Map. St OMER 1/80000
Ref: Operation Order No 2
by A.D.M.S. LAHORE DIVⁿ
dated 23/10/14

1. Capt MITCHELL R.A.M.C
will proceed in command
of ½ Bearer Division
+ will accompany the
Advance Guard which will
be clear of the Starting point
at 5.30 a.m.

2. Starting point will be
cross road 600 yds S.E
of the F in BELLE CROIX

about 1½ miles SE of METEREN.

3. The remainder of F.A. will accompany main body which will pass the above point at 5.45 a.m.

4. Asst Surgeon PINTO will march in rear of Ma. vance guard. to report to A.Q.M.G or his representative for billets

J Wray Lt Colonel
     D.A.M.S

Issued personally
4.15 a.m.
To O Cs A + C Sections

85

Appendix 8

LOCON
26.10.14
12.45 pm

Ref. Maps
St OMER & ARRAS 80,000

1. Please send ½ B.D. to LE DRUMEZ to relieve ½ B.D. under Capt BOYD IDIS No 113 IFA. who should fall back on his unit in LA GORGUE.

2. All ambulance waggons of your unit should report today for duty to Capt. LANE at Town Hall LA GORGUE

BM Gryfith
Coal
ADMS

Personally to O.C. No 7 B Fa
at 12-50 pm

No 4 F.A. orders by Lt-Colonel L.
WAY. R.A.M.C. O.C. No 7 B.F.A.
LA LACON
26/10/14.

Ref: maps.
ST OMER & ARRAS 1/80,000.

Ref: order by A.D.M.S. LOCON
26/10/14

1. Capt MITCHELL, R.A.M.C. will
proceed with 1/2 B.D. to LEDRUNE
and relieve 1/2 B.D. No 113 / F.A
under Capt BOYD I.M.S who
will join him at/in LA GORGUE

2. He will take cooked
rations today and rations
for tomorrow

Personally   L Way Lt Colonel
to Capt MITCHELL   R.A.M.C.
1.50 p.m.   O.C. No 7 B.F.A.

Appendix 9

Appendix 10

MESSAGES AND SIGNALS.

"A" Form. Army Form C. 2121.

TO — O.C. No 7 B.F.a

AAA

Send out Bearer Division to establish Advanced Dressing Station at Le DRUMEZ. The bearers and wagons should proceed to via ROUGE CROIX to cross roads at A in RUE DU BACQUEROT & collect casualties from regtl aid posts of GORDON Highd - SUFFOLKS - MIDDLESEX - CONNAUGHTS - BHOPAL Infty, & laidry from FAUQUISSART to farm house 400 SE of X in ROUGE CROIX. Motor ambulances will be at Le DRUMEZ at 10-30 to evacuate wounded to

O.C. N° 4 B.4.a

URGENT

"A" Form. Army Form C. 2121.
MESSAGES AND SIGNALS.

LA GORGUE where you are open to receive them. G.O.C. 8th Indian Bde. has been notified. Report compliance to me.

From ADMS Lahore Divn
Place ESTAIRES
Time 4.20 PM 30th/10/14

No 5 F.A. orders by Lt Col L. WAY
RAMC O.C. No 7 B.F.A.
Appendix 11

La Gorgue
30-10-14

Def Map St OMER & LILLE
1/80000
Ref: orders by A.D.M.S LAHORE DIV^N 30/10/14

1. MAJOR BARTLETT and CAPT M^cARTUR will proceed to LEDRUMEZ with ½ Bearer Divⁿ and establish an Advance Dressing Station.

2. They will proceed with 5 Ambulance wagons via ROUGE CROIX to cross roads at A in RUE DE BACQUEROT and collect casualties from regimental aid posts of GORDON HIGHLDERS - SUFFOLKS MIDDLESEX - CONNAUGHTS - BHOPAL Infantry extending from FAUQUISART to farm house S.O.E. of X in ROUGE CROIX.

3. Motor ambulances will be at LEDRUMEZ at 10.30 to evacuate wounded to LA GORGUE Tent Division of No 7 B.F.A. in ECOLE LIBRE RUE DE HINETIERE

4. One days rations will be taken

Reports to be sent to Tent Division Personally at 5.35 p.m.

L. Way Lieut Colonel RAMC

to MAJOR BARTLETT
CAPT M^cARTHUR O.C. No 7 B.F.A

Appendix 12

"A" Form.   Army Form C. 2121.
MESSAGES AND SIGNALS.

TO — O.C. No. 7 D.F. a

Our dressing station & rendezvous for wagons for tonight remain as last night. Troops on front you work over are from right to left beginning at house 300 yds S.W. of X in Rouge CROIX — CONNAUGHTS — SUFFOLKS — MIDDLESEX.

From
Place ESTAIRES
Time 3-15   31.10.14

Appendix 13

No 6 F.A. Order by Lt Colonel L. WAY. RAMC
O.C. No 7 B. F.A.

LA GORGUE
31-10-14

Ref: Map ST OMER & LILLE 1/80,000.

Ref: orders by A.D.M.S. LAHORE Divⁿ dated 31/10/14

1. The Dressing Station and rendez-vous for wagons for tonight remain as last night.

2. Troops on front are from right to left beginning at house 300 yds S.W. of X in ROUGE CROIX — CONNAUGHT RANGERS — SUFFOLKS — MIDDLESEX.

3. Reports to be sent to 7enth Division

L Way Lt-Colonel
RAMC
O.C. No 7 B.F.A.

Sent by hand to
MAJOR BARTLETT
4.20 p.m.

War Diary
of
No. 7 British Field Ambulance

From 1-11-14
To 30/11/14

(Pp 29 to 40
Volume I

VOL 3

LIEUT. COLONEL L. WAY RAMC
O.C. No 7 BRITISH FIELD AMBULANCE

WAR DIARY FROM 1-11-14 TO 30-11-14

INTELLIGENCE SUMMARY. No 7 BRITISH F/E BASE AMBULANCE
I.E.F. — A

(Erase heading not required.)

Instructions regarding War Diaries and Intelligence Summaries are contained in F.S. Regs., Part II, and the Staff Manual respectively. Title pages will be prepared in manuscript.

Army Form C. 2118.

Stamps:
- ADJUTANT / 32 War Divn / 9 DEC 1914 / BASE AMBULANCE OFFICE
- No 3 Section A.G's Office at Base I.E. Force — Passed to General S. Sectn on 10.12.14

Hour, Date, Place.	Summary of Events and Information.	Remarks and references to Appendices.
1-11-14 LA GORGUE	Evacuated 18 officers and 2 wounded to Clearing Hospital at BETHUNE — Motor Ambulance requisitioned in Wellington Dumps for Heavy Artillery Corps Units — Beaven Duffin sent to LEPRUMEZ Dispatched report 2 — Diary to A.G. BASE (Indian)	
2-11-14 LA GORGUE	Wounded and 6 sick New SUFFOLK REGT Evacuated to Clearing Hospital BETHUNE — 1 man 1st CONNAUGHT RANGERS admitted M.D. — Received two Motor Ambulances (General duty) and S.A.S.C. Drivers reported themselves — 1 Indian Bearer Dvn JDH and oc Divn Stores at LEDRUMEZ — One A.B. Corps wounded. Neither first + wounded DW	
4 p.m.	Sent Digby to No. 112 B'y yesterday. Sizes at LEDRUMEZ.	
3-11-14 LA GORGUE	1 Officer and 7 men 1st CONNAUGHT RANGERS and 1 Sergeant 1st R. SCOTS FUSILIERS wounded and received from Dressing Station at LEDRUMEZ in the course of the night. The wounded men & Lieut H.T. HEWITT, who was suffering from a gun shot wound (severe) in the left knee — WBt to A.G. BASE.	Appendices 14 – 15 attached
10.210 PM M. CAHILL, 1st CONNAUGHT RANGERS, expired from haemorrhage — wound abdomen.	
9 a.m.	BASE — Evacuated 1 officer and & wounded to the Clearing Hospital at BETHUNE of 9 officer — Beaven Duffin is still on duty at Dressing Station at LEDRUMEZ — Sent R + D Vondree Jnr to 27 British heavier Carts reserve which were distributed to the BASE COMMANDANT, MARSEILLES — 1st ADMS. LAHORE DIVN on 21st and 3rd — 30 cases (all) Jerrigts Sectn 111 F.A. wot	
3.30 pm	Evacuated to this unit. Three Juncab Cavalry soldiers slightly wounded from the Dressing Statn of LEDRUMEZ at 3.30 p.m.	
4 p.m.	No. 10210 Pte M. CAHILL 1st CONNAUGHT RANGERS was interred in the Cemetery at LAGORGUE at 4 p.m. — 2 sick from 4E	
4 p.m.	MIDDLESEX REGt admitted at 4 p.m. — 1 A.B. Corps man found dead in Billet — Divn with no grass of A.W. BACQUEROT A.D.M.S for Behar Divn made attention to this. Neither time wounded. UN	

WAR DIARY or INTELLIGENCE SUMMARY.

Army Form C. 2118.

No 7 B.F.A.

Hour, Date, Place.	Summary of Events and Information.	Remarks and references to Appendices.
4-11-14 LA GORGUE	No 3504 Bearer JODHA - A.B.C. this Unit was wounded by shell fire last night at RUE DU BACQUEROT and was admitted to No 112 I.F.A. During the night 1 Officer and 14 wounded were admitted to the Dressing Station of EDRU-MEZ. 17 sick about 40 wounded during light, 2nd LIEUT R. HARRISON 1st R. SCOTS FUSILIERS admitted. They are suffering with slight wounds of the right leg, one of them 2nd LIEUT C. GRAHAM 1st R. SCOTS FUSILIERS admitted to be taken with Pneumonia to the Clearing Hospital.	Appendices 16-17 attached
9 a.m.	at BETHUNE. 3 French Soldiers were sent to the FRENCH HOSPITAL at BETHUNE. 1 m. A.B.C. sent	
6.15 p.m.	returned to duty. One large fun No.112 I.F.A. Received orders from A.D.M.S. LAHORE DIVN to Evacuate Division to be at BACQUEROT at 8 p.m. Eight were admitted 16-17 attached - W-d to A.G. BASE 2nd LIEUT R. HARRISON 1st R. SCOT FUSILIERS wounded - 7 wounded and 11 sick admitted from Dressing Station at	
10 p.m. to midnight	LEDRUMEZ. Weather raining, heavy.	
5-11-14 LA GORGUE	No 3504 Bearer JODHA A.B. Coy died of wound (gunshot) at 10.30 a.m. 4-11-14 - 1 Officer CAPT. O. UNDERHILL- FAITHORNE 1st CONNAUGHT RANGERS admitted with gunshot wound thigh and 36	Appendices 18 to 19 attached
10 a.m.	at 1 a.m. - W-d to A.G. BASE. Evacuated 26 Officers and 36 men to Clearing Hospital at BETHUNE - 5.10 p.m. Send Orders to Bearer Division near At 5 DMS side appd.	
9 a.m. to 4 p.m.	Divs 18-19 - Bearer Division at LEDRUMEZ - 4 p.m. Instructed Dressing Station at LEDRUMEZ. Admitted 1 Officer + 17 men wounded and sick during the day 1/2 MAJOR J. M. HALLOWS 15th INDIAN LANCERS sick wounded left hand severe - W-d to A.G. BASE LW. Weather foggy and cold.	

WAR DIARY or INTELLIGENCE SUMMARY.

Army Form C. 2118.

No 7 B.F.A.

(Erase heading not required.)

Instructions regarding War Diaries and Intelligence Summaries are contained in F. S. Regs., Part II, and the Staff Manual respectively. Title pages will be prepared in manuscript.

Hour, Date, Place.	Summary of Events and Information.	Remarks and references to Appendices.
6-11-14 LA GORGUE 6.30 p.m.	Evacuated 10 sick and 4 men to Clearing Hospital at LEDRUMEZ-BETHUNE — B/ Division. Bearer Division on receipt of orders from A.D.M.S. at 6.30 p.m. proceeded to Field Ambulance 20+21 attached to 22nd admitted during the 24 hrs. 9 wounded and 11 sick. Weather foggy & cold.	Appendices 20 & 21 attached.
7-11-14 9 a.m. LA GORGUE 9.45 a.m.	Evacuated 16 cases to the Clearing Hospital at CHOCQUE - 10 were sick and 6 wounded. No 10520 19 Corpl. F. McGOW AN 2nd ROYAL SCOTS died of multiple shell wounds at 9.45 a.m. and was buried in the Cemetery at LA GORGUE. West to D.A.Q. 3rd ECHELON BASE — Sent in return for clothing for the Qr ending 31-8-1916 — No 1032 Pte N. WHITTLES 1st MANCHESTER REGt and N 1104 Pte H. ROYLE 1st MANCHESTER REGt awarded 4 days field punishment No 2 and fined one days pay for drunk — No 3278 BEARER TIRTHA — A.B.C. awarded 7 days field punishment No 2 for entering a dwelling house without permission & obtaining 3.30 p.m. grapes. N.C.O. SURGEON GENERAL MACPHERSON 6-14 p.m. inspected the Hospital — 9 cases admitted to B. Division on arrival — 8 days pm. A.D.M.S. at 6.14 p.m. all attended — H.33 admitted — 3 killed during the day. Weather foggy & cold.	Appendices 22 & 23 attached.
8-11-14 LA GORGUE	Evacuated 4 cases to Clearing Hospital at CHOCQUE — B/ord A.D.M.S. Bearer Division returned from LEDRUMEZ. All attended with the exception of 3 men who were written Divisional Establishment have been notified in writing by B.S. — 4 admissions & one sick during the 24 hrs. Weather foggy & cold. L.W.	

Gulab Singh & Sons, Calcutta — No. 22

Army Form C. 2118.

4 32

WAR DIARY
or
INTELLIGENCE SUMMARY. No 7 B.F.A.

(Erase heading not required.)

Instructions regarding War Diaries and Intelligence Summaries are contained in F. S. Regs., Part II, and the Staff Manual respectively. Title pages will be prepared in manuscript.

Hour, Date, Place.	Summary of Events and Information.	Remarks and references to Appendices.
9-11-14 LA GORGUE	Evacuated 2 wounded and 4 sick to Clearing Hospital at MERVILLE – 12 cases admitted today, 3 being wounded and 9 medical cases. Weather foggy & cold. WN.	
10-11-14 LA GORGUE	Evacuated 1 wounded and 3 medical cases to Clearing Hospital MERVILLE today. Evidence handed over to Ordnance for scrap clothing etc. A.H. Corps and A.B. Corps – The following were awarded for breaking out of camp:– No29789 D⁰ Cash Aj No34180 D⁰ Gover A – A.S. CORPS No10766 P⁰ S. Watson 3 days field punishment No2 – No10866 P⁰ S. Watson 1st West Riding Regt 3 days field punishment No2 – No9124 P⁰ W. Morgan 1st West Riding Regt 7 days field punishment No1 – Weather foggy & damp. cold. WN	
11-11-14 LA GORGUE	Evacuated 8 wounded to the Clearing Hospital at MERVILLE – 1 gunshot wound and 3 sick admitted. Weather very stormy and raining, cold. WN	
12-11-14 LA GORGUE	Evacuated 4 wounded and 2 sick to the Clearing Hospital at MERVILLE – CAPT ALEXANDER of MULE CORPS wounded the units attached to this Hospital A.D.M.S inspected the hospital – No5804 P⁰ W. WHEWELL 1st CONNAUGHT RANGERS died of shell wound of right femur, and was buried in LA GORGUE cemetery. 13th Private to D.A.G. ECHELON BASE – 9 wounded and 5 sick admitted today. Weather wet and stormy. WN	

WAR DIARY or INTELLIGENCE SUMMARY. No 7 B.F.A.

Army Form C. 2118.

33

Hour, Date, Place.	Summary of Events and Information.	Remarks and references to Appendices.
13-11-14 LA GORGUE	Evacuated 7 wounded and 1 sick to No 6 Clearing Hospital at MERVILLE – MAJOR C.A. JAMIESON 9th BHOPAL INFANTRY suffering from Bronchitis and CAPT G. STACK. R.E. suffering from rheumatism admitted to field hospital. Transferred to No 6 Clearing Hospital at MERVILLE – LIEUT A. DONALDSON 34th SIKH PIONEERS admitted with Dysentery. 17 sick and 12 wounded admitted. – Pte JOHN BURNAM 56th GERMAN INFANTRY – 7th WEST PHALIAN CORPS wounded admitted with two bayonet and one gunshot wounds. 2/Lt LIEUT E. MORRIS, 1st CONNAUGHT RANGERS admitted with gunshot wound of cheek slight. Weather wet and cold. LW.	
14-11-14 LA GORGUE	Evacuated 3 officers to No 6 Clearing Hospital at MERVILLE – evacuated 4 sick + 10 wounded. Returned to MERVILLE Hospital 4 sick discharged to duty. LIEUT R. BROWN 1st MANCHESTER REGT admitted with gunshot wound of left eye severe – one boy sent with horse and dulie. A & C received Divine services. 1 sick + 1 wounded admitted. Weather very stormy cold with rain. LW.	
15-11-14 LA GORGUE	Admitted 2 Lieut HENDERSON, 1st MANCHESTER REGT gunshot wound left arm. Wired to D.A.G. 3rd ECHELON BASE – Lieut 790's CORPL W. DYER 1st CONNAUGHT RANGERS died at 9 a.m. from gunshot wound of knee and buried in LAGORGUE Cemetery. German wounded Pte admitted on 13th evacuated to Clearing Hospital No 6 at MERVILLE	

Army Form C. 2118.

WAR DIARY
or
INTELLIGENCE SUMMARY.   No 7 B.F.A.

(Erase heading not required.)

Instructions regarding War Diaries and Intelligence Summaries are contained in F. S. Regs., Part II, and the Staff Manual respectively. Title pages will be prepared in manuscript.

Hour, Date, Place.	Summary of Events and Information.	Remarks and references to Appendices.
15-11-14 LA GORGUE	Received 1 transfer from No 14 FIELD AMBULANCE – Admitted 12 wounded and 46 sick – Evacuated to No 8 Clearing Hospital at MERVILLE sick – 19 wounded. Weather cold and wet.	
16-11-14 LA GORGUE 12.a.m.	Received working instructions from A.D.M.S. to move to ZELOBE – LOCON the hospital (school) where to be found (killed – have been found on the Unit) near sent MAJOR B.S. BARTLETT to select billets etc. at 12 noon – Admitted 9 wounded and 3 sick – Evacuated 6 wounded and 12 sick to No 6 Clearing Hospital at MERVILLE. Order received from A.D.M.S. to be prepared to move during the night. Weather wet and cold. W.N.	
17-11-14 10 a.m LA GORGUE LOCON 12 noon	Marched for LOCON at 10 a.m. and arrived at 12 noon. The hospital was opened for sick. Unit in billets. Weather very cold & hard frost at night.	
LOCON. 18-11-14.	No 9293 Pte W. MARTIN 1st WEST RIDING REGT awarded 4 days Field Punishment No 2 and P.C. returning to Cell for swearing and for being drunk in camp. AMC Cpt admitted to hospital sick. Hospital closed. Weather freezing with occasional snow.	
LOCON 19-11-14 20-11-14		

Army Form C. 2118.

7 35

WAR DIARY
or
INTELLIGENCE SUMMARY. No 7 B. F.A.

(Erase heading not required.)

Instructions regarding War Diaries and Intelligence Summaries are contained in F. S. Regs., Part II, and the Staff Manual respectively. Title pages will be prepared in manuscript.

Hour, Date, Place.	Summary of Events and Information.	Remarks and references to Appendices.

21-11-14 LOCON

9 a.m. ambulances better. Motor Army Corps Order sent in Ambulances to division has had a wrecked car and were unable to attempt Received Instructions to furnish Motor Ambulance cars attached to convoy from the A.S.C. Drivers attached—
1 A.B. Cav. Bde have sent back to 112 I.F.A. an ambulance Waggon which was sent out with two Major J.D. Beaumond Woolwright, ADMS, B.S. BARTLETT and CAPTN D.H.G. MACARTHUR to reconnoitre ground over which Bde. Cav. were going to attack on 23-11-14. Cav. were held to have suspended operation in held up on ordinance — Received instructions from A.D.M.S. to take over MESPLEUX FARM to open Hospital on 23-11-14. — Weather freezing & very cold. LW.

22-11-14 LOCON

Two six horse Ambulances waggons attached to this Unit- in order by A.D.M.S. attached to the BAD. Cavalry Brigade Field Ambulance. SECUNDERABAD. Cavalry Brigade Field Ambulance. Sickness A.S.C. attached; one was sent out on sick transport duty one three hospital it was often he was left present to No 8 B.F.A.— Weather very cold and frosty. Moved to MESPLAUX FARM today. Medical Stores arrived today from Advance Medical Depot.

WAR DIARY or INTELLIGENCE SUMMARY. No 7 B, F.A.

Army Form C. 2118.

P 36

(Erase heading not required.)

Instructions regarding War Diaries and Intelligence Summaries are contained in F. S. Regs., Part II, and the Staff Manual respectively. Title pages will be prepared in manuscript.

Hour, Date, Place.	Summary of Events and Information.	Remarks and references to Appendices.
23-11-14 2 p.m. LA CASSAN.	Marched to LA CASSAN from LOCON and opened A and C sections at MESPLAUX FARM – 2 b.w. carried orders from A.D.M.S. re evacuation of wounded to LE TOURET. Issued orders for opening 24 + 25 attached LIEUT: F. VON-STEGLITZ and LIEUT C.H.M DENNYS 1st CONNAUGHT RANGER admitted and transferred to the LAHORE CLEARING HOSPITAL at LILLERS. CAPT J.F. BOYD I.M.S admitted (rheum) 2 + sick 1st CONNAUGHT RANGERS admitted and transferred to Clearing Hospital LAHORE at LILLERS.	Appendices 24 + 25 attached
12 midnight	LIEUT R.I.M DAVIDSON 1st MANCHESTER REGt admitted at midnight [unclear] wounded by fragment of shell and died at 12.20 a.m. 8 sick and 6 wounded admitted at midnight – LW	Four cases of frostbite 2nd CONNAUGHT – that was killed in division was admitted as sick
24-11-14 10 a.m. LA CASSAN.	LIEUT W.L. FARWELL 2nd GHURKA RIFLES admitted with sprain of hand and was transferred to LAHORE CLEARING HOSPITAL at LILLERS. – CAPT J.F. BOYD I.M.S evacuated to LAHORE CLEARING HOSPITAL 5 wounded and 9 sick evacuated to LAHORE CLEARING HOSPITAL – LIEUT R.I.M. DAVIDSON was buried at LOCON cemetery at 4 pm (R.C.) Wink	Two cases of frostbite admitted to hospital – Nature of which was sick
4 p.m.	G.D.A.Q. 3rd ECHELON at BASE. – No 9124 Pt. W TRAYNOR 1st WEST RIDING REGt awarded 10 days R.P. No 2 for absence from duty. – No L.D.T. 5 Dr BRADBURY R. A.S.C awarded 4 days F.P. No 2. for absence from duty.	

Army Form C. 2118.

WAR DIARY
or
INTELLIGENCE SUMMARY. No 7 B.F.A.

(Erase heading not required.)

Hour, Date, Place.	Summary of Events and Information.	Remarks and references to Appendices.
24-11-14 LA CASSAN 8.30 AM 5 PM	1 Six horse ambulance wagon issued to O.C. 18th Brigade R.F.A. in place of A.D.M.S. – Capt. G.P. R. WHEATLEY S + T No 2 Coy. A.S.C. admitted to hospital 1 wounded and 16 sick admitted to hospital – Orders received from A.D.M.S. – Lahore Division at 5 p.m. issued. Vide appendices 26 + 27 – Weather cold and thawing.	Appendices 26-27 attached
25-11-14 LA CASSAN	Capt E.A. TRAFFORD 52nd SIKHS attached JULLUNDER BRIGADE AMMUNITION COLUMN admitted 24th in and transferred to LAHORE Clearing Hospital at LILLERS at 6 p.m. previous run. 9 sick Connaught Rangers 5 sick – 1 wounded and 12 sick transferred to Lahore Clearing Hospital at LILLERS – No 10066 Pte J. KITSON 1st WEST RIDING REGT was awarded 14 days F.P. No 2 for being absent without leave from 12 noon to 12 midnight on 23/24. Duties reinstated from 18th Brigade R.F.A in place of ADMS. sent order to Bearer Division the appendices 26+29 5 wounded and 30 sick admitted to hospital (2amb). Weather cooler – No frost. LN	Appendices 28 + 29 attached
26-11-14 LA CASSAN 1.45 P.M	Capt G.P.R. WHEATLEY S+T att'd 2nd Coy A.S.C who had been suffering from malarial fever discharged to duty. Lieut H.N. URMSTON 59th SEIND RIFLES admitted 1st 1.45 p.m. with gunshot wound of head (moderate) (dangerous) wire to D.A.G. 3rd ECHELON BASE – Several others to Base Division. high appendices 30 + 31 attached. Received 184 wagons Sowal Present. + Lewis A.B. Coy of personnel issued 121 other men attached as butlers to O/C Dulhi Div ? at LILLERS Wounded evacuated 1 wounded + 12 sick (with) admitted 26 sick + wounded to train (sqdn). Weather wet & pouring. LN	Appendices 30 + 31 attached

WAR DIARY
INTELLIGENCE SUMMARY. No 7 B, F.A.

Army Form C. 2118.

Hour, Date, Place.	Summary of Events and Information.	Remarks and references to Appendices.
27-11-14 LACASSAN	180 fm wind wanted work received from ordnance and issued to A.B.C and A.H.C. – Pte J. Spode Cough referred hospital & slightly on sick list from hospital – 19 sick and 2 slightly wounded discharged from hospital to duty.	Appendices Nos 32 & 33 attached.
6.15 p.m.	No. 2099 Pte H. WINDLE 1st MANCHESTER REGt died at 6.15 p.m. from shell wound of abdomen. LIEUT H.N. IRMITON 69th SCINDE RIFLES stated in hospital as he unfit to move to Base at present. To proceed next to Bearer Division held appendices 32 & 33 attached. MAJOR J. CORLET 15th INDIAN LANCERS	
9 p.m.	admitted 9 p.m. with shrapnel wound left foot. LIEUT A.C. MOUTRAY 1st CONNAUGHT RANGERS admitted	
9.30 p.m.	with a severe gunshot wound (b) at 9.30 p.m. Admitted 7 wounded and 29 sick – 2 wounded and 13 sick, 1–3 goods Corps reported have discharged from hospital – Brought 2 stretcher bearer wounds left knee in shrapnel & the slightly & not. Reling June – weather milder & a bit not.	
28-11-14 4 a.m. LACASSAN	LIEUTt F.E. BULLER 3rd SAPPERS + MINERS admitted with gunshot wound of buttock at 4 a.m. No. 2099 Pte H. WINDLE 1st MANCHESTER REGt was buried in LOCON cemetery. – 5 A.B.C. bearers reported on duty from hospital – Admitted 3 wounded and 39 sick. – Evacuated 4 wounded 5 sick and 14 wounded men and 18 sick to later Clearing Hospt by L/LCRS. – Discharged 1 slightly wounded & 6 sick to duty. Send down to Bearer Division ride appendices 34 & 35 attached. Weather mild, windy twp.	Appendices 34 & 35 attached. Appendices 36 & 37 attached. J.N.

WAR DIARY

or

INTELLIGENCE SUMMARY. No 7 B.F.A. # 39

Army Form C. 2118.

(Erase heading not required.)

Instructions regarding War Diaries and Intelligence Summaries are contained in F. S. Regs., Part II, and the Staff Manual respectively. Title pages will be prepared in manuscript.

Hour, Date, Place.	Summary of Events and Information.	Remarks and references to Appendices.
29-11-14. 8:00 a.m. LA CASSAN	No. 8974 Pte T. MARTIN 1st CONNAUGHT RANGERS was buried at 8:30 a.m. in a graveyard surrounded by hedge & trees in Richebourg l'Avoué N. of CON cemetery at 4 p.m. Ambulance wagon + two horses rejoined Draw.	I send orders to Brewer Division Appendices 36 & 39 attached
4.40 p.m.	A.D.S. + T.W. No. 2 A.D.M.S. – CAPT. H.E. GROWSE 15th SIKHS admitted with gunshot wound of head at 4.40 p.m. – Admitted 19 sick and 4 wounded – Discharged 2 sick and AH.C. + A.B.C. men have been supplied with for hand carts. Weather mild, showering and returned.	
30-11-14. 1:30 p.m. LA CASSAN	Wire to D.A.G. 3rd ECHELON BASE & CAPT GROWSE No. 7877 Pte F PARROT 2nd LEICESTER REGT died. No. 9495 Pte A DAVIS 2nd LEICESTER REGT died & also a gunshot wound of head at 5:30 a.m. – while there were only 2 found wounded at 1.30 p.m. – While there were 2 own Reported at GORRE – Drew Draws 37 – for the Field Hospital & Field Fund in lieu of payment drew two orderlies which I send orders to Brewer Division with the approvals – 38 & 39 attached – 10 Conf with Horse drive letter – order – & form associate with orders – returned to O.C. LAHORE DIV. TRAIN – one a man was letter – #SIKHS kept in Hospital for two days – CAPT. H.E. GROWSE 15th SIKHS kept in Hospital – Capt. H.E. GROWSE 15th SIKHS admitted at 9 p.m. Benefitting from 9 a.m. CONNAUGHT RANGERS admitted at 9 p.m. an oppressive the result of overstrain an oppressive in the trenches from	Attendees 38 & 39 attached.

Gulab Singh & Sons, Calcutta.—No. 22 Army C.—6-9-14.—1,07,000.

Army Form C. 2118.

£ 40

WAR DIARY

or

INTELLIGENCE SUMMARY. No 7 B.F.A.

(Erase heading not required.)

Instructions regarding War Diaries and Intelligence Summaries are contained in F. S. Regs., Part II, and the Staff Manual respectively. Title pages will be prepared in manuscript.

Hour, Date, Place.	Summary of Events and Information.	Remarks and references to Appendices.
30-11-14 LA CASSAN	Admitted 18 sick and 4 wounded — Evacuated 3 wounded and 10 sick — Discharged 28 sick to duty — The prevalent disease is myalgia owing to exposure to cold & in the trenches in wet weather. L Watson Lieut Colonel RAMC O.C. No 7 B.F.A.	

Appendix 15

No 6 7.A. Orders by Lt-Colonel L. Wray
O.C. No 7 B.7.A.
LAGORGUE
3-11-14

Ref: Map ST OMER Sheet 1/80000

Ref: Order A.D.M.S. LAHORE DIVN 3/11/14

1. The whole Bearer Division with wagons will be at A in BACQUEROT at 8 p.m. tonight.

2. Reports will be sent to Divisions at LAGORGUE.

L Wray Lt. Colonel
R.A.M.C.
O.C. No 7 B.7A

By hand 4.40 p.m.

MAJOR BARTLETT
R.A.M.C.
CAPT McARTHUR.

Appendix 16

I. A. F. Z201
P.—Corps.
G.—Depts.

MEMORANDUM

FROM: The ADMS Lahore Divn

TO: The OC. No 7 B.F.A

No. _____ Station _____ Date 3-11-14

Position of Bearer Division and Waggons tonight at 8 p.m.

No 7 B.F.A. — Whole bearer division and waggons at A in BACQUEROT.

The bearer Division and Waggons must be at A in Bacquerot by 8 p.m.

WMGray(?)
Colonel ADMS

To
The O.C.
No: 7 B79

Appendix 16

MEMORANDUM.

From: The ADMS Lahore Divn   To: The OC No 7 BFA

No. _____   Station _____   Date 4-11-14

Position of Bearer Division and Waggons tonight:—

No 7 B.F.A.   Whole bearer division and waggons at <u>A</u> in RUE-du-BACQUEROT.

The bearer Division and Waggons must be at the above place by 8 p.m. tonight.

The portion of my letter No 179 of 4-11-14 ordering to relieve Major Bartlett from the Dressing Station is cancelled.

[signature]
Colonel I.M.S.
A.D.M.S.

O.H.M.S.

To OC
No 7 SFA

No 7 F.A. Appendix 17 Orders by Lieut-Colonel L. Wayram
O.C. No 7 B F.A.

LA GORGUE
4-11-14.

Ref: map ST OMER Sheet 1/80000

Ref Order A.D.M.S. LAHORE DIV N. 4/11/14

1. The whole Bearer Division with wagons will be at A in BACQUEROT at 8 p.m. tonight.

2. Reports will be sent to Tenth Division at LA GORGUE

L Wayram Lt-Colonel
RAMC
O.C. No 7 B F.A.

By hand 6.35 p.m.
MAJOR Bartlett
RAMC
CAPT McARTHUR
RAMC

"A" Form. Appendix 18 Army Form C. 2121.
MESSAGES AND SIGNALS.

TO — OC. N/ 4 B/a

Orders re bearers & waggons same as last night. Troops on right of your front in place of composite battalion are 9th Bhopal Inf - 57th Rifles & 129th Baluchis holding ground from house 300 yds S.E. of IX in ROUGE CROIX to a point 400 yds S.W. Remaining troops on left unchanged - OC 7th Bde. asked to communicate with bearers at 9 in RUE du BACQUEROT at 8 pm.

Im Sloan
Maj
for ADMS

From
Place ESTAIRES 5.11.14
Time 3-30 pm

Appendix 19   8

No. 7. A. orders by Lt-Colonel L. Way RAMC
O.C. No 7 B. 7. A.
LA GORGUE
5-11-14

Ref: map ST OMER sheet 1/80000

Ref: orders by A.D.M.S. LAHORE DIVN
dated 5/11/14.

1. The whole Bearer Division with wagons will be at A in RUE DU BACQEROT at 8 p.m. tonight.

2. The area for collecting wounded will be from Kohee 300 yds S.E of X in ROUGE CROIX to a point 400 yds S.W.

3. O.C Bearer Divn will get into touch with G.O.C. 7th BRIGADE who has been asked to communicate at A in BACQUEROT.

4. Reports will be sent to Tent Division at LA GORGUE

By hand at 5:10 p.m.   L. Way Lt Colonel
To MAJOR BARTLETT   RAMC
   CAPT MAC ARTHUR O.C. No 7 B. 7. A

Appendix 20

I. A. F. Z2011.
P.—Corps.
G.—Depts.

MEMORANDUM.

From The ADMS
Lahore Divn

To The O.C.
7oy B.F.A.

No. 248   Station _____   Date 6-11-14

Orders regarding bearers and waggons same as last night ie 8 p.m. at the A in RUE-du-BACQUEROT.

Jn Sloan
Major RAMC
for ADMS

Appendix 21

No.q 7.A orders by Lieut-Colonel L. Wray
O.C. No 7 B.F.A.   R.Art.

                                LA GORGUE
                                6-11-14
Ref: Map, ST OMER sheet   1/80000
Ref: order No 248 A.D.M.S. LAHORE DIV Nd/6 11/14

1. The whole Beauv. Division with wagons
will be at A in RUE DU BACQUEROT
at 8 p.m. tonight.

2. Reports will be sent to Jaunt
Division at LA GORGUE

                            L Wray Lt Colonel
                                 R.Art.
                            O.C. No 7 B.F.A.
By hand 6.30 p.m
    MAJOR BARTLETT
    CAPT: MACARTHUR.

Appendix "A" Form 22 — Army Form C. 2121.

MESSAGES AND SIGNALS.

Prefix	Code	Words	Charge	This message is on a/c of:	Recd. at m.
Office of Origin and Service Instructions		Sent			Date
		At m.		Service.	From
		To			
		By		(Signature of "Franking Officer.")	By

TO — O.C. No 4 Bre

| Sender's Number | Day of Month | In reply to Number | A A A |

Bearers & Waggons at 8 P.m to A in RUE du BACQUEROT regiments in trenches asked to communicate with bearers at rendezvous are EAST SURREYS – DEVONS – D.C.L.I. who relieve R. SCOTS FUSILIERS in night –

Jn Sloan
Maj
for adms

From
Place ESTAIRES 4/11/14
Time 4.40 pm

The above may be forwarded as now corrected. (Z)

Appendix 23.   11

No 10 7. Orders by Lieut- Colonel
L. Way RAMC. O.C. No 7 B.F.A.

                                LA GORGUE
                                7-11-14.

Ref: map ST OMER sheet $\frac{1}{80,000}$.

Ref: Orders by A.D.M.S. LAHORE DIVⁿ 7f

<u>1</u> Bearers and wagons will be at A u
RUE DU BACQUEROT at 8. p.m toni;

<u>2</u> Regiments in the trenches asked to
communicate with the bearers at the
rendezvous.

<u>3</u> Reports will be sent to Lieut Divis
at LA GORGUE

                              L Way Lt Colonel
                                RAMC
By hand at 6.45 p.m O.C. No 7 B.F.A.
MAJOR BARTLETT
CAPT: MACARTHUR

"A" Form.   Army Form C. 2121.
MESSAGES AND SIGNALS.   No. of Message_____

Prefix___ Code___	Words	Charge	This message is on a/c of:	Recd. at___ m.
Office of Origin and Service Instructions.				Date___
Approved	Sent At___ m.		......Service.	From___
	To			
	By		(Signature of "Franking Officer.")	By___

TO — O.C. No 4 B/A

| Sender's Number | Day of Month | In reply to Number | A A A |

77 Fd. Ambs. should proceed to MESPLAUX and open there for reception of wounded by three pm. today AAA Bearer Division should form dressing station at LE TOURET Bearers & waggons to rendezvous tonight at 6 pm at Cross roads immediately W of R. in RUE de L'EPINETTE & at Cross roads 400 yds N of F in FESTUBERT AAA Motor ambulances will be at LE TOURET at seven p.m. AAA. Bearers should get touch with MANCHESTER Regt. at RUE de L'EPINETTE and with CONNAUGHTS near FESTUBERT AAA. Report tonight to ADMS at ~~LOCON~~ CHATEAU DURAULT & tomorrow to LOCON

From Place DURAULT   23/11/14
Time   10 am

No 11, 7. A ~~Order by Lt-Colonel~~ L. W ay
R.A.M.C. ~~Appendix 25~~
O.C. No 7 B.F.A.

LA CASSAN
23-11-14

Ref map

Ref order No 77 dated 23/11/14 by A.D.M.S LAHORE Divn

1. The Bearer Division will form a Dressing Station at LA TOURET

2. The Bearers and wagons will rendezvous tonight at 6 p.m. at crossroads immediately W of R in RUE DE L'EPINETTE and at crossroads 400 yds N of F in FESTUBERT

3. Bearers will get in touch with Units at RUE DE L'EPINETTE and FESTUBERT.

4. Motor ambulances will be at LE TOURET at 7 p.m.

5. Reports will be sent to Head Division at MESPLAUX FARM

By hand 2 p.m.
MAJOR B.S. BARTLETT
CAPT D.H. MACARTHUR

L W ay Lt Colonel
R.A.M.C.
O.C. No 7 B.F.A.

"A" Form.　　　　　　　　Army Form C. 2121.

MESSAGES AND SIGNALS.　　No. of Message _____

| Prefix ____ Code ____ m. | Words | Charge | This message is on a/c of: | Recd. at ____ m. |
| Office of Origin and Service Instructions | Sent At ____ m. To ____ By ____ | 26 (Signature of "Franking Officer.") | Service. | Date ____ From ____ By ____ |

Appendix

TO — O.C. No 4 B.F.A.

Sender's Number	Day of Month	In reply to Number	**A A A**
82	24		

Orders for waggons and bearers same as last night AAA.

Sgn Sloan
Maj
for advance

From
Place LOCON
Time 4-30 pm

No 7 B7A

<u>Appendix 27</u>

14

No 17. 7. A. order by Lt Colonel L. Way
RAMC. O.C No 7 B.F.A

LA CASSAN
24-11-14

Ref map MERVILLE-LE BASSÉ 1/4000

Ref: order No 83 dated 24/11 by A.D.M.S LAHORE DIVn

1. The Bear Division will form a dressing station at LE TOURET.

2. The Bearers & wagons will rendezvous tonight at 6 p.m at crossroads immediately W of R in RUE DE L'EDINETTE and at crossroads 400 yds N of E in FESTUBERT.

3. Bearers will get in touch with Units at RUE DE L'EPINETTE and FESTUBERT.

4. Motor ambulances will be at LE TOURET at 7 p.m.

5. Reports will be sent to 7 end Division at MESPLAUX FARM.

By hand 5 p.m.
MAJOR B.S. BARTLETT
CAPT D.H. MACARTHUR

L Way Lt Colonel
RAMC
O.C No 7 B.F.A

"A" Form. Army Form C. 2121.

MESSAGES AND SIGNALS.

TO — O.C. No 1 B.F.A.

Sender's Number	Day of Month	In reply to Number	AAA
92	25		

Orders for rendezvous of bearers and waggons as for last night AAA Return of admissions for previous 24 hours must reach this office not later than 10 am this morning if necessary all surgical cases to be shown as remaining

From
Place LOCON
Time 2-55 PM

Appendix 29

No 13 F.A. order by Lt Colonel L. Waystone
O.C. No 7 B.F.A.

LA GASSAN
25-11-14

Ref. map MERVILLE – LE BASSE 1/40000
Ref. order No 92 dated 25/11 by A.D.M.S.
LAHORE DIVISION

1. The Bearer Division will form a dressing station at LE TOURET.

2. The Bearers and waggons will rendezvous tonight at 6 p.m. at cross roads immediately W of R in RUE DE L'EPINETTE and at cross roads 400 yds N of E in FESTUBERT.

3. Bearers will get in touch with Units at RUE DE L'EPINETTE and FESTUBERT.

4. Motor ambulances will be at LE TOURET at 7 p.m.

5. Reports will be sent to Tent Divn at MES PLAUX FARM.

By hand 4.30 p.m.
MAJOR BARTLETT
CAPT MACARTHUR
L Waystone
R.A.M.
O.C. No 7 B.F.A.

"A" Form.   Army Form C. 2121.

MESSAGES AND SIGNALS.

Prefix	Code	m.	Words	Charge	This message is on a/c of:	Recd. a	m.

Office of Origin and Service Instructions

Appendix 30

Sent At ___ m.
To
By
(Signature of "Franking Officer.")

Date
From
By

TO { O.C. 1 B.F.A.

Sender's Number	Day of Month	In reply to Number	AAA
98	26/16		

Orders for rendezvous bearers and wagons B for last night

From
Place LOCON
Time

The above may be forwarded as now corrected. (Z)

Censor. Signature of Addressee or person authorised to telegraph in his name.

Recd 1945
A.D.M.S.

Appendix 31

No 119. 7.A orders by Lt. Colonel L. Wray, repeat
O.C. No 7. B. F.A.

LA CASSAN
26-11-14.

Ref: map MERVILLE — LE BASSE 1/40000.
Ref: order No 98 dated 26/11 by A.D.M.S LAHORE DIVn

1. The Bearers and wagons will rendezvous and carry out the orders laid down in my No 13 7.A order dated 25/11/14.

L Wray Lieut Colonel
Raine
O.C. No 7 B.F.A

By hand 4.45 p.m.
MAJOR BARTLETT
CAPT MACARTHUR

"A" Form. Army Form C. 2121.
MESSAGES AND SIGNALS.

TO O.C. 7 B.F.A.

Sender's Number: 101
Day of Month: 27

AAA

Orders for rendezvous bearers and waggons as for last night

From: ADMS Lahore Div

Appendix 32

No. 15. 7. Order by Lt-Colonel L. Way
R.A.M.C. O.C. No 7 B.F.A.

LA CASSAN
27-11-14
Ref map MERVILLE—LE BASSÉE 1/40000
Ref. order No 101 dated 27/11/14 by A.D.M.S.
LAHORE Divⁿ

1. The Bearers and wagons will
rendezvous and carry out the
orders laid down in my No 13
F.A. orders dated 26/11/14

L Way Lieut-Colonel
R.A.M.C.
O.C. No 7 B.F.A.

By hand 4.45 pm
MAJOR BARTLETT
CAPT MACARTHUR

"A" Form.   Army Form C. 2121.

MESSAGES AND SIGNALS.

Prefix ___ Code ___ Words ___ Charge ___ This message is on a/c of: ___ Recd. at ___ m.
Office of Origin and Service Instructions.
Sent At 2 m.
To
By   (Signature of "Franking Officer.")
Date ___ From ___ By ___

TO O.C. No 7 B. F. A.

Sender's Number	Day of Month	In reply to Number	A A A
103	28		

Orders for rendezvous convoys and wagons as for last night AAA Refilling point for tomorrow same as today

From ADMS Lahore Divn
Place
Time

Signature: [signed] Colonel ADMS

Appendix 35.

No 15 F.A order by Lt-Colonel L. Way
R.Awe O.C. No 7 B. F. A.

LA CASSAN
28 - 11 - 14

Ref: map MERVILLE - LE BASSÉ $\frac{1}{40000}$

Ref: order No 103 dated 28/11/14 by A.D.M.S LAHORE DIVⁿ

1. The Bearers and wagons will rendezvous and carry out the orders laid down in my No 13 F.A. Orders dated 25/11/14

L. Way Lieut-Colonel
R.A.M.C.

By hand 4.30 p.m.
MAJOR BARTLETT
CAPT MAC ARTHUR.

"A" Form. Army Form C. 2121.

MESSAGES AND SIGNALS.

TO — O.C. No. 7 B.F.A.

Sender's Number	Day of Month	In reply to Number	AAA
107	29		

Orders for rendezvous bearers and wagons as for last night AAA Refilling point for tomorrow as today at 10 a.m.

From A.D.M.S, Lahore Division
Place
Time

Col. ImS
A.D.M.S

YB 7a

017 + A. Order by Lt-Colonel L. Way
Paine, O.C. No 7 B.F.A.

       LACASSAN.
       29-11-14

Ref maps MERVILLE LABASSÉ 1/40000

Ref order No 107 dated 29/11 by A.D.M.S. LAHORE DIVN

1. The Bearers and wagons will rendezvous and carry out the orders laid down in by No 13 F.A. orders dated 25/11/14

          L Way Lieut-Colonel
              Paine
      O.C. No 7 B.F.A.

By hand 4.30 p.m.
MAJOR BARTLETT
CAPT MACARTHUR.

No 16. F.A. Orders by Lt Colonel L. Way
RAMC   O.C. No 7 B. F.A.

LA CASSAN
30-11-14

Ref map MERVILLE - LE BASSÉ 1/40000

Ref order No 111 dated 30/11/14 by A.D.M.S.
MORE DIVN

1. The Bearers and wagons will rendezvous and carry out the orders laid down in my No 12 F.A. orders dated 25/11/14

L Way Lt Colonel
RAMC
O.C. No 7 B.F.A.

By hand 4:30 pm
MAJOR BARTLETT
CAPT MACARTHUR.

"A" Form. Army Form C. 2121.

MESSAGES AND SIGNALS.

TO	O.C., 7 B.F.A.
O.C., 112 F.A.
O.C., 111 F.F.A.

Sender's Number	Day of Month	In reply to Number	
111	30th	—	A A A

Orders for rendezvous bearers and wagons as for last night AAA Refilling point tomorrow same as today at 10 a.m.

From: A.D.M.S., Lahore Division

7 B. 7. a.

War Diary of
No 7. British Field Ambulance

From 1-12-14
To 31-12-14.

Volume I
Pp 41 to 50.

Army Form C. 2118

LIEUT-COLONEL L. WAY, R.A.M.C.

VOLUME 4.

WAR DIARY or **INTELLIGENCE SUMMARY.**

O.C. No. 7 BRITISH FIELD AMBULANCE. From 1-12-14 to 31-12-14

No. 7 BRITISH FIELD AMBULANCE

(Erase heading not required.)

Instructions regarding War Diaries and Intelligence Summaries are contained in F. S. Regs., Part II, and the Staff Manual respectively. Title pages will be prepared in manuscript.

Hour, Date, Place.	Summary of Events and Information.	Remarks and references to Appendices.
1-12-14 LA CASSAN	All cases evacuated and lorry sent to the LAHORE CLEARING HOSPITAL at LILLERS – CAPT R. PAYNE 1st CONNAUGHT RANGERS and CAPT H.E. GROWSE 15th SIKHS evacuated for Clearing Hospital LILLERS today. Send order to Bearer Division rejoining tomorrow – 40 admitted – LIEUT H.T.D. HICKMAN 34th SIKH PIONEERS admitted for fever N.Y.D. – Admitted 11 wounded and 16 sick. Evacuated to 6 wounded and 7 sick – 5 cases discharged to duty. – Weather warm and almost dry. JW	Appendices 40 & 41 attached
2-12-14 12.30am LA CASSAN 10.0am	Hospital inspected today by SIR JAMES WILLCOCKS G.O.C. Indian Army Corps and he expressed himself very well pleased with the LIEUT H.T.D. HICKMAN 34th SIKH PIONEERS was evacuated to LAHORE Clearing Hospital today. O.C. case of Pneumonia was admitted 15 gt Highland L.I. and evacuated to LAHORE Clearing Hospital today – Issued orders that Bearer Division who rejoin 42 + 43 – Admitted 8 wounded and 1 Gurkha wounded PTE R. KAUFEMANN 170th RGt 9th BADEN CORPS gunshot wound of left thigh severe – 18 sick admitted. Evacuated 8 wounded and 4 sick – 3 men discharged to duty. Weather stormy, wet and wild. JW	Appendices 42 & 43 attached
3-12-14 LA CASSAN	War diary for November despatched to A.G. BASE. Issued orders to Bearer Division re appendices 44-45. Order received from A.D.M.S. LAHORE DIVN to proceed for shelter and appendix 46 attached and to proceed to ZELOBE and other appendix. Rifle attached – CAPT W.M. THOMSON SEAFORTH HIGHLANDERS admitted with a bullet wound of neck (severe) –	Appendices 44 & 45 attached and other appendix attached

Army Form C. 2118

WAR DIARY
or
INTELLIGENCE SUMMARY. N° 07 B.F.A.

42

(Erase heading not required.)

Hour, Date, Place.	Summary of Events and Information.	Remarks and references to Appendices.
3-12-14 LACASSAN	Admitted 9 wounded and 12 sick — Evacuated 10 wounded and 5 sick — 15 sick discharged to duty. Weather wet and comparatively mild — LW.	
4-12-14 LACASSAN 12 noon 1.30 p.m.	Evacuated 10 Officers and 8 wounded including the German prisoner mentioned in diary 2-12-14. Evacuated 14 sick — 7 sick discharged to duty — Closed Hospital and marched to ZELOBE — Arrived at ZELOBE and opened Hospital (A + C Sections) in a large house. Some hundred wounded were brought in but the ground floor being unsuitable (cement) [illegible] were attended to and sent on — Admitted 1 wounded (officer) and 5 sick including 1 pneumonia case and 5 sick — 1 attached to 91st Battery R.F.A. — Weather wet — mild — LW.	
6-12-14 ZELOBE	Admitted one accidental gunshot wound of head (severe case) was evacuated to Chauny hospital after being dressed — Admitted 4 sick and evacuated 4 sick — Weather wet — stormy — mild — LW	
6-12-14 ZELOBE	Admitted 4 sick and evacuated 4 sick — ASST SURGEON C. A. EMILE I.S.M.D. reported his arrival for duty 110 BATTY R.G.A. — Gun. wag. Corps handed over to 14 division + the A.S.C. attached to this Unit — Weather heavy wet — mild and stormy. LW.	
7-12-14  ZELOBE	CAPT A.T.J. MITCHELL R.A.M.C. has been granted 7 days leave to LONDON by the G.O.C. INDIAN ARMY CORPS.	

Army Form C. 2118

43

WAR DIARY
or
INTELLIGENCE SUMMARY. No 7 B.F.A.

(Erase heading not required.)

Instructions regarding War Diaries and Intelligence Summaries are contained in F.S. Regs., Part II, and the Staff Manual respectively. Title pages will be prepared in manuscript.

Hour, Date, Place.	Summary of Events and Information.	Remarks and references to Appendices.
7-12-14 ZELOBE	Admitted 8 sick, and evacuated 6 sick to duty — Weather wet, stormy and mild	LN.
8-12-14 ZELOBE	Asst Surgeon H.V. DEWEY I.S.M.D. proceeded on 10 days leave to LONDON granted by the G.O.C. INDIAN ARMY CORPS. — 2nd LIEUT A. KNIGHT-BRUCE 32nd BATTY R.F.A. admitted with fever. N.Y.D. and evacuated to LAHORE Clearing Hospital. 6 I.A.B.C. joined this Unit on transfer from the 8 INFANTRY BRIGADE — Admitted 6 sick and evacuated 8 sick to Clearing Hospital. By order of A.D.M.S. 3rd Br. Division 1st Asst Surgeon to report for duty for supply of this Unit near BETHUNE — Weather shower, wet.	LN.
9-12-14 ZELOBE	The two R.A.M.S. general duty orderlies who were attached to this Unit have been transferred to the A.D.S + T just duty in the RESERVE PARK in lieu of 2 R.A.M.S. — Admitted 7 sick + evacuated 7 sick — Three of the evacuated cases were N.Y.D. fever and were supposed of pneumonia. All preventive measures were taken + were sent to the O.C. LAHORE Clearing Hospital drawing his attention to these cases — Weather mild, stormy + windy.	LN.
10-12-14 8 p.m. ZELOBE	Received an order from the A.D.M.S. to evacuate the sick forenoon and march at 12 noon to BETHUNE and that the Hospital in the SEMINARY (COLLEGE ST VAAST) for which admitted 15 sick, evacuated 11 sick, and three were forward to duty — Weather, wet and stormy.	LN.

Army Form O. 21
44

WAR DIARY
or
INTELLIGENCE SUMMARY. No 7 B.F.A.

(Erase heading not required.)

Instructions regarding War Diaries and Intelligence Summaries are contained in F. S. Regs., Part II, and the Staff Manual respectively. Title pages will be prepared in manuscript.

Hour, Date, Place.	Summary of Events and Information.	Remarks and references to Appendices.
11-12-14. ZELOBE 12 noon BETHUNE 2 p.m.	Admitted 7 sick; evacuated 17 sick and 1 wounded. Marched to BETHUNE at 12 noon. Arrived at BETHUNE at 2 p.m. and opened at C.S.'s billets in the SEMINARY (COLLEGE ST VAAST). Brought 2 sick and 2 wounded (hundred) with us from ZELOBE. — Weather very wet and stormy.	
12-12-14 BETHUNE	A.S.C. Driver reported on discharge from hospital. All Wards in this hospital have been disinfected & fumigated by sulphur and lysol dressings in the past week. 8 sick and wounded 4 other ranks. — Weather fine & mild. J.W.	
13-12-14 BETHUNE	Admitted 6 sick and evacuated 7 sick to clearing hospital. — Weather wet, mild & stormy. J.W.	
14-12-14 BETHUNE	CAPT T.J. MITCHELL R.A.M.C. returned from 7 days leave to ENGLAND — Admitted 10 sick and evacuated 4 sick to Clearing hospital. — 1 man discharged to duty. — N° 9450 Pte E. ROLPH 1st WEST RIDING REG. was awarded 4 days F.P N° 2 for being improperly dressed. — Weather wet, mild & stormy. J.W.	
15-12-14 BETHUNE	MAJOR M.F. SHEA R.A.M.C. proceeded on the sick leave (N.Y.D) & was transferred to N° 4 CLEARING HOSPITAL LILLERS — 1 Driver A.S.C. returned to H.Q Coy A.S.C. being unfit for battle establishment	

WAR DIARY or INTELLIGENCE SUMMARY. No 7 B.F.A.

Army Form C. 2118
45

Hour, Date, Place.	Summary of Events and Information.	Remarks and references to Appendices.
15-12-14 7.30 p.m. BETHUNE	Operation orders received from A.D.M.S. LAHORE DIVISION for Bearer Division to go out to AUBIGNY and RUE DS BETHUNE. Left Appendices 46 & 47 after Scout Cars (47th?) Admitted 8 wounded to British - evacuated 4 sick & wounded to Clearing Hospital - Weather heavy - mostly mild Dry	Appendices 46 & 47 attached.
16-12-14 BETHUNE	Bearer Companies proceeded and worked at 2.30 a.m. No1801 Pte WARWICK 1st MANCHESTER REGT gunshot wound about died about 4.30 a.m. he was buried in the cemetery at BETHUNE - CAPT A.C. SANDERS 1st SAPPERS & MINERS and CAPT E.M. GRANT 1st H.L.I. admitted with multiple wounds. Shell wounds and transferred to No4 CLEARING HOSPITAL at LILLERS - MAJOR F.P.C. REILLY 125th NAPIERS RIFLES was admitted with gunshot wound & to No4 CLEARING HOSPITAL LILLERS. No 8148 Pte J. CRIEVEY 1st H.L.I admitted with shell wound & the knee died at 7.15 p.m —	
7.15 p.m.	Admitted 12 wounded and 6 sick - evacuated 12 wounded and 19 sick to Clearing Hospital at LILLERS, 4 sick to Clearing Hospital to be disposed of. Nothing of importance — Weather dry - mild - S.W. wind in the afternoon	
17-12-14 BETHUNE	CAPT C.A.G. MONEY 129th RIFLES I.A. admitted with gun shot wound (head) (slight) - No.4 to D.A.Q. & ECHELON BASE - 23 Officer belonging British Brigade wounded were telegraphed for instructions from O Quarter Mr LAHORE DIV.	

Army Form C. 2118.

46.

WAR DIARY

or

INTELLIGENCE SUMMARY. No 7 B.F.A.

(Erase heading not required.)

Instructions regarding War Diaries and Intelligence Summaries are contained in F. S. Regs., Part II, and the Staff Manual respectively. Title pages will be prepared in manuscript.

Hour, Date, Place.	Summary of Events and Information.	Remarks and references to Appendices.
17-12-14. BETHUNE	No 38 Driver A. GREENMAN and 1304 Driver F. BATT A.S.C. were admitted to hospital 8.45 A.M. No 2 F.A. being in BETHUNE without A.S.C. drivers on this wake sent by the A.P.M. to watch A.C. horses that delay in the meanwhile was witty. Admitted 10 sick — Neither not doing well. J.N.	
18-12-14. BETHUNE	No 9149 Pt. J. GRIEVEY 1st M.L.I. was buried in BETHUNE cemetery at 9.30 am — Lieut Surgeon H.V. DEWEY 15MB reported for duty on arrival for today's work, proving as always a great and immediate Strength — I have checked F in duty — M Laycock not so well. Admitted 9 sick.	
19-12-14. BETHUNE	Pt. J. PARADISE 2nd NORTHUMBERLAND FUSILIERS brought in dead (suicide) to the Clearing Hospital by fourteen from the result of overdose of Strychnine in solution (clearly accidentally while cleaning an abscess of the mouth) I A.B.Sgt was transferred to 112 I.F.A. N.Y.D. LIEUT (temporary) S. CROSS R.A.M.C. reported his arrival for duty, having been posted for temporary medical duty 1/ Manchester Regt by order of A.D.M.S. LAHORE DIV.— Capt C.D.K. SEAVER R.A.M.C. admitted with severe N.Y.D.— Capt J.D. SCALES 69th SCINDE RIFLES admitted with a gunshot wound of right leg (severe) wired to D.A.G. 3 Echelon Base.— Capt E.K. SQUIRES 34 Sappers & Miners admitted with a severe new penetrating wound of Right hand — Admitted 11 sick and wounded. — Neither met well today. Capt C.D.K. SEAVER R.A.M.C. & Capt J.D. SCALES 69th SCINDE RIFLES evacuated to No 4 Clearing Hospital LILLERS. J.N.	

WAR DIARY or INTELLIGENCE SUMMARY. No 7 B.F.A.

Army Form C. 2118.

47

(Erase heading not required.)

Hour, Date, Place.	Summary of Events and Information.	Remarks and references to Appendices.
20-12-14. BETHUNE	MAJOR B.S. BARTLETT R.A.M.C. reported back on transfer to No 17 B.F.A. MEERUT DIV. LIEUT'S CROSS R.A.M.C. reported from temporary duty with 1ST MANCHESTER REGT. contributed. Bearer Divisions 1) dressed out to RUE DE BETHUNE in order. D.A.D.M.S. vide appendices 48 + 49 attached. Admitted 5 Sick - 5 men wounded and 2 sick - Evacuated 6 wounded 5 Officers sick - 5 sick officers - Admitted 39 wounded and 24 sick - Evacuated 27 wounded & 26 sick. 1 man died of wounds - 1 man died 1 SCONN. AUGHT RANGERS died & was buried in the cemetery at BETHUNE - 8 wounded Germans prisoners admitted 1 man from 170th INFANTRY and 7 from the 56th INFANTRY in cattle wagons. LN	Appendices 48 + 49 attached
5 pm		
21-12-14. 5am BETHUNE	The Bearer Division returned at 5 am to BETHUNE Appendices 50+ ordered to RUE DE BETHUNE at 2-p.m. the Bearer DIV 51 attached adv. by A.D.M.S. appendices 50 + 51 attached. Sick + wounded of 1ST British Division were admitted Admitted 19 wounded officers and 19 sick officers 12 - Admitted 212 wounded and 125 sick - Evacuated 138 wounded and 17 sick - 1 man died of wounds 3 men died of wounds + were buried in BETHUNE Cemetery. Evacuated 7 German wounded - 1 German wounded died + was buried in BETHUNE Cemetery. LN	Appendices 50+ 51 attached

WAR DIARY
or
INTELLIGENCE SUMMARY. No 7 B.F.A.

Army Form C. 2118.

48

(Erase heading not required.)

Hour, Date, Place.	Summary of Events and Information.	Remarks and references to Appendices.
22-12-14 – 1.45 pm BETHUNE 2 p.m.	Bearer Division returned at 5 a.m. – CAPT MACARTHUR R.A.M.C. joined for duty with 1/1 YD Force – A.D.M.S gave orders that all cases were to be sent to civil hospital BETHUNE (on admission after 2 p.m.) – Admitted 6 (1) wounded and 3 sick – Admitted 116 wounded and 18 sick – Wounded French soldier O/142 INFANTRY admitted – Evacuated 11 wounded & 1 sick and 2 and evacuated 186 wounded more than 133 wounded soldiers –	
12 noon	Order received for A.D.M.S to move to BURBURE tomorrow – weather cold & raining –	
23-12-14 BETHUNE	CAPT D.H.O. MACARTHUR R.A.M.C. left W.Y.D Force to the Hospital Train at BETHUNE – Admitted (with Medical Officer) 3 wounded and 17 sick – Evacuated 3 wounded and 21 sick – wounded sent to No 8 Hospital Train – Wounded & sick sent to Bodegais died in Hospital at BETHUNE Canadian (No 14236 Pt J. BRICKLEY, 1st S.W. BORDERERS) wounded French soldier admitted – The Field Ambulance closed down. Permission obtained for A.D.M.S to march tomorrow – Weather cold & overcast	
12 noon		
24-12-14 10 a.m BETHUNE AUCHEL 6 p.m.	Marched to BURBURE at 10 a.m. Morning received orders from A.D.M.S to billet at AUCHEL – Arrived at AUCHEL at 6 p.m. had to search for billets Supt & lodging was not settled till 9 p.m. Wounded French men	

WAR DIARY or INTELLIGENCE SUMMARY.

Army Form C. 2118.

No 7 B.F.A. 49

(Erase heading not required.)

Hour, Date, Place.	Summary of Events and Information.	Remarks and references to Appendices.
24-12-14 AUCHEL	One Gurkha wounded. Report still in. Enquiry instituted. Orders issued for distribution by O.C. Divisional Troops. Parade conducted by A.D.M.S. 7th Division. Weather wet & fine. LW.	
25-12-14 AUCHEL	Field Ambulances closed and functioned as Hospitals. Two wounded. 1 hand, 1 foot — Westminster Pending disposal. LIEUT J.C. PYPER RAMC joined the unit for duty and has been posted to D. Section. Weather cold & frosty. LW.	
26-12-14 AUCHEL	Unit notified and ordinary routine work carried on. Horses having rough shoes screwed in frosts. M.R.H. PRINCESS MARY's gifts received and distributed. Weather cold but fine. LW.	
27-12-14 AUCHEL	Ordinary routine. Weather wet & stormy. LW.	
28-12-14 AUCHEL	CAPT W.H. O'RIORDAN reported his arrival for duty from BOULOGNE today vice MAJOR H.F SHEA proceeded on duty to RAWAL PINDI BRITISH GENERAL HOSPITAL. No 9424 Pt W. TRAYNOR 1st WEST RIDING REGT was awarded 21 days F.P. No 1 and fine according to Green Book entries for being drunk and disorderly and violating and abusing a sentinel on Infantry S/ J.G.C. Bolger. Weather wet and stormy. LW.	
29-12-14 AUCHEL	Ordinary routine — One horse sent in to [?] horses still in hospital horse disposal. Weather cold & frosty. LW.	

Army Form C. 2118.

WAR DIARY
or
INTELLIGENCE SUMMARY. No 7 B. 7. A.

(Erase heading not required.)

Hour, Date, Place.	Summary of Events and Information.	Remarks and references to Appendices.
30-12-14 AUCHEL	All Officers of the Unit attended today Bridal Taylor, Mess Corps at 9/10 a to be interviewed by Army Commander - Sir J. Willcocks K.W. Weather wet + stormy -	
31-12-14 AUCHEL	Ordinary routine - Weather wet + stormy.	

Lt. Col Ireland
Rann
O.C. No 7 B.7.A.

"A" Form. Army Form C. 2121.
MESSAGES AND SIGNALS.   No. of Message _____

Prefix ____ Code ____ m. | Words | Charge | This message is on a/c of: | Recd. at ____ m.
Office of Origin and Service Instructions. | Sent At ____ 40 m. To ____ By ____ | | Service. (Signature of "Franking Officer.") | Date ____ From ____ By ____

TO { OC. No 7 B F A

Sender's Number: 112 | Day of Month: 1/12 | In reply to Number: | AAA

Orders for rendezvous bearers and wagons as for last night AAA Refilling point tomorrow same as today

From: ADMS Lahore Divn
Place:
Time:

Colonel ADMS

no 7 NFA

Appendix 41

No 19 F.A. order by Lieut-Colonel L. Way
RAMC O.C. No 7 B.F.A.

LA CASSAN
1-12-14.

Ref: map MERVILLE - LE BASSÉ
1/40000.

Ref: order No 112 dated 1-12/14 by A.D.M.S
LAHORE DIVN.

1. The Bearers and wagons will
rendezvous and carry out the
orders laid down in my No 13. F.A
orders dated 25-11/14.

L. Way Lt-Colonel
RAMC
O.C. No 7. B.F.A.

By hand 4.30 p.m.
MAJOR BARTLETT
CAPT. MACARTHUR.

"A" Form. Army Form C. 2121.

MESSAGES AND SIGNALS.

Prefix	Code	m.	Words	Charge	This message is on a/c of:	Recd. at	m.
Office of Origin and Service Instructions.			Sent At ___ m. To By		___ Service. (Signature of "Franking Officer.")	Date From By	

TO { O.C.
7 B.F.A.

Sender's Number	Day of Month	In reply to Number	AAA
	2		

Orders for rendezvous bearers and wagons as for last night AAA Refilling point tomorrow same as today

From A.D.M.S. Lahore Div'n
Place
Time

Sd. Ivan Hoar
Major
for A.D.M.S.

The above may be forwarded as now corrected. (Z)

Censor. Signature of Addressor or person authorised to telegraph in his name

*This line should be erased if not required.

Appendix 4.   26

No 20 F.A. order by Lt-Colonel L. Way
DAwe. O.C. No 7 B. F. A.

LA CASSAN
2-12-14

Ref: map MERVILLE - LE BASSÉ $\frac{1}{40000}$

Ref: order No 118 dated $2\frac{12}{14}$ by A.D.M.S
LAHORE DIVⁿ

1. The Bearers and wagons will
rendezvous and carry out the
orders laid down in my No 13 F.A.
order dated $25\frac{11}{14}$.

L Way Lt-Colonel
RAMC.
O.C. No 7 B. F.A.

By hand 4.30 p.m.
MAJOR BARTLETT
CAPᵀ MACARTHUR.

"A" Form. Army Form C. 2121.
MESSAGES AND SIGNALS.

TO: O.C., No 7 B.F.A.

Sender's Number: 139
Day of Month: 3rd

AAA

Orders for rendezvous bearers and wagons same as last night. The bearer divisions and ambulance wagons of the Lahore Division will clear the whole wounded from trenches tonight.

From
Place: LOCON

Colonel IMS
A.D.M.S

No 22 F.A.O ~~Appendix 45~~ Wray
2nd issue O.C. No 7 B.F.A.

LA CASSAN.
3-12-14

Def work MERVILLE – LEBASSÉ

Dist: order No 139 dated 3/12/14 by A.D.M.S. 40000/1
LAHORE DIVN.

1. The Bearers and wagons will ~~~~ rendezvous and carry out the orders laid down in my No 13 F.A. order dated 25th/14

2. All wounded of LAHORE DIVISION will be cleared from the trenches tonight.

3. Reports to be sent to Tent Division

By hand 4.35pm Wray Lieut Colon
MAJOR BARTLETT   RAMC
CAPT MACARTHUR   O.C. No 7 B.F.A

"A" Form.   Army Form C. 2121.
MESSAGES AND SIGNALS.

TO — OC No 7. B F A

Sender's Number: 84   Day of Month: 13   AAA

Stretcher bearers and ambulance wagons of your field ambulance should be distributed tonight as follows AAA One half should rendezvous at road South of Rue d BETHUNE and remainder half a mile West of ~~Gui~~ Auchy-lès-LaBASSE on the BEUVRY-LaBASSE Road at 5 am. AAA These must be prepared to cooperate respectively with Ferozepore & Jullundur Brigades AAA Wounded will be evacuated to your Unit at BETHUNE and thence to CHATÉ GORRE and 112 F A BETHUNE. AAA Scale 1 over 40,000.

From: ADMS Lahore Divn

Recd. 4.30 pm.

Appendix 47

No 23 7. A. order by Lt Colonel L. Nay
office O.C. No 7 B.F.A.

BETHUNE
15-12-14

Ref: map MERVILLE - LA BASSÉE 1/40000

Ref operation order No 184 dated 15/12/14 by
A.D.M.S LAHORE DIVISION

1. CAPT MACARTHUR RAMC with half the Bearer Division and 3 ambulance wagons will rendezvous at the road South of RUE DE BETHUNE at 5 a.m on 16/12/14.

2. MAJOR BARTLETT RAMC with half the Bearer Division and 3 ambulance wagons will rendezvous half a mile west of AUCHY-LES-LA-BASSÉE on the BEUVRY-LA BASSÉE road at 5 a.m on 16/12/14.

3. These will be prepared to co-operate respectively with FEROZEPORE and JULLUNDER BRIGADES.

4. They will evacuate British wounded to last division in BETHUNE — Indian wounded to CHATEAU GORRE and 112/FA at BETHUNE.

5. Bearer Division will parade at 2.30 a.m & march at once

6. Reports to Field Division at BETHUNE

Signed 8 p.d MAJOR BARTLETT
CAPS

"A" Form. Army Form C. 2121.

MESSAGES AND SIGNALS.

| Prefix | Code | Words | Charge | This message is on a/c of: | Recd. at | m. |
| Office of Origin and Service Instructions. | | Sent At m. To By | | Service. (Signature of "Franking Officer.") | Date From By | |

TO { O.C. No 7 B.F.A.

Sender's Number	Day of Month	In reply to Number	AAA
24	20		

please despatch bearers and stretchers under an officer to RUE-DE-BETHUNE wounded should be collected and concentrated at CHATEAU GORRE where motor ambulances will take them over AAA all hand wounds in your field amb: should be evacuated at your own discretion I will sign any descriptive roll you please in the morning

From ADMS Lahore Div
Place
Time 4.25 pm

Jan Stoan
Major
for ADMS

OC
T.B.F.A

Appendix 49

No 24 F.A. Order by Lt-Colonel L. Way
B.Awe O.C. No 7 B. F.A
BETHUNE
20-12-14

Ref: map MERVILLE - LE BASSÉE 1/40000.

Ref: Operation Order No 224 dated 20/12/14 by
A.D.M.S. LAHORE DIVISION.

1. CAPT. MACARTHUR R.A.M.S with the Bearer
Division and 4 Ambulance Waggons will
proceed at once to the RUE DE BETHUNE

2. He will get into touch with the Regimental
Medical Units collect the wounded and
transfer them to the CHATEAU GORRE

3. Motor ambulances will take over wounded
at CHATEAU GORRE & transfer them
to the 7ent Division at BETHUNE
COLLEGE St VAAST.

4. Reports will be sent to 7ent Division

J. Way Lt Colonel
B.Awe
O.C. No 7 B.F.A.

By hand 5 p.m.
CAPT MACARTHUR.

"A" Form.
Army Form C. 2121.

MESSAGES AND SIGNALS.

Prefix	Code		Words	Charge		This message is on a/c of		Recd. at	m.
Office of Origin and Service Instructions.			Sent At	m.		Service.		Date	
			To					From	
			By			(Signature of " Franking Officer.")		By	

TO { OC No 7 FA

Sender's Number	Day of Month	In reply to Number	AAA
229	21		

Send out immediately ambulance waggons with bearers and stretchers to FORK of roads South of DE of RUE DE BETHUNE AAA wounded from FESTUBERT should be evacuated to your Unit.

From ADMS Lahae Dom
Place
Time 1.5 am

The above may be forwarded as now corrected.   (Z)

Censor.   Signature of Addressor or person authorised to telegraph in his name

Appendix 5

No 25-7. A. Order by Lt-Colonel L. Way
R.A.M.C. O.C No 7 B.F.A.

BETHUNE
21-12-14.

Ref: Map MERVILLE - LE BASSÉE 1/40000
Ref: Operation Order No 229 dated 21/12/14 by A.D.M.S. LAHORE DIVISION.

1. LIEUT S.S. CROSSE R.A.M.C. will proceed at once with the Bearer Division and 4 Ambulance wagons to FORK of roads South of DE of RUE DE BETHUNE

2. He will get into touch with the Regimental Medical Units at FESTUBERT and collect the wounded.

3. He will evacuate the wounded to the Tent Division at the COLLEGE ST VAAST at BETHUNE.

4. Reports will be sent to the Tent Division

L Way Lt-Colonel
RAMC
O.C. No 7 B.F.A.

By hand 1.30 p.m.
LIEUT S.S. CROSSE R.A.M.C.

WAR DIARY

of

No 7 British Field Ambulance Lahore Division.

From 1st January 1915 To 31st January 1915

121/44 D1
Jan 1915

LIEUT-COLONEL L. WAY　　VOLUME-1　From 1-1-1915
RAMC
O.C. No 7 BRITISH FIELD AMBULANCE　　to

Army Form C. 2118

WAR DIARY
or
INTELLIGENCE SUMMARY. No 7 BRITISH FIELD AMBULANCE.

J.E.F.A

Instructions regarding War Diaries and Intelligence Summaries are contained in F. S. Regs., Part II, and the Staff Manual respectively. Title pages will be prepared in manuscript.

(Erase heading not required.)

Hour, Date, Place.	Summary of Events and Information.	Remarks and references to Appendices.
1-1-15 AUCHEL	Received orders from A.D.M.S. to hold two Sections in readiness to proceed at a moments notice. - Detailed C and D Sections - Weather cold wet & windy. LW	
2-1-15 AUCHEL	Two sick horses were returned & admitted to Vet'y hospital under Vet'y Officer later Division yesterday and two have been laboured to replace them from the Transport. Weather wet & cold. LW	
3-1-15 AUCHEL	Lt. L WAY RAMC proceeded on 9 days leave to ENGLAND. 2 Cord Surg. V I Pack Store Sergt. proceeded on 10 days leave to ENGLAND. I assumed command of No 7 British Field Ambulance today. J Ratcliff Col RAMC	
4-1-15 AUCHEL	Received notes from ADMS re two Sections of Field Ambulance to accompany Yorkshire Brigade - if move ordered. Two sections to form with No 112 97A a mixed Field Ambulance. C & D sections detailed. J.R.	
5-1-15	Nothing of note to record re above. Lieut (Paul) SS Corps RAMC was admitted to hospital suffering from NYO Ichyo	

Army Form C. 2118

VOLUME - 1
WAR DIARY from 1-1-1915 to
INTELLIGENCE SUMMARY.
NO 7 BRITISH FIELD AMBULANCE
I.E.F. — A.

(Erase heading not required.)

Instructions regarding War Diaries and Intelligence Summaries are contained in F. S. Regs., Part II, and the Staff Manual respectively. Title pages will be prepared in manuscript.

Hour, Date, Place.	Summary of Events and Information.	Remarks and references to Appendices.
AUCHEL 6-1-15	No 3436 Naik SHIV NATH No 3 A.B.C was severely reprimanded for being intoxicated on duty.	JG Mitchell (?) Rawe
AUCHEL 7-1-15	No 3551 Bearer KISHEN SINGH No 3 A.B.C and No 3507 3rd gr. bearer servant RAM BHAROS, A.H. Corps were placed under arrest for theft and remanded for Commdt. mulcted. JM	M Bennett Capt RAMC
AUCHEL 8-1-15	CAPT. A.M. BENETT R.A.M.C. reported his arrival and assumed temporary command of the unit. Summons of evidence taken against the above prisoners. Copt I Mitchill and put in charge of the hutting arrangements for Sirhind Brigade.	M Bennett Capt RAMC
AUCHEL 9-1-15	Lt A.R. Allen RAMC reported his arrival for temporary duty.	M Bennett Capt RAMC
10-1-15 AUCHEL	I returned from 7 days leave to England last night. 2 G.S. wagons and 1 supply wagon sent to the H.Q. A Company LAHORE DIVISIONAL TRAIN for infantry to the ARMY CORPS COMMANDER - Walker not returning. I Mar Holland Rawe O.C. No 7 B.F.A.	

Army Form C. 2118

WAR DIARY

INTELLIGENCE SUMMARY. No 7 B. F. A.

(Erase heading not required.)

Hour, Date, Place.	Summary of Events and Information.	Remarks and references to Appendices.
11-1-15 AUCHEL	No 9156 Pte J. OLDFIELD. 1st WEST RIDING REGt was admitted to 1/1st B.F.A. suffering from Gonorrhoea. 1 man A.H.C. + 1 man A.B.C. slightly ill also admitted. Received and evacuated one accidental B+ No 111 F.A. Confidential orders from A.D.M.S. to detail 3 light cable 2 light cable 9 M.H.S. to accompany the Brigade + ordered to the place of deaths each Battery to be attached to 3 sections) I/A were mised. 2 W.S. Ambulance— Detailed B.Section to No 111 F.A., C. Section to 112 F.A., + D. Section to No 111 F.A. Via a finishing 1 attached. Weather very stormy with sleet and rain. LW	Appendices 1 attached
12-1-15 AUCHEL	One A.B.C. was admitted to No 111 F.A. suffering from Gonorrhoea. No 3507 3rd Grade Ward Servant RAM BHAROS A.H.C. and No 35551 Bearer KISHEN SINGH A.B.C. having tried by Summary Court-Martial charged with theft of a watch + revolver stolen from Capt. I... was fully. Sentenced and our Paloltre Surgeon returned here — 10 days leave to England. Weather very stormy. LW	
13-1-15 AUCHEL	Summary Court-martial finished its sittings. No 35551 KISHEN SINGH A.B.C. found guilty of theft (Stealing a watch and revolver was sentenced to I yr R.I. (rigorous imprisonment in civil lines) and sentenced to undergo 6 months and stoppage... LW	

VOLUME – 1
WAR DIARY
or
INTELLIGENCE SUMMARY. No 7 B.F.A.

(Erase heading not required.)

Army Form C. 2118.

4

Instructions regarding War Diaries and Intelligence Summaries are contained in F. S. Regs., Part II, and the Staff Manual respectively. Title pages will be prepared in manuscript.

Hour, Date, Place.	Summary of Events and Information.	Remarks and references to Appendices.
14-1-15 AUCHEL	Captain A.M. BENETT. R.A.M.C. transferred to the No 4 Clearing Hospital at LILLERS suffering from fever. N.Y.D. - 3507 3rd Grade Ward Orderly RAM BHAROS A.H.C. tried by Summary Courtmartial for theft and receiving stolen property, was acquitted. One mutiny orderly No 8768 Pt C.P. SELL Y+L. REGT ordered home the Base as unfit for active service.	Appendix 2 attached
6 p.m.	Urgent orders received from A.D.M.S. Jn Div to march to VIELLE CHAPELLE tomorrow and to open confirmed and Advances with Nos 112 and 113 I.F.A. in rôle of offensive 2 attached. Weather wet and showery.	
15-1-15 AUCHEL 8 a.m.	Hand and 1 [?] case transferred to No 8 B.F.A by order of A.D.M.S. Stable Duc. Marched to VIELLE CHAPELLE at 9 a.m. Arrived there during the morning Q.M.S. (no JULLUNDUR and SIRHIND Brigades Sir Welter Latulippe).	Appendix 3 attached
16-1-15 ZELOBE	Opened a combined advance dressing station for British and Indian troops wounded at RICHBOURG ST VAAST. Sent Divisions of No 7 B.F.A opened at ZELOBE and Sent Division of No 113 I.F.A. opened at VIELLE CHAPELLE. No 112 I.F.A Littaker in reserve at PARADIS in accordance with instructions of A.D.M.S. Yumo Collection with wounded by Brigades at Hullets of 2 Division attached by Brigadier. Hullets of 2 Division attached to 9 Army. JULLUNDUR + SIRHIND Bugler [?] wet and covered. Sent Division of No 7 B.F.A attached to 1st Brigade Meerut Benn Division at RICHBOUR ST VAAST N.W	Appendices 4+5 attached

Army Form C. 2118

VOLUME - 1
WAR DIARY
or
INTELLIGENCE SUMMARY N°7 B.F.A.
(Erase heading not required.)

Instructions regarding War Diaries and Intelligence Summaries are contained in F. S. Regs., Part II, and the Staff Manual respectively. Title pages will be prepared in manuscript.

Hour, Date, Place.	Summary of Events and Information.	Remarks and references to Appendices.
17-1-15 ZELOBE	LIEUT J.C. PYPER R.A.M.C (Special Reserve) reported from N°. 7 Field Amb. - with BETHUNE sick late N.V.D. reinforcement. Evacuated to N°1 Clearing Hospital. I.S.M.D. proceeded to N°1 Clearing Hospital BETHUNE suffering from severe N.V.D. 1.A.B.C. was admitted to N°113 I.F.A. Admitted 4 wounded and 15 sick. Evacuated 11 Sick and 1 wounded to N°1 Clearing Hospital at BETHUNE - North West from Half Beau Division at RICHEBOURG ST VAAST.	
18-1-15 ZELOBE	Issued instructions on Medical arrangements to JULLUNDUR and SIRHIND Brigades on the Brigades changing over on 19-1-15 - Vide Appendices 6+7 attached - 1 A.H.C. was admitted sick to N°113 I.F.A - Admitted 3 wounded and 28 sick (75) there were cases of) (frostbite). Evacuated 4 wounded and 24 sick to N°1 Clearing Hospital BETHUNE. Dull clear followed by rain was the day. W.N.	Appendices 6+7 attached
19-1-15 ZELOBE	1541 P⁹⁴ H. ROSS 4ᵗʰ SEAFORTH HIGHLANDERS admitted with gunshaft wound of abdomen (penetrating) last night - died at 11 A.M. - 9 sent witness to M O³ of Admiral Drawing Station about Medical arrangements when Brigade change over to go into trenches, same arrangements before. Vide appendices 6+7 & 8-1-15 - and Appendices 8 and 9 attached - 1 A.B.C. was sent sick to N°113 I.F.A - 3 sick being evacuated to N°1 Clearing Hospital at BETHUNE - 9 sick admitted & 1 wounded 20 sick evacuated to N°1 Clearing Hospital - HOQUE Division at RICHEBOURG ST VAAST. W.N.	Appendices 8 + 9 attached

Army Form C. 2118

VOLUME – 1
WAR DIARY
or
INTELLIGENCE SUMMARY. No 7 B.A.A.
(Erase heading not required.)

Instructions regarding War Diaries and Intelligence Summaries are contained in F. S. Regs., Part II, and the Staff Manual respectively. Title pages will be prepared in manuscript.

Hour, Date, Place.	Summary of Events and Information.	Remarks and references to Appendices.
20-1-15 ZELOBES	11 a.m. No 1541 Pt. H. Ross 4th SEAFORTH HIGHLANDERS who died of gunshot wound of abdomen was buried at VIELLE CHAPELLE at 11 a.m. – 4 A.B.C. who were admitted sick to No 113 I.F.A. No 14612 Dr. R. CARTER 44 BRIGADE R.F.A. AMMUNITION COLUMN 2nd DIVISION died out of Hospital with cerebral haemorrhage – 3 wounded admitted and sick – 6 wounded & sick – 3 were discharged to duty and rejoined Units. Weather wet and mist. J.W.	
21-1-15 ZELOBES	8 a.m. Operation Order No 61 received by G.O.C. LAHORE DET dated 21st Jany 15 – received at 8 a.m. Appendix 10 att. Field – White lectured officers and n.c.os Appendix 11 att taflet. One sick and one wounded officer admitted and 3 other ranks evacuated to No 1 Cavalry Clearing Station BETHUNE. Admitted 26 sick and evacuated 3 wounded and 1 sick who were detained to duty. Advanced dressing stations at RICHEBOURG ST VAAST had to be closed owing to bright moonlight and moved to LA COUTURE evening. Shelled by shrapnel – Weather wet and mild. J.W.	Appendix 10 attached. Appendix 11 attached.
22-1-15 ZELOBES	8.30 a.m. No 112 I.F.A. moved at 8.30 a.m. to RAIMBERT. 10 a.m. No 14612 Dr. R. CARTER 44 K B. R.F.A. was buried at VIELLE CHAPELLE at 10 a.m. His sentence of six months rigorous imprisonment awarded to No 5351 Bearer KISHEN SINGH, A.B.C. on the 13-1-15 had been commuted by G.O.C. LAHORE DIV to 30 lashes. Unit handed at 12 noon opposite FESTUBERT promulgated - SIRHIND BRIGADE moved out 12 noon for the neutral area	

VOLUME – 1
WAR DIARY
or
INTELLIGENCE SUMMARY. No 7 B.D.A.

Army Form C. 2118
7

Hour, Date, Place.	Summary of Events and Information.	Remarks and references to Appendices.
22-1-15- 12 noon ZELOBE	GARHWAL BRIGADE MEERUT DIVN marched into LACOUTURE at noon. I notified the Brigade I had 12 attached. of the Brigade of the medical arrangements made for receiving the sick and wounded. (see Appendix)	Appendix 12 attached.
2 p.m.	1/39 attached. CAPT. B.E. ANDERSON 69th SCINDE RIFLES admitted with gunshot wound right knee (severe) at 3 p.m. and was evacuated to No. Cavalry Clearing Station at 3.30 p.m. – Admitted 3 wounded	
3.30 p.m.	and 11 sick – Evacuated 16 sick to No.1 Cavalry Clearing Hospital BETHUNE – Weather fine + frosty. JW.	
23-1-15- ZELOBE	No 35511 Bearer KISHEN SINGH A.B.C. received 80 lashes by the A.P.M. Lahore Division – 5 cases of men charged w/ use of SEAFORTH HIGHLANDERS who reported to the No. 1 Cavalry Clearing Hospital BETHUNE – Advanced Dressing Station – were sent from LA COUTURE to make room for Wd for JULLUNDUR BRIGADE – Bearers + wagons of not returning wounded with medical officers from No 7 D.A. + No 11 9 D.A. to collect wounded from Aid Posts at usual No 10066 PT J. KITSON 1st WEST RIDING REGT. observed 7 a.m F.P. No 2 for neglect of duty. Section 19 B.A. + No 127 FA. MEERUT DIVN admitted 3 wounded 8 sick. Admitted 9 sick - Evacuated 3 wounded and 8 sick to Cavalry Hospital No 1 BETHUNE, 3 heavy draped Co's 9 wagons (wound) to No 19 B.D.A. and Hospital shell 1 A.B.C. to N.W. attached to No 113 F.A, No 128 D.A. for first week	

Army Form C. 2118

VOLUME - I
WAR DIARY
or
INTELLIGENCE SUMMARY. No 7 B. F. A.

(Erase heading not required.)

Instructions regarding War Diaries and Intelligence Summaries are contained in F. S. Regs., Part II, and the Staff Manual respectively. Title pages will be prepared in manuscript.

Hour, Date, Place.	Summary of Events and Information.	Remarks and references to Appendices.
24-1-15 ZELOBE	3rd Cl. Asst. Surgeon E.M. CUZENS I.S.M.D through to Sub-medical charge 1st MANCHESTER REGT. Handed over duties of S.M.O to Lt-Colonel HAMILTON I.M.S. and Unit marched to VENDIN at 10.a.m. & going to will be in route to AUCHEL - in a hospital in a hospital girls school - Weather unchanged LN	
VENDIN.		
25-1-15 VENDIN 10.45am AUCHEL 11.30pm	Marched at 10.45 a.m. for AUCHEL and arrived at 1.30pm Received orders from A.D.M.S. to be prepared to move at short notice. Appendix 13 attached. Unit billeted in the HOTEL DE VILLE. LIEUT A. WILSON (Veterinary) R.A.M.C reported on arrival for duty - LIEUT A.R ALLAN R.A.M.C (Temp) also failed to rejoin having been detached for duty to supervise bathing and disinfection of clothing by order of A.D.M.S - Weather unsettled LN.	Appendix 13 attached
26-1-15 AUCHEL. 8.30pm	No25764 Pte J. DAVENPORT 2nd NORTHUMBERLAND FUSILIERS. awarded 7 days F.P. No 2 for being absent from billets after roll call - Orders from A.D.M.S at 8.30 p.m to return in a state of constant readiness to move also weapons finished & cleaned Appendix 14 Hotel Asst Surgeon C. A. Quin EMILE sent to No 8 B.F.A. for Asst Surgeon A.R. D'ABREU reporting his arrival for duty. Weather unsettled LN.	Appendix 14 attached
27-1-15 AUCHEL	11.a.m Orders from A.D.M.S. that constant readiness to move should be observed - ambulances were present at 11 a.m. 3rd Cl Asst Surgeon C A Quin attached 8 F.A. Orders received from SIRHIND BRIGADE - LAHORE DIVISION to state of readiness to move to FEROZEPORE	Appendix 15 attached

Gulab Singh & Sons, Calcutta—No. 22 Army C.—5-8-11—1,07,060.

Army Form C. 2118.

9

VOLUME — 1
WAR DIARY
or
INTELLIGENCE SUMMARY. No 7 B.F.A.
(Erase heading not required.)

Instructions regarding War Diaries and Intelligence Summaries are contained in F.S. Regs., Part II, and the Staff Manual respectively. Title pages will be prepared in manuscript.

Hour, Date, Place.	Summary of Events and Information.	Remarks and references to Appendices.
27-1-15 AUCHEL	BRIGADE Orders of this nature not attached — issued — Field Ambulances have all asked for Brigade award vide Appendix 17 attached. 2 1st grade Conges and 1 hrs half public servants to No III I.F.A. — Permanent offr detail from A.D.M.S. return 8 - 160 Up Park to the Base Reserve upright on the Transport cadge, wagons + 1 draughthorse and just to the English Veterinary Section — LW. Weather cold and fine.	Appendix 16 attached Appendix 17 attached
28-1-15 AUCHEL	No. L.D.T. 5. Dr. R. BRADBURY A.S.C. awarded 7 days F.P. No.2 for refusing to obey an order given by N.C.O. Route March — and Wells being carried out daily. Received one Riding Pony from Indian Ruts Corps Lahore Divisional weather cold & fine. T.J. Mitchell Capt Raine for O.C.	
29-1-15 AUCHEL	Capt W.H. O'RIORDAN, R.A.M.C. proceeded on Seven days leave. No 2323 PTE WALKER J. 2nd N.T. awarded 7 days F.P. No.2. for Breaking out of Billets & remaining absent until 4 a.m. 29-1-15. Lt. Col. L. WAY R.A.M.C. placed on the sick list. 3 followers were admitted to ho 111 I.F.A. & one A.S.C. driver admitted to ho 8 R.F.A. Parade for hooking up & loading of 1 leading led on wagons and was ready to move in 25 minutes. Weather cold & fine. T/h	
30-1-15 AUCHEL	Received orders from the A.D.M.S. re-allotment of Field Ambulances to Brigades. 4 days Special Surg. A.R. D'ABREU. I.S.M.D attached to the medical charge of Indian Contacts of 129th BALUCHIS. Pte A.B.C. man returned to court from 111 I.F.A. Weather bright but milder	Appendix 18 attached T/h

VOLUME - 1
WAR DIARY

or

INTELLIGENCE SUMMARY. No. 7 B.F.A

Army Form C. 2118.

10.

(Erase heading not required.)

Instructions regarding War Diaries and Intelligence Summaries are contained in F. S. Regs., Part II, and the Staff Manual respectively. Title pages will be prepared in manuscript.

Hour, Date, Place.	Summary of Events and Information.	Remarks and references to Appendices.
AUCHEL 31-1-15	One Indian Sepoy attached to this F.A. from the 9th Infantry - to change the arms of men admitted to hospital. One A.S.C. driver arrived to draft. Lt Col L WAY RAMC taken off the Sick list. Orders received at 8.30 p.m. for the march to the New Billeting Area vide appendix attached. Weather cold & snowy. 7/pm	Appendix 19 attached.

L J Mitchell Capt
R A M C
for O.C. No 7. B.F.A.

Appendix 10.

COPY NO. 6

OPERATION ORDER No. 61.
by
Major-General H.D'U KEARY, C.B. D.S.O. Commanding Lahore Detachment.

21st
~~20th~~ January 1915.

1. The LAHORE Detachment will be relieved by a similar detachment of the MEERUT Division as detailed in the attached March Table.

2. The Companies of Sappers & Miners attached to Brigades will march with their Brigades.

3. The Senior Medical Officer will arrange for 3 ambulance wagons (for the carriage of sick men only) and a due proportion of personnel to accompany each Brigade.

The 112th Indian Field Ambulance will march at 6-30 a.m. on 22nd January by PACAUT – HINGES – LABBOY and CHOCQUES to RAIMBERT The 113th Indian Field Ambulance and No.7 British Field Ambulance will march on 24th on relief by MEERUT Division to CHOCQUES and VENDIN respectively where billets will be arranged for them by JULLUNDUR Brigade.

4. Arrangements have been made to pick up the medical unfits in lorries and to convey them to AUCHEL on the 22nd and to ALLOUAGNE on 24th. The lorries will stop at VIEILLE CHAPELLE at 9-30 a.m. pick up the sick there and then proceed to LA COUTURE and pick up sick there. The lorries will then proceed via LE TOURET and ESSARS and CHOCQUES. Men will be sent to the refilling point at LESTREM at 9 a.m. to guide the lorries to where they will pick up sick.

5. After 11-45 a.m. the LOCON-LA COUTURE-VIEILLE CHAPELLE Road (Sq.X.5) will be reserved for all traffic moving West and the FOSSE – LA COUTURE-RICHEBOURG Road (Sq.R.35) for that moving East.

The General Officer Commanding SIRHIND and JULLUNDUR Brigades will post police at 11-45 a.m. at LOCOBER, FOSSE, the Road Junctions (3) at E. side of VIEILLE CHAPELLE the 2 Western and 1 Southern Road Junction at LA COUTURE and the Road Junctions at
RICHEBOURG

2.

RICHEBOURG Sq.B 1 and Sq.C 7(b).

The police should be furnished with written instructions as to the route traffic is to take.

6. Refilling points as shown in the attached table.

7. Brigadier General A.B.SCOTT,C.B.,D.S.O.Commanding MEERUT Detachment will take over command of the defensive area from the General Officer Commanding Lahore Detachment at 10 a.m. on the 24th January 1915.

H. DePree
Lt Col.
General Staff, Lahore Detachment.

Issued at ..8... a.m.

Copy No. 1 to G.O.C. Sirhind Brigade.
Copy No. 2 to G.O.C. Jullundur Brigade
Copy No. 3 to C.R.Engineer.
Copy No. 4 to A.A.M.G.
Copy No. 5 to A.D.M.S.
Copy No. 6 to S.M.O.Lahore Dett; ✓
Copy No. 7 to 1st Corps.
Copy No. 8 to Meerut Division.
Copy No. 9 to A.D.S & T.
Copy No.10 War Diary.
Copy No.11 War Diary.

MARCH TABLE

DATE	Unit	LEAVES	ROUTE	BILLETS at	Remarks
22nd Jan.	SIRHIND Brigade and 20th Coy. S&Ms.	VIEILLE CHAPELLE and LA COUTURE at 12 noon	VIA ZELOBES - LOCON - HINGES - VENDIN Baggage Train to follow Brigade closely.	Bt. limits OBLINGHEM - VENDIN IN. limits - CHOCQUES	
23rd Jan.	— do —	OBLINGHEM - VENDIN and CHOCQUES at 9-30 A.M.	VIA LA PUGNOY and MARLES	AUCHEL and FERFAY	
23rd Jan.	JULLUNDUR Bde. and 21st Coy. S&Ms.	Trenches and RICHEBOURG ST. VAAST.		VIEILLE CHAPELLE and LA COUTURE	
24th Jan.	JULLUNDUR Bde. and 21st Coy. S&Ms.	VIEILLE CHAPELLE and LA COUTURE at 12 noon.	VIA ZELOBES - LOCON - HINGES - VENDIN - Baggage train to follow Brigade closely.	Bt. limits OBLINGHEM - VENDIN IN. limits - CHOCQUES	
24th Jan.	LAHORE Detachment Headquarters and Signal Company.	LES LOBES at 10-30 a.m.	LOCON - HINGES - VENDIN	LOZINGHEM	
25th Jan.	JULLUNDUR Bde. and 21st Coy. S&Ms	OBLINGHEM - VENDIN and CHOCQUES at 9-30 a.m.	VIA	ALLOUAGNE	

Copy No 5.

Operation order No. 39./S.M.O.
by
Lieut- Colonel L. WAY R.A.M.C; S.M.O. Lahore Detachment

21st January 1915.

Reference Map ARRAS 1/80,000

Reference operation order No 61 dated 21.1.1915 by G.O.C. LAHORE DETACHMENT.

1. The O.C. No 112 I.F.A. will detail 3 ambulance wagons, 1 sub. assistant Surgeon, 6 A.B.C. men, 1 ward orderly, 1 sweeper with blankets, medical comforts, field medical Companion and haversack to accompany the SIRHIND BRIGADE on the march on the 22.1.1915 from VIEILLE CHAPELLE and LA COUTURE at 12 noon. They will report to the Brigade Major at Brigade Head Qrs at 11 a.m. Two days rations will be carried.

2. The O.C. No 113 I.F.A will detail 1 ambulance wagon, 1 sub. assistant Surgeon, 2 A.B.C. men, 1 ward orderly, 1 sweeper with blankets, medical comforts, field medical Companion and haversack to accompany the JULLUNDUR BRIGADE on the march on the 24.1.1915 at 12 noon

The O.C. No 7 B.F.A. will detail 2 ambulance wagons, 1 assistant Surgeon, 1 nursing orderly, 1 ward servant, 1 sweeper, and 4 A.B.C. men with blankets, medical Comforts, field medical Companion and haversack to accompany the JULLUNDUR BRIGADE on the march on the 24.1.1915 at 12 noon.

They will report to the Brigade Major at Brigade Head Qrs at 11 am. Two days rations will be carried.

3. The 112th I.F.A. will march at 8.30 A.M. on 22nd January by PACAUT- HINGES- LANNOY and CHOCQUES to RAIMBERT.

2.

The 113th I.F.A. and no 7 B.F.A. will march on 24th on relief by MEERUT DIVISION to CHOCQUES and VENDIN respectively where billets will be arranged for them by JULLUNDUR BDE.

4. Ambulance wagons and personnel will rejoin their units on termination of Brigade movements.

5. Refilling points as in attached table.

6. March Table is attached for information.

7. British sick on the march to be transferred to no 8 B.F.A. ALLOUAGNE, and Indian sick to No 111 I.F.A. at LOZINGHEM.

Issued at 5 pm.

Lieut Colonel
S.M.O. Lahore Detachment

Copy no 1 to A.D.M.S.
Copy no 2 to OC. 112 I.F.A
Copy no 3 to OC. 113 I.F.A.
Copy no 4 to OC. No 7 B.F.A
Copy no 5 War Diary.

Appendix 12.

46 S.M.O.
22-1-1915.

From S.M.O. Lahore Det
ZELOBES.
To Brigade Major
Garhwal Brigade

The following are the arrangements for sick and wounded.

No 7 BRITISH FIELD AMBULANCE at ZELOBES. and No 113 INDIAN FIELD AMBULANCE at VIEILLE CHAPELLE

2 Medical Officers of both the above units with bearers and ambulance wagons get into touch with medical officers of units at the AID POSTS morning and evening to clear wounded from the trenches

3 Ambulance wagons are sent to Brigade Headquarters LA COUTURE and RICHEBOURG ST. VAAST every morning to collect sick of British and Indian units by 9 am.

4. Please communicate these arrangements to your units.

L W ay
Lt Col Raure
S.M.O. LAHORE DETT.

"A" Form.   Army Form C. 2121.

MESSAGES AND SIGNALS.

TO	O.C. No 7 BFA			

Sender's Number	Day of Month	In reply to Number	AAA
34	25		

your	Unit	should	be	ready
to	move	at 2 hours	~~short~~	notice
AAA	These	orders	are	issued
on	account	of	the	heavy
gun	fire	heard	this	morning
near	BETHUNE			

From A.D.M.S. Lahore Divn

Colonel
A.D.M.S

MESSAGES AND SIGNALS.

Prefix ____ Code ____ Office of Origin and Service Instructions.

URGENT

TO: O.C. No 7 B.F.A.

This message is on a/c of: Appendix 14

Sender's Number	Day of Month	In reply to Number	AAA
39	26		

Please hold your Unit in constant readiness to move and all leave cancelled.

From: ADMS Lahore Divn
Place:
Time: 7.10 pm.

Colonel
ADMS

"A" Form.

MESSAGES AND SIGNALS.

Prefix	Code	Words	Charge		
Office of Origin and Service Instructions.		Sent At ___ m. To ___ By ___	This message is on a/c of: ___ Service. (Signature of "Franking Officer.")	Recd. at ___ m. Date ___ From ___ By ___	

TO: O.C. No 7 B.F.A.

Sender's Number	Day of Month	In reply to Number	AAA
44	27		

My 39 of yesterday aaa
The state of constant readiness
is related to one of
being able to turn out
at two hours notice

From A.D.M.S. Lahore Divn
Place
Time 9.20 am.

The above may be forwarded as now corrected.   (Z)

Colonel

Appendix 16

No. 163-B.M.   H/eadquarters, Sirhind Brigade,
                         dated 27th January 1915.

Copy of a telegram from the Headquarters, Lahore Divn,
to the Headquarters, Sirhind Brigade, No.G-407, dated 27th
January 1915.

....

Under orders from First Army only LAHORE Division will
be kept in a state of readiness. Of Lahore Division one
Brigade (FEROZEPORE) will be ready to march at two hours
notice remainder will carry on training as usual but
arrangements must be made for minimising delay in turning
out remainder of Division. Separate orders being issued regarding grant of leave.

....

Memorandum.

    Forwarded for information.
    Transport may now be dispersed and unloaded.

                                    Ridgeway
                                        Captain.
                        Brigade Major, Sirhind Brigade.

To,
    The Officer Commanding,
            1/B.F.A.
    ....

Appendix 17 27.1.15

The following is the allotment of Field Ambulances for Brigade work in future.

Ferozepore Brigade.
No 111 I.F.A. + 2 secs No 8 B.F.A. under the command
of Lieut-Col. G.A. Frost, IMS

Jullundur Brigade.
No 112 I.F.A. + 2 secs No 8 B.F.A. under the command
of Lieut-Col. J.de B. Wheir, RAMC

Sirhind Brigade.
No 113 I.F.A. + 2 secs No 7 B.F.A. under the command
of Lieut-Col. L. Way, RAMC

Divisional Area
2 sections No 7 B.F.A.

[signature]
Colonel, IMS
ADMS, Lahore Divn.

To.
Gen Staff, Lahore Divn
O.C. Ferozepore Bde
  Jullundur "
  Sirhind "
O.C. No 7 B.F.A.
     8 "
     111 I.F.A.
     112 "
     113 "
A.D.S.T.

Appendix 18   50 12
                               30.1.15

In supersession of this Office No.46 dated 27th January 1915, the following is the re-allotment of Field Ambulances for Brigade areas in future:-

Jullundur Brigade

No 8 B.F.A. & No 112 I.F.A. The Senior Officer in the two field ambulances will be the S.M.O. of the Brigade.

Sirhind Brigade

No 7 B.F.A. & No 113 I.F.A. The Senior Officer in the two field ambulances will be the S.M.O. of the Brigade.

Ferozepore Brigade

No 111 I.F.A. under the command of Lt Col G.H. Frost I.M.S. who will be the S.M.O. of the Brigade.

                               [signature]
                               Colonel M.S.
                               D.D.M.S. Lahore Divn

To Genl Staff Lahore Divn
   OC. Lahore Divl Train
   GOC R.A. Lahore Divn
   "   Jullundur Bde
   "   Ferozepore "
   "   Sirhind   "
   OC. No 7 B.F.A.
   "   No 8   "
   "   No 111 I.F.A
   "   " 112   "
   "   " 113   "

Appendix 19

OPERATION ORDER NO. 10.
by
Lt.Colonel A.H.Dennys, Commanding Sirhind Brigade,

Copy 8

Dated 31st January 1915.

Reference Map $\frac{1}{80,000}$ and Squared Sheet $\frac{1}{40,000}$

1. The Troops in the SIRHIND BRIGADE AREA will march tomorrow the 1st February 1915, to new billeting areas vide attached March Table.

2. The new SIRHIND BRIGADE AREA is as follows:-
ROBECQ (exclusive) – South and East CLARENCE R. – LE PETIT PACAUT (exclusive) – LE GRAND PACAUT (exclusive) – GRAND CHEMIN DE BETHUNE inclusive – D'AIRE – LA BASSEE CANAL. Also ROBECQ CALONNE Road from road junction North of CARVIN to CALONNE exclusive.

3. Baggage Section of the SIRHIND BDE group will follow <u>immediately</u> in rear of the last unit of the group without any interval.
The baggage wagons of the 20th Coy, S and M. will join the train of the group (immediately in rear of the wagons of the ~~15th Brigade, R.F.A.~~ *1/1st G.R.*) at the cross roads LOZINGHEM.
The baggage wagons of the 34th Pioneers will march with the unit to the cross roads LOZINGHEM where they will join No.1 Coy train.
Supply Section will refill on the road between Cross roads S.W. of ALLOUAGNE and HAUT RIEUX at 12 noon being careful not to arrive at the refilling point till the Division is clear. After refilling they will follow the route laid down for the SIRHIND Bde group.
Rendezvous for meeting Supply wagons – ROBECQ Church, *except for 1st H.L.I and 1/4th G.R for which Rendezvous is PONT LEVIS Sq Q 32 a*

4. ~~15th Brigade, R.F.A. and~~ Each unit in the group will be halted independently by its Commander at 10 minutes before each clock hour and will move on again at the hour.
In the event of there being any serious gap in the Column, the O.C. Unit in front of which the gap has occurred, will report accordingly to SIRHIND BRIGADE HEAD QUARTERS at the hourly halt.

5. Reports to head of group on march, on arrival in new area to *House near Church in Sq Q 9 b*

A. Ridgway
Captain,
Brigade Major, Sirhind Brigade.

Copy No.1 to O.C., 1st H.L.I.
Copy No.2 to O.C., Connaught Rangers.
Copy No.3 to O.C., 1/1st G.R.
Copy No.4 to O.C., 1/4th G.R.
~~Copy No.5 to O.C., 15th Brigade, R.F.A.~~
Copy No.6 to O.C., 20th Coy, S and M.
Copy No.7 to O.C., 34th Pioneers.
Copy No. 8 to O.C., No.7 B.F. Ambulance.
Copy No.9 to O.C., No.113 I.F. Ambulance.
Copy No.10 to O.C., No.4 Coy A.S.C.
Copy No.11 to Headquarters, Lahore Division.
Copies 12 and 13 War Diary.

Handed to Signal Section at 8.10 p.m.

Confdl

O.C. No. 7 B.F.A.
   111 I.F.A.
   112 "
   113 "

Appendix 1

In the event of the Brigades of Infantry of the divn being sent away in busses to the fighting line, mixed field ambulances on a light scale in lorries in busses will accompany them, the remainder of the field ambulances following on.

For the Sirhind Bde - One section No 7 British & three sections No 112 Indian Field Ambulance under the command of Major G Browse I.M.S.

For the Ferozepore Bde - One section No 7 British & three sections No 113 I.F.A. under command of Lt Col L. Way R.A.M.C.

For Jullundur Bde - One section No 7 British & 3 sections No 111 I.F.A. under command of Lt Col G.A. Frost I.M.S. or the next senior officer attached to No 111 I.F.A.

The following is the scale of equipment & personnel for each

        mixed

Field Ambulance to be taken in lorries & busses.

O.C. must be prepared to move quickly on receipt of orders & make ~~prospective~~ necessary arrangements for the prospective move.

PERSONNEL

British Sec		Indian Sections	
Officer	1	Officers	3
Asst Surgeon	1	Sub Asst Surgeons	3
British Nursing Orderlies	2	Ward Orderlies	3
Ward Servants	2	Cooks	3
Cook	1	Water Carriers	2
Water Carrier	1	Sweepers	3
Sweeper	1	A.B.C. Men	70
Bearers	30	Hospl Store Keeper	1
Pack Store Sergt	1	to work for mixed Fd Amb.	

Equipment

British Sec		Indian Sections	
Fd Medl Panniers prs	1	Fd Medl Panniers prs	6
Medl boxes light	5	Medl boxes light	15
S+T boxes light	6	S+T boxes light	15

As the medical & S+T boxes were re-equipped in India on new scale Officers Comdg Field Ambulances will use their own discretion in taking medl & S+T boxes on light scale & such ordnance equipment and stores as are absolutely necessary for

for immediate requirements.
Five busses & one lorrie will be allowed for each mixed field ambulance.

B M[...]
Colonel AMS
ADMS

"A" Form.   Army Form C. 2121.
                MESSAGES AND SIGNALS.   No. of Message ____

Prefix ___ Code ___ m. | Words | Charge | | Recd. at ___ m.
Office of Origin and Service Instructions. | | | This message is on a/c of : | Date
                              Sent
                              At ___ m.   Service.   From
                              To
                              By   (Signature of "Franking Officer.") | By

TO { O.C. NO 7 B.F.A.

Sender's Number | Day of Month | In reply to Number | A A A
      22 | 14 | |

Your field Ambulance complete will
march to VILLECHAPELLE in time
to open for reception of British
sick and wounded of
Sirhind and Jullundur Bdes by
evening of fifteenth January
if possible aaa On arrival
at VILLECHAPELLE two sections
of your field Ambulance will
join NO 112 I.F.A. to make
a mixed field Ambu-
lance under your Command and
two sections will join No 113
I.F.A. to make a mixed field
Ambulance under Command Major
BRADLEY IMS aaa Report to
G.O.C. Sirhind Brigade and G.O.C.

From
Place
Time

"A" Form.
MESSAGES AND SIGNALS.

Army Form C. 2121

Jullundur	Brigade	and	Report	also
to	A.D.M.S.	Second	Division	Locon
under	whose	orders	you	will
be	AAA	Orders	to	112
and	113	JFA	issued	separately
and	they	are	marching	
same	day			

From: A D M S Lahore Div
Time: 3-45

Colonel
ADMS

"A" Form.   Army Form C. 2121.

MESSAGES AND SIGNALS   No. of Message ____

Prefix __ Code __ m.	Words	Charge		Recd. at __ m.
Office of Origin and Service Instructions			This message is on a/c of:	Date __
	Sent At		Service	From __
	To			By __
	Y		(Signature of "Franking Officer.")	

TO { O.C. No. 7 B.F.A.

| Sender's Number | Day of Month | In reply to Number | |
| 29 | 14 | | AAA |

During the operations of the Sirhind & Jullundur Brigades you will be S.M.O. and do the administrative duties in connection with two mixed field ambulances aaa GOC Divn and some of his Staff will be at LES of LESLOBES aaa if you find that Command of the mixed field ambulance interfere with your administrative duties but Major Browne IMS in Command of the field ambulance

From: ADMS Lahore Divn

Place:

Time: 7.45 pm

Signature: MMGuy M
Colonel
ADMS

Appendix 4.

2 S.M.O.
16.1.1915.

From   S.M.O. Sirhind and Jullundur
                                    Bdes.
To   The Staff Captain
                Jullundur Bde.

Memo,
To inform you that No 7 B.F.a.
is opened at ZELOBES for reception
of sick and wounded of British
Troops of your Brigade and no 113
I.F.a. is open for Indian troops at
VIEILLE CHAPELLE.

2. Two ambulance wagons have been
detailed for No 7 B.F.A to attend
at your headquarters at 9 am
daily to collect sick of British
units and 2 wagons from
113 I.F.a. to collect the sick
of Indian units.

3. Will you please notify units
of this arrangement.

L Way
Lt Col Raine
S.M.O

Appendix 5.

3 S.M.O.
16.1.1915.

From.   S.M.O. Sirhind & Jullundur Bde

To,   The Staff Captain
                Sirhind Bde

Memo. The following is the arrangement made now for sick and wounded of your Brigade. No 7 B.F.a. has opened at ZELOBES for reception of British sick and wounded, No 113 I.F.A. has opened at VIEILLE CHAPELLE for Indian Troops

2. All sick from units will report at 9 a.m. daily at ADVANCED DRESSING STATION for British and Indian Troops which has been opened at the mayor's house RICHEBOURG ST. VAAST. on the site occupied by the old dressing station of No 5 B.F.A.

3. Please direct artillery Bdes to send their sick & wounded to No 7 B.Fa, ambulance wagons with Bdes of artillery should be utilised for this purpose or application made to No 7 B.Fa. for the required transport.

4. Please notify to all concerned the position of advanced dressing station & field ambulances.

Lt Col R—
S.M.O.

appendix 6.

16 S.M.O.
18-1-1915

From S.M.O. Lahore Detachment
To   The Brigade Major
                Sirhind Bde

Memo.

The following will be the arrangement for collection of sick of your Brigade when they leave the trenches. One ambulance wagon will call at the Brigade headquarters at 9 am daily for sick of the British unit billeted in LACOUTURE another wagon will be at No 113 I.F.A, VIEILLE CHAPELLE from the same ambulance for sick of the British unit billeted in VIEILLE CHAPELLE.

2. The OC. No 113 I Fa. has been instructed to send two ambulance wagons daily to Brigade headquarters for collection of sick of Indian units.

3. Please notify to all concerned

4. Ambulance wagons will be sent for R.Fa. if applied for from No 7 B.Fa. at ZELOBES.

Lt Col Ram c.
S.M.O.

Appendix. 7.

No 17 S.M.O.
18.1.1915

From S.M.O. Lahore Detachment

To Brigade Major, Jullundur Bde

Memo.

The following will be the arrangement for the collection of sick and wounded of your bde while at the trenches. All sick of units will report at 9 a.m. daily at the advanced dressing station for British and Indian troops which has been opened in the house next to the Church in RICHEBOURG ST. VAAST.

2. Medical Officers in charge of advanced dressing station has been instructed to get into touch with regimental aid posts at 8pm daily and they will also attend there at 8am daily if they are instructed to do so by telephonic instructions from headquarters of units, kindly let me know if this meets with your approval.

3. Sick and wounded of artillery Bdes should be sent to No 7 B. Fd. ZELOBES, ambulance wagons with Bdes of artillery being utilised for this purpose or application made to No 7 B.F.A for required transport.

4. Please notify to all concerned the position of the advanced dressing station.

L. W. a?
S.M.O.
Lt Col Ram...

Appendix 8.

URGENT.

No 20 S.M.O.
19.1.15.

From SMO
JULLUNDUR & SIRHIND BRIGADES

To O.C. No 113 I. F.a.

On the JULLUNDUR and SIRHIND Brigades changing over the medical arrangements for collection of sick and wounded will be the same as arranged before. I have communicated with Brigade Majors of both brigades. Please direct the medical officer in charge of the advanced dressing station to communicate with the Brigade Major JULLUNDUR BRIGADE and medical officers of units and point out position of advanced dressing station

LWay
Lt Col Rame
S.M.O.

Appendix 9.   URGENT   105/19.1.15

From O.C. No 7 B.F.A.
To. Lieut A. R. ALLAN.
                   R A M C.
       In charge advanced dressing station

On the JULLUNDUR and SIRHIND Brigades changing over the medical arrangements for collection of sick and wounded will be the same as arranged before.

2. Please see Brigade Major JULLUNDUR Brigade and Medical officers of units and point out position of your dressing station and arrangements for clearing of sick and wounded.

3. I have communicated with Bde Major JULLUNDUR Brigade.

4. Please acknowledge on this and return.

LWay
Lt Col Ramc
O.C. No 7 B. F. a.

"March Table"

Group	Unit in order of march	Starting Point	Time	Route to Starting Point	Destination	Route from Starting Point	Serial No	Remarks
SIRHIND BRIGADE GROUP	H.G.R.	Ry. crossing near Bde H.Q. Auchel - LOZINGHEM	8.no. 8·55	Main Street Auchel	LE CORNET MALO	HAUT and BAS RIEUX-BUSNETTES-GONNEHEM-LANNOY-LECAURON, LES HARISOIRES-PONT LEVIS	1.	
	1st H.L.I.	-No-	9·0	-No-	RIEZ de VINAGE	As No 1.	2.	
	C.R.	-No-	9·7	RAIMBERT AUCHEL ROAD	BAQUEROLLES & RUES DES VACHES	HAUT and BAS. RIEUX BUSNETTES. L'ECLEME-PONT LEVIS-ROBECQ.	3.	
	1/1 G.R.	-No-	9·14	Main Street Auchel	RUE DE CALONNE	As No 3	4.	
	½ 20th Sn	Cross roads LOZINGHEM	9·43	MARLES LOZINGHEM ROAD	L'ECANGTME	As No 3	5.	Join 1st Bn at Balomont. Lately on Pont of the B.A.A.
	No.9 B.A.A.	Ry. Crossing near Bde H.Q. Auchel LOZINGHEM RDS	9·23	Via AUCHEL church and main Street	BAQUEROLLES and RUES DES VACHES	As No 3	6.	
	No 113 F.A.	-No-	9·27	-No-	-No-	As No 3	7.	
	No 4 Coy Train	-No-	9·31	As for unit	H.Q. South of CALONNE	H.Q. as No 3. Baggage train as for units.	8	OC No 4 Coy will march off the baggage train except that of 34th which will decompany until to its starting point.
Auxil H.Q. Group	34th Pioneers H.Q. Group	Cross roads LOZINGHEM	10·34	RAIMBERT-AUCHEL and LOZINGHEM Rd	?	—	9	Come under orders of Air H.Q. Group on reaching starting point.

Serial No 34.

121/4/219

WAR DIARY
with Appendices.

No 7 British Field Ambulance.

1st February 1915 to 28th February 1915

KR/F/S

Army Form C. 2118

Vol. 2. A.I.

I. E. F. A.

WAR DIARY

or

INTELLIGENCE SUMMARY. No Y.B.F.A.

(Erase heading not required.)

Instructions regarding War Diaries and Intelligence Summaries are contained in F. S. Regs., Part II, and the Staff Manual respectively. Title pages will be prepared in manuscript.

Hour, Date, Place.	Summary of Events and Information.	Remarks and references to Appendices.
AUCHEL 1-2-15	1. Col. L. Way R.A.M.C. proceeded on seven days leave to ENGLAND. Sick – 31 from 1/H.L.I. Y 4 from 2/C.R. collected Y evacuated 6. N.4 Casualty Clearing Station – LILLERS. Baths for troops were closed Y message received from A.D.M.S. that O.C. Lahore Divisional Train has arranged for the removal of the occupants – that purchaser should accompany it to new area. Left AUCHEL at 9.23 a.m. and arrived at new billets in RUES DES VACHES Square Q.14.c reference sheet BETHUNE 1:40,000 at 3.15 p.m. Weather bright Y mild. L.J. Mitchel Capt R.A.M.C. for O.C. No Y.B.F.A.	[Stamp:] No 3 Section A. G's Office at Base I.E. Force Passed to S. Sectⁿ on 5-3-15
RUES DES VACHES – 3.15 p.m. 2.2.15	One A.B.C. man missing from the march from AUCHEL. One A.B.C. man admitted direct to the Lahore Division Clearing Hospital at LILLERS. 14 British Y 60 Indian Personnel were inoculated against Enteric. Was sorry for jam forwarded to Base. Received Brigade orders to march to CALONNE SUR LA LYS. Y other Y.A. for such of the Brigade. Weather dull Y wet. LJM	
CALONNE SUR LA LYS 3.2.15	Marched from RUES DES VACHES at 9 am arrived at 9.30 am. Y.A. opened for sick in the Church Y State School. The General Surgeon two British Y 134 Indian Personnel are still billeted in the RUES DES VACHES. One charger horse admitted to the Mobile Veterinary Section. Brigade ordered to hold itself in readiness to turn out on two hours notice from 4-2-15. 15. Sick admitted to hospital. Weather bright Y mild. LJM	

Army Form C. 2118

WAR DIARY

or

INTELLIGENCE SUMMARY.

(Erase heading not required.)

No Y B.F.A.   Vol 2 r 2

Instructions regarding War Diaries and Intelligence Summaries are contained in F. S. Regs., Part II, and the Staff Manual respectively. Title pages will be prepared in manuscript.

Hour, Date, Place.	Summary of Events and Information.	Remarks and references to Appendices.
CALONNE SUR LA LYS 4-2-15-	Sgt CHRISTIE W proceeded on 5 days leave to ENGLAND. Lieut I.R.M. ALLAN R.A.M.C. posted to medical charge of the CONNAUGHT RANGERS by order of the A.D.M.S. 11 sick admitted, 23 evacuated to No 6 Casualty Clearing Station MERVILLE, one French interpreter from 1/4 GURKHAS admitted & evacuated - suffering from N.Y.D. Faces the missing A.D.C. man has rejoined. weather bright & mild. 49 h	
CALONNE SUR LA LYS 5-2-15-	Capt W.H. O'RIORDAN R.A.M.C. has reported his arrival from leave. 86 Indian Personnel vaccinated - one dose - 100 anti-typhoid Vaccine. One officer MAJ T.L. SEEDS - 59th SCINDE RIFLES and 15 men admitted to Hospital. 3 A.B.C. men awarded twelve Strokes by APM. weather bright & mild. 49 h	
CALONNE-SUR-LA-LYS. 6-2-15-	Capt D.H.C. MACARTHUR R.A.M.C. rejoined from sick leave. 9 sick admitted. 1 officer & 20 sick evacuated by No2 Amb. Convoy to No 6 C.C.S. MERVILLE weather dull & damp. 49 h	
CALONNE-SUR-LA-LYS 7-2-15-	1 2nd Surgeon, 1 2/followers joined the unit - 1 follower admitted to hospital. 1 officer & 11 sick evacuated by Mo2M.A.C. to No 4 C.C.S. LILLERS - 3 men discharged to duty. Received SIRHIND BRIGADE OPERATION ORDER No 10 at 7.21G. re march to new area made of further attached. weather bright & mild. 49 h	Appendices 1. Vol 2 attached
CALONNE-SUR-LA-LYS 8-2-15-	No 14.11 Acting Sergt MERCER R 1st MANCHESTERS transferred Sergt & had transferred to 4 C.C.S. LILLERS. One follower admitted 6 H2.97A - 1 officer & 9 men admitted to hospital. One officer & 14 men evacuated to No 4 C.C.S LILLERS. No men discharged to duty. weather dull & damp.	

WAR DIARY
or
INTELLIGENCE SUMMARY. No 7 B 74 Vol 2 A 3

Army Form C. 2118

(Erase heading not required.)

Instructions regarding War Diaries and Intelligence Summaries are contained in F. S. Regs., Part II, and the Staff Manual respectively. Title pages will be prepared in manuscript.

Hour, Date, Place.	Summary of Events and Information.	Remarks and references to Appendices.
CALONNE-SUR-LA-LYS 9-2-15.	Hospital closed. Marched at 8.20 am to VIELLE CHAPELLE. Arrived there at 10.15am. Opened level in School House for Sick & wounded. Admitted with SMD 10 class GARHWAL BRIGADE of Sick evacuated - Indian & British. N/D WAY RAMC. Recruited Sick cases from 5-2-15 to 14-2-15. Admitted 4 wounded & 21 sick - 11 sick evacuated. Weather fine turning flurry - damp afternoon. 7/k.	
VIELLE CHAPELLE 10-2-15	One Offer Surgeon joined for duty. Sergt W CHRISTIE rejoined from base. GARHWAL BRIGADE closed of Sick & wounded. Admitted Y 20 men from hosp & 20 men Sick admitted. 2 wounded & 3 - Ok A evacuated to MERVILLE. Y 5 Ok A evacuated for twenty big other. Weather Bright & cold. 7/k	
VIELLE CHAPELLE 11-2-15	Colonel Surgeon A.R D'ARRIEU IS M.O rejoined this hosp. A.D.M.S. inspected Y reported on hand cases in hospital. Sick 1 evacuated from GARHWAL BRIGADE. Red Poste closed at 9pm, adinomining Y 1Office 1 y mer Sick. JULLUNDER BRIGADE returned GARHWAL BRIGADE. Regained evacuated 2 Officers Y 16 men. Acting Segt MERCER returned to duty. Weather Bright Hard Frost. 7/k	
VIELLE CHAPELLE 12-2-15.	1 man (Bag C.R.) died from wounds received in action. 4 ABC men sent to 113 F.A. 1000 sets of underwear, vests, shirts, socks (new) received for issue as dry clothing for men in relief from the trenches. Admitted 2 wounded Officers Y 14 men sick. Evacuated 4 wounded 1 Officer Y 7 men sick to MERVILLE. 2 men discharged to duty weather Dull & damp with light intervals. 7/k	
VIELLE CHAPELLE 13-2-15.	Y ABC men joined this unit. Capt W.H. O'RIORDAN RAMC posted to temporary medical charge of 1st H.L.I. Lieut R.M. ALLAN RAMC rejoined unit from the C.R. Received order by wire to distribute his clothing & wash and clothing of Scotland Brigade - from DAA'DMS. Sent wire to R.AA RSMS stating no previous order had been received re arrangements for washing clothes that the MEERUT DIVISION were using the baths. Second wire from DAA'DMS. stating MEERUT DIVISION had arranged to wash the clothes. Admissions 6 wounded 1 Officers Y 17 men. Sick Evacuated wounded 2 Y 1 sick 1 Officer Y 8 N.C. men. 3 men rejoined for land. Case retained for ADMS. Inspection Weather damp cold 7/k	

Army Form C. 2118

WAR DIARY
or
INTELLIGENCE SUMMARY. No 7 B.F.A. Vol 2 – p4.

(Erase heading not required.)

Instructions regarding War Diaries and Intelligence Summaries are contained in F. S. Regs., Part II, and the Staff Manual respectively. Title pages will be prepared in manuscript.

Hour, Date, Place.	Summary of Events and Information.	Remarks and references to Appendices.
VIELLE CHAPELLE 14-2-15	15 men of unit evacuated with autolyphoid vaccine. Serjt W. ROLANDS granted four days leave to England. CHAND awarded 12 strokes by A.P.M. Total admissions from AMM 19 N/S to include clothing etc. 150 Seh to 11 N.C.R. 425 hand over ordes from GARHWAL BRIGADE – a maximum number of Seh 150 p. day. Bathing establishment of MESEROY DIVISION to wash all duty clothes. Admissions – 1 wounded. 11 officers, 15 men Sick. Evacuated 1 wounded, 3 Sick. 1 officer, 10 men, 6 men discharged to duty. A.D.M.S. inspected hand cart. Weather foggy, damp, misted. 7/h.	
VIELLE CHAPELLE 15-2-15	Lieut A. WILSON RAMC detailed by A.D.M.S. for medical charge of Heavy Battery LAHORE DIVISION. One ASC man admitted to No 113 IFA. Admissions, wounded 2 Sick. 1 officer. 18 men. Evacuated 1 wounded 13 Sick. Discharged 4 men. Weather bright with some rain. 7/h.	
VIELLE CHAPELLE 16-2-15	Nothing of note. Admissions, wounded. 1 officer. 1 Head Intelpets 42 men. Sick. 11 men – Evacuated – 2 officers 42 men wounded. 1 officer 17 men Sick. Discharged to duty 3. Weather bright misted 7/h.	
VIELLE CHAPELLE 17-2-15	20 men of 114 RGA from 61 wounded evac and lyphoid vaccine notified A.P.C. that a Sick horse was left in a farm house at LOCON 7 LESTOBES ROAD. Capt W.H. O'RIORDAN reported sick for duty. Admitted 1 wounded. 6 Sick. Evacuated 3 wounded 14 Sick. Discharged 6 duty, 2 Sick. Weather damp, rainy. 7/h.	
VIELLE CHAPELLE 18-2-15	One ABC man admitted & to 113 IFA. Lieut L. WAY RAMC with Pleuralis. Major, 1 one AMC has joined the unit. Lt Col L. WAY RAMC granted extension of leave from 16.2.15 to 28.2.15 – Admissions. 10 wounded, 113 Sick. Evacuated 10 wounded, 10 Sick. 1. Discharged to duty. Weather damp misted. 7/h.	
VIELLE CHAPELLE 19-2-15	Serjt N. ROLANDS rejoined the unit from leave. Admissions 2 officers, 12 men wounded, 15 Sick. Evacuated 9 Sick. Discharged to duty 2. Weather bright & mild. 7/h.	

Army Form C. 2118

No 7 B 7a Vol 2 p 5

WAR DIARY
or
INTELLIGENCE SUMMARY.

(Erase heading not required.)

Instructions regarding War Diaries and Intelligence Summaries are contained in F. S. Regs., Part II, and the Staff Manual respectively. Title pages will be prepared in manuscript.

Hour, Date, Place.	Summary of Events and Information.	Remarks and references to Appendices.
VIELLE CHAPELLE 20-2-15	2 A.B.C men reported sick from Hospital. One Asstd. Surgeon joined for temporary duty. One Gunshot wound Rght hand admitted. Admissions 4 wounded, 1 officer 16 men sick. Evacuations - 2 officers 10 men wounded - 1 officer 10 men sick. No man discharged to duty. Two cases were discharged 20 wounds. No 1/c civils informed I ADMS, civ bearers forwarded to them. Weather dump rained 7th.	
VIELLE CHAPELLE 21.2.15.	GARHWAL BRIGADE relieved the SIRHIND BRIGADE. Wounded collected from area occupied by JULLUNDUR BRIGADE & GARHWAL BRIGADE throughout the day. H.Q. LAHORE DIVISION to remove our clothing from Rolle & No One. Admissions - 5 wounded - 1 officer 10 men sick. Evacd to C.C.S.A. N.R.C. 1 officer 7 men sick. 2 wounded. Discharged to duty 7 men. Weather kept raind with bright intervals. 7/n	
VIELLE CHAPELLE 22.2.15:	A. A.B.C men admitted 6 to 113 IFA. Evacd sick wounded from JULLUNDUR & GARHWAL BRIGADES. Collected one case of Gunshot wound R hand from HQ. 59 S.Rs. case handed over to HQ 113 IFA. Ambulance Wagon despatched all necessary precaution taken. Admissions 12 officers 15 men sick - Evacuated 6 wounded 12 officers 15 men sick - Discharged to duty 2. Weather cold frosty. 7/n	
VIELLE CHAPELLE 23.2.15:	Clothing from Rolls Establishmnt handed over to O.C. & O.C. Coffs shown to conveyance to ROBECQ. One asstd and Surgeon transferred to Labor Branch Stn LILLERS. Received orders to C/re sick wounded of JULLUNDUR & GARHWAL and DEHRA DUN BRIGADES from ADMS. Brigades classed by sick two wounded 2 ABC men aggregate in no 113 IFA. Evacd to 9 ABC Total 56 Ambro Spinal Meningitis case evacd on 22.2.15. 9 ABC Total 6 Civil. One case suspious Cerebro Spinal Meningitis admitted from no 1 Co. ASC attached to no 94 H Bat. R.F.A. ADMS informed by wire. Admissions wounded 8 sick. 10 Evacd 1/2 sick. 2 men discharged duty. Weather cold raind with bright intervals. 7/n	

Army Form C. 2118

Volume 2 - page 6.

WAR DIARY
or
INTELLIGENCE SUMMARY. No 7 B/72

(Erase heading not required.)

Instructions regarding War Diaries and Intelligence Summaries are contained in F. S. Regs., Part II, and the Staff Manual respectively. Title pages will be prepared in manuscript.

Hour, Date, Place.	Summary of Events and Information.	Remarks and references to Appendices.
VIELLE CHAPELLE 24-2-15.	Case of Cerebro Spinal Meningitis evacuated to No 18 Stationary Hospital N°OMER admissions 3 sick. Evacuated 8 sick – Sick 4 – discharged to duty. 3. one hand case transferred to AD 19 BFA. Hospital closed at 12 noon. Relits handed over to No 19 BFA. Two hand cases took on ambulance wagons to ROBECQ with unit. Unit marched to ROBECQ at 2pm & arrived at ROBECQ 5.30pm. Oral officers billeted.	APPENDIX 2 Pt 2 attached
ROBECQ 24-2-15.	& cleaning billets. Stand a school well. NO 113 JFA. Lieut H J WARWICK attached for temporary duty. Weather cold Field 7pm. admitted 3 sick.	
ROBECQ 25-2-15.	Lieut WARWICK detailed to see sick of 40th How Bark at ECLEME (appointed temporary medical charge of 18th Bde. R.F.A. & 40th How Batty. Lieut R M ALLAN detailed by ADMS take charge of Brigade Baths YMCA men admitted to Hospital. 3HC found unit. Weather cold. Snow 7pm 7pm.	
ROBECQ 26-2-15	4 Sick/Wounded men handed over to C18 Section which were detailed to remain in ROBECQ. AYB section marched to CALONNE's jungle instructions from ADMS. AYB section are to billeting handed over by JULLUNDUR Brigade entrained in building suitable for a hospital. AYB Section remained closed ADMS notified by wire. Remd Evacuation ADMS detailing AYB Section. Brenau closed. Capt C.D.K. SEAVER RAMC. Joined the unit for duty. Weather cold & frosty.	
CALONNE-SUR-LE LYS 27-2-15.	Unit AYB Section undergoing training & equipment overhauled weather – Damp & cold. 7pm.	

Army Form C. 2118.

WAR DIARY
or
INTELLIGENCE SUMMARY.   VOL 2 - page 7

(Erase heading not required.)

Instructions regarding War Diaries and Intelligence Summaries are contained in F. S. Regs., Part II, and the Staff Manual respectively. Title pages will be prepared in manuscript.

Hour, Date, Place.	Summary of Events and Information.	Remarks and references to Appendices.
CALONNE - SUR - LYS 28.2.15	No 9293 Pte W MARTIN 1st W RIDING REG. sent to LILLERS. 2nd BATT W. RID. REG. 1 about Surgeon posted to had charge of Battery R.H.A. and continues to training equipment to sing overhauled. Weather bright - frosty. Steno off. J. Mitchell Capt. R.A.M.C. for O.C. to Y.B.F.A.	

Gulab Singh & Sons, Calcutta—No. 22 Army C.—5·8·14—1,07,000.

SECRET and URGENT.

OPERATION ORDER No.10.
by
Brigadier General W.G.Walker,V.C.,C.B.,Commanding Sirhind Bde.
dated,7th February 1915.

1. The SIRHIND Brigade will march to LA COUTURE tomorrow, the 8th instant. March table attached.

2. Baggage Section of the SIRHIND Brigade Group will follow immediately in rear of the last unit of the group without any interval.

   Supply wagons will refil at present Refilling Point on morning of the 8th instant. The order re wagons carrying half loads is cancelled during the move of units.

3. Billeting officers must preceed their units tomorrow and meet the Staff Captain at Starting point at 8 a.m.

   A billeting Officer from each Ambulance will meet the Staff Captain at 3 p.m. tomorrow at ZELOBES road junction.

4. No.7 British F.A. and No.113 Indian F.A. will move on 9th instant to billets in VIEILLE CHAPELLE and ZELOBES, respectively — Route to be followed is via LE PETIT PACAUT — PARADIS — LA CIT HARNUSE — ZELOBES To march so as to be ready to open at MIDDAY the 9th instant.

5. Reports to Head of Column on March — In LA COUTURE to house on main road now occupied by Headquarters, GARHWAL Brigade.

   Ridgeway
   Captain.
   Brigade Major, Sirhind Brigade.

Copy No. 1 to O.C., 1st H.L.I.
Copy No. 2 to O.C., C.Rangers.
Copy No. 3 to O.C., 1/1st G.R.
Copy No. 4 to O.C., 1/4th G.R.
Copy No. 5 to O.C., 34th Pioneers.
Copy No. 6 to O.C., No.7 B.F.A.
Copy No. 7 to O.C., ;o. 113 I.F.A.
Copy No. 8 to O.C., No.4 Coy, A.S.C.
Copy No. 9 to Headquarters, Lahore Division.
Copies 10 and 11 War Diary.

Handed to Signal Section for despatch at 8 p.m.

"March Table"

Unit included in march	Starting Point	Time Route to Starting Point	Destination	Route to Destination	Serial No.	Remarks
1/4 G.R.	Cross roads in Sq. Q.28d	8.45	N.W. part of LACOUTURE	LES OF LES LOBES – ZELOBES – VIEILLE CHAPELLE – Road through Sq. R.28c and R.34a.B' and d.	1.	
1st H.L.I.	— No —	8.50	via LE CORNET MALO	VIEILLE CHAPELLE	As in 1 to VIEILLE CHAPELLE	2.	
6. Cameronians	Western of the two roads junctions in Sq. Q.27a	8.30	road in Sq. Q.21c	S.E. part of LACOUTURE	As in 1 to VIEILLE CHAPELLE Thence by road through Sq. R.34a.C and d.	3.	
1/1 G.R.	— No —	8.37	via CARVIN Sq. Q.19.20	S.W. of LACOUTURE	As for 3	4	
HighlandersNo 4 confr train	Cross roads in Sq. Q.28d	9.4	As for unit	H.Q. ZELOBES Baggage wagon with unit	As for unit	5	O.C. Moycof will arrange to march and march off the baggage wagons in the following order:- 1/4G.R., 1/1G.R. & J.H.

Note:- Each unit will leave a representative at VIEILLE CHAPELLE to guide the baggage wagons.

MESSAGES AND SIGNALS.

Army Form C. 2121.

Prefix	Code	m.	Words	Charge		This message is on a/c of:	Recd. at	m.
Office of Origin and Service Instructions			Sent				Date	
			At	m.		Service.	From	
			To				By	
			By		(Signature of "Franking Officer.")			

TO: No 7 B.F.A.
No 113 S.F.A.
G.O.C. Jullundur Bde.

Sender's Number	Day of Month	In reply to Number	AAA
63	20		

The field ambulance under your command will march from VIEILLECHATEAU to ROBECQ on 24th February 1915 via FOSSE - S of LESTREM - R 13 B - L'EPINETTE AAA Time of march will be about midday on relief by field ambulances of Meerut Divn AAA

Copy for information to
G.O.C. Jullundur Bde

From: ADMS Lahore Divn
Place:
Time:

The above may be forwarded as now corrected.

(Z)
Censor. Signature of Addressor or person authorised to telegraph in his name

Colonel
ADMS

WAR DIARY

OF

No. 7. British Field Ambulance; Lahore Division.

From 1st March 1915 to 31st March 1915

Army Form C. 2118.

page 1.

WAR DIARY
or
INTELLIGENCE SUMMARY.

(Erase heading not required.)

VOLUME 3

No 7 B.F. AMBULANCE.
LAHORE DIVN.
9 E. F. A.

Instructions regarding War Diaries and Intelligence Summaries are contained in F. S. Regs., Part II, and the Staff Manual respectively. Title pages will be prepared in manuscript.

Hour, Date, Place.	Summary of Events and Information.	Remarks and references to Appendices.
CALONNE SUR-LA-LYS 1-3-15.	Headquarters & "B" Sections are at CALONNE. C & D Sections are alone for Sick at ROBECQ - admissions 4 sick - Evacuated 2. Discharged 2. Weather bright & fine. W/Mitchell Cpl RAMC	
CALONNE-SUR-LA-LYS 2-3-15.	No 1411 L/Cpl MERCER R. reverted to Regimental Duty. Was placed by No 9616 Cpl MORAN J. 2nd C.R. one having orderly reported from the Base. One A.S.C. man admitted to No 113 F.A. Evacuated 2. Still continues. Admissions 1 sick. Weather bright & frost. JPM	
CALONNE SUR-LA-LYS 3-3-15.	No 34499 Pte SHAW J. No 1 A.S.C. by forfeits 8 days pay for being in neglect articles of equipment. Relating two A.S.C. men forfeited 5 days pay & awarded 5 days extra duty. Admissions 4 sick including one case evacuated from 10 C.R. Evacuated 3 sick. Two A.S.C. men sent to No 113 F.A. one since day since trans- 1 nursing orderly transferred to No 8 B.F.A. Weather bright & frost. JPM	
CALONNE SUR-LA-LYS 4-3-15.	Two ambulance began work on the road well of 4th BLACK WATCH 1 A.S.C. man 11 A.M.C. sent to No 113 F.A. 1 cook 1st E. WARWICK R. rejoined the unit. Admissions 2 sick. Evacuated 4. Weather mild & dull. JPM	Sick 8 sick admissions 1 officer Evacuated 1 officer
CALONNE SUR-LA-LYS 5-3-15.	Nothing of note. Weather chill and damp. JPM	

Army Form C. 2118

VOL III page 77
No 4 BFA
LAHORE DIVISION

WAR DIARY
or
INTELLIGENCE SUMMARY.
(Erase heading not required.)

Title pages will be prepared in manuscript.

Instructions regarding War Diaries and Intelligence Summaries are contained in F. S. Regs., Part II, and the Staff Manual respectively. Title pages will be prepared in manuscript.

Hour, Date, Place.	Summary of Events and Information.	Remarks and references to Appendices.
CALONNE-SUR-LA-LYS 6-3-15	One A.B.C. man posted to duty. 6 ADMS's office. One batman awarded minor punishment. Surplus kit of unit stored in ROBECQ. Weather damp & dull 7ph.	
CALONNE-SUR-LA-LYS 7-3-15	One AHC joined the unit. Operation order No 17 JULLUNDUR BRG. and 6 telated two sections to open in the School CALONNE and two sections in ROBECQ. No offensive 1 Vol III. Received orders from ADMS to collect cart from JULLUNDUR BRIGADE Hqrs. offensive 2 Vol III. Weather, cloudy & dull 7ph.	Offensive 1 Vol III attached Offensive 2 Vol III attached SAB F and BCD sections attended 2 officers & 4 men. Emerald 2 officers & 3 men.
CALONNE-SUR-LA-LYS 8-3-15	Arrived to School CALONNE at 8-15 am. AVB sections open for inspection at Sch. One ASC man admitted to No 10 N.Z.A. claim for damage referred to Hanson through ADMS location rest. showery with dull 7ph Zeal.	Sch & Sch CVD AVB sections attended 4 Emerald —
CALONNE-SUR-LA-LYS 9-3-15	W L & L Pay Rank ??? continuous of Sick leave from 1-3-15 to 31-3-15. Received note from ADMS LAHORE DIVISON ordering two sections to be attached to Transport Bryce. One offensive 3 Vol 3. Received note from ADMS LAHORE DIV attaching sections on ROBECQ to hand cards, my command to L'EPINETTE refer for Sch from JULLUNDUR BRG by 9am on 10-3-15. Note offensive 4 V.3 One case of measles from No 4 Coy ASC. Weather cloudy & cold 7ph	Offensive 3 Vol 3 attached Offensive 4 V 3 attached Sch attached AVB section attended 2887 Mann 3 men Emerald 1 officer 9
ROBECQ 6 am	Took over command of CVD Section R 136 at 10 am offered for Sch Square R 136. Weather Damp & Cold 7ph	Stab of Sch Advance camp at 7/13 No different 1 Maven officers 13 men
L'EPINETTE - LA CIX MARMUSE ROAD 10-2-15 Bellrave west 1-4000 Square R. 136		Emerald 1 off 724 men personnel duty 3

Army Form C. 2118

VOL III A III
No. 7. B.7.A.
LAHORE DIVISION

WAR DIARY
or
INTELLIGENCE SUMMARY.
(Erase heading not required.)

Instructions regarding War Diaries and Intelligence Summaries are contained in F. S. Regs., Part II, and the Staff Manual respectively. Title pages will be prepared in manuscript.

Hour, Date, Place.	Summary of Events and Information.	Remarks and references to Appendices.
L'EPINETTE Square R 13.6. 11-3-15.	Received orders by wire from A.D.M.S. MEERUT DIV. 4:30 p.m. to detail bearer subdivision to relieve Bearer Division of No 20 B.7.A. at advanced dressing station Square S.6. line between A.T.B. Vide appendix V attached. Ordered Cpl O'RIORDAN R.A.M.C. with bearer subdivision of C.T.D. to march out at 5:45 p.m. to relieve No 20 B.7.A. C.T.D. tent subdivision open for wounded (appendix VI attached) weather dull, misty & damp.	Appendix V attached. Appendix VI attached. State of Sick A.T.B. C.T.D. admission 9 186 - 3 own Evacuated 3 183 Brun
L'EPINETTE Square R 13.6. 12-3-15.	A.T.B. sections joined the unit at Gorre under instructions from A.D.M.S. Vide appendix VII attached. Bearer subdivision of C.T.D. still at advanced dressing station. One field Surgeon tore sadly cut to carrie at advanced dressing station. 22 wounded admitted from 7/14 K.I. were admitted for evacuation to the base weather bright, mild with rain in the evening. Tyler received partial instructions from D.A.D.M.S. Lahore Division to evacuate German wounded & hand cases remaining in hospital.	Appendix VII attached. State of Sick remained admission - wounded 60 own +1 German Sick 54- including 22 Prisoners & Enfils. Evacuated 60 wounded + 16 Sick.
L'EPINETTE Square R 13.6. 13-3-15.	7.10 a.m. Received orders from the A.D.M.S. Lahore Division to send 2 bearer subdivisions to assist evacuation (Ferozepore SIRHIND BRIG) location of Brigade to be ascertained from LAHORE REPORT CENTRE Vide appendix VIII attached - Cpl C.D.K. SENVER R.A.M.C. detailed with bearer subdivision of A.T.B. below - also attached TX attached. They left at 8.20 p.m. Reported sick and sent to A.D.M.S Lahore Division at 10:45 a.m. Bearer subdivision of C.T.D. below under Cpl O'RIORDAN R.A.M.C. returned this Division on relief at dressing station by No 112. I.F.A. Two lorries dispatched received from A.D.R.S. one D.I. Horse on exchange for sick - one from No 1 Coy A.S.C. Lahore Divisional Train weather bright & fine.	Appendix VIII Y IX attached. State of Sick - wounded admissions or sick own Evacuated - 1 German wounded two hand cases (Me) wounded Sick 41 including 22 hand cases Y Discharged to duty

Army Form C. 2118

Vol III Page IV
3 No Y.R.F.A.
LAHORE DIVISION

WAR DIARY
or
INTELLIGENCE SUMMARY.
(Erase heading not required.)

Instructions regarding War Diaries and Intelligence Summaries are contained in F. S. Regs., Part II, and the Staff Manual respectively. Title pages will be prepared in manuscript.

Hour, Date, Place.	Summary of Events and Information.	Remarks and references to Appendices.
L'EPINETTE R.136. 14-3-15.	A113 Bearer Sub division still at advanced dressing station. One sect. Surgeon detailed two sub sections charge of 1st Manchesters Regt. Much relief from A.D.M.S. Lahore Division. Bearers sub division to still at advanced Dressing Station. The Rev. F. O. JERVIS C of E posted to unit. One horse and Douglas Klemony Sidecar. Weather fine and mild. Tyler.	Sub Officer Sect. admissions 9 Wounded 1 Evacuated nil
L'EPINETTE R.136. 15-3-15.	One ABC man admitted S/to 112 I.F.A. Bearer Subdivision A113 still at advanced Dressing Station. Weather fine and chilly. Tyler.	Sub Officer admitted 2 Wounded nil
L'EPINETTE R.136. 16-3-15.	Bearer Sub division of A113 Sections rejoined unit. Services of Rev F. O. JERVIS. lent aboard goods from the Lahore provided to Rev F. O. JERVIS. 9the A.D.M.S. Lahore Division. Weather bright thaw. Tyler.	Sub Officer Sect. admitted 4 Sect. Evacuated 1wounded 112 Sect. Discharged Duty 3 men
L'EPINETTE R.136. 17-3-15.	3 A.B.C. admitted to No. 112 I.F.A. One suffering from mumps. 3 A.B.C. man joined the unit. Saving Jejuni Column - Sub. Seidler. Rout. I tent. March. Weather. bright Thaw. Tyler.	
L'EPINETTE R.136. 18-3-15.	Saving Jejuni column - weather bright thaw. Tyler.	
L'EPINETTE R.136. 19-3-15.	Saving Jejuni column - weather bright thaw with sleet. Tyler.	

Army Form C. 2118

No Y B.F.A Vol III Page V

WAR DIARY
or
INTELLIGENCE SUMMARY.
(Erase heading not required.)

Instructions regarding War Diaries and Intelligence Summaries are contained in F. S. Regs., Part II, and the Staff Manual respectively. Title pages will be prepared in manuscript.

Hour, Date, Place.	Summary of Events and Information.	Remarks and references to Appendices.
L'EPINETTE 20-3-15.	Looking after horses. Weather bright frosty 9°F.	
L'EPINETTE 21-3-15 to 23-3-15	Nothing of note. Weather bright frosty. Landed over supply command of unit to Lt Col A.C.R. HIME, R.A.M.C. 9°F. Took on charge of Petrol "Wimsishnue"	
L'EPINETTE 24-3-15.	Taking in the sick of rest division horses. Capt. T.J. Mitchell R.A.M.C. proceeded on 7 days leave to England. St. F. Warwick R.A.M.C. transferred to 108 Rn. Fd. Ambly., 4 Ors. Surgeon WINDSOR (S.M.R.) reported his arrival this day for duty. Three sick in hospital. Dull & showery all day.	1/16
L'EPINETTE 25-3-15.	Promoted 19616 Cpl. J. MORAN "Connaught Rangers" (Transport nco.) to be a Sgt. Capt. O.D.K. SEAVER, R.A.M.C. reported his departure this day on transfer to No. 141 Secunderabad Indian Cavalry Field Ambulance 2nd Ind. Cav. Division. Three sick in hospital. Dull + times heavy all day.	1/16

Army Form C. 2118

WAR DIARY
or
INTELLIGENCE SUMMARY.

(Erase heading not required.)

No 7 Br: Fd. Ambulance

(Vol. III, page VI.)

Instructions regarding War Diaries and Intelligence Summaries are contained in F. S. Regs., Part II, and the Staff Manual respectively. Title pages will be prepared in manuscript.

Hour, Date, Place.	Summary of Events and Information.	Remarks and references to Appendices.
26.3.15. L'EPINETTE.	Transport proceeded for their periodic route-march. – Followers continue daily instruction in stretcher-drill & also have day route-march. – 1 Rny. sick of while Burour & Co. SIRHIND BDE: from today. Evacuated a case of CEREBRO-SPINAL MENINGITIS in a Pt: of MARCHES -TER REGT:. He was located in Regt: Aid Post of CONNAUGHT RANGERS. Notified A/D.M.S. LAHORE DIVN.	Sick State:– Admitted 15 Transferred 8. Discharged 2. Remaining 8 K6
27.3.15. L'EPINETTE.	Some G.S.-wagons received this morning in exchange for 4 from A.T. carts, returned to BURGETTE. No 34499 Dr. SHAW, A.S.C. granted 7 days leave to ENGLAND from 28.3.15. Evacuated a case of Epilepsy case, which was left at CONNAUGHT RANGERS Aid Post, was transferred to ST: OMAR at 10 P.M. 15 mjds by Motor Ambulance. 5 Pakali Wheelie attached to this Ambulance sent to No 113 F.A. from with their dresser prior to return to India. Occidental G.S.W. was admitted. Snow fell night & day.	Stk:g Sick:– Admitted 1 Officer 11 men Transferred 1 Ofr 6 men Discharged 2 Remaining 11 K6
28.3.15 L'EPINETTE	Head Quartered Centre & Spinal fever was not a case of their disease. A.D.M.S. inspected the case of accidental G.S.W. hand. Snow during night – and again day.	Sick State:– Admitted 6 Transferred 9 Discharged 3 Remaining 6 K6

Army Form C. 2118

N° 7 Br: Fd: Amb:

Vol: III   p. VII

WAR DIARY
or
INTELLIGENCE SUMMARY.

(Erase heading not required.)

Instructions regarding War Diaries and Intelligence Summaries are contained in F. S. Regs., Part II, and the Staff Manual respectively. Title pages will be prepared in manuscript.

Hour, Date, Place.	Summary of Events and Information.	Remarks and references to Appendices.
29.3.15. L'EPINETTE.	Lt: STRODE, R.A.M.C. reported his arrival from N° III Ind: Fd: Amb: at 12 noon. Training of Bearers & exercises of horses as usual. No case of Measles admitted from CONNAUGHT RANGERS — transferred 3 C.C.S. CHOQUES. 1 Bearer admitted to Hospl: - normal piv.	State of Sick. Admitted 18 Transferred 9 Discharged 5 Remaining 13
30.3.15. L'EPINETTE.	Received orders for Ambulance to move to VIEILLE CHAPELLE on 31.3.15, & to fit for receipt of sick & wounded from SIRHIND & FEROZEPORE Bdes. Fine bright day — with cold South wind.	State of Sick Admitted 10/ffg 13 men Transferred 10/ffg 14 men Discharged 1 " Remaining 18
31.3.15. VIEILLE CHAPELLE.	Left L'EPINETTE 2p.m. & arrived VIEILLE CHAPELLE 4p.m. Passed N°55 R.F. Amb: en route. Took over schools & Villa from N° IX R.F.A. also from patients. Capt: MITCHELL R.A.M.C. returned from 7 days leave to England last evening & Lt: ALLAN R.A.M.O. departs on 7 days leave to ENGLAND. Commenced surrounding Regtl: Aid Posts of FEROZEPORE and SIRHIND Bdes. Bright, fine, cold day.	State of Sick Admitted 10/ffg 22 men Transferred 10/ffg 16 men Discharged 1 " Remaining 10 "

Operation Order No. 17   Copy No. 12

By

Brig-General E. P. Strickland C.M.G., D.S.O

Commanding Jullundur Bde

7th March 1915

1. The Bde and No. 3 Coy Train, less 15th Sikhs, will march this evening to an area South of LESTREM.

2.   47th Sikhs
       59th Rifles
       1st Manchester Regt, less 1 Coy.
       1st Line Transport
       No. 3 Coy Train

Rear Guard

1 Coy 1st Manchester Regt.

The head of the above column will pass the cross roads on the CHEMIN DE BETHUNE square Q5b at 7.30 pm and will march via point 19 thence via the road in squares Q12c and 'd' to L'EPINETTE thence due South to the Road junction in square R.13b. North, and from this point units will march direct to their billets.

3. The Transport Officer, 1st Manchester Regt will be in charge of all 1st L.T

4. The 15th Sikhs will join the SIRHIND Bde under separate orders.

5. Bde Headquarters in the new area will be between the two road junctions in square R.13.d North.

6. Field Ambulances will be situated as follows:-

No. 7 BFA will open two sections at the School CALONNE and two Sections in ROBECQ.

No. 8 BFA will concentrate at ST FLORIS

No. 111 SFA will remain at   LAMIQUELLERI

     112 SFA   "   "   CALONNE

     113 SFA   "   "   ROBECQ

7. Reports to head of Column.

H. Still, Major
Brigade Major Jullundur Bde.

Copy No 1   1st Manch R.   7. O/c Bde Reserve SAA
        2   15th Sikhs   8 D Sec Lahore Sig Coy
        3   59th Rifles   9 & 10 Diary
        4   47th Sikhs   11 No. 7 BFA
        5   No. 3 Coy Train   12 No. 8 BFA

"A" Form.
Army Form C. 2121.

MESSAGES AND SIGNALS.

TO — OC No 7 BFA

Sender's Number	Day of Month	In reply to Number	AAA
74	7		

The two Secs under your Command near CALONNE will march tomorrow morning to CALONNE and open in the School behind Church for Bdewick of the Jullundur Bde which should be collected each afternoon at 2pm till further orders aaa Location of Brigade will be communicated separately. aaa Your Unit should arrive at CALONNE by 9am

From — ADMS Lahore Divn
Place —
Time — 2.50 pm

Jul Shaw
Colonel
Jort DMS

"A" Form.   Army Form C. 2121

MESSAGES AND SIGNALS.

app iii Volume III

TO: Ferozepore Bde

Sender's Number	Day of Month	In reply to Number	AAA
78	9		

Reference para seven of operation order no 66 dated sixth March by GOC Lahore Divn aaa the medical units allotted to your Brigade are No 112 I.F.A. and two Secs No 7 BFA at present in CALONNE aaa major BROWSE IMS will act as SMO of Brigade aaa addressed Ferozepore Bde copy to field ambulances concerned

From: ADMS Lahore Divn

Time: 9.45 am

Colonel
ADMS

"A" Form.   Army Form C. 2121.
MESSAGES AND SIGNALS.

Prefix	Code	m.	Words	Charge	This message is on a/c of :	Recd. at	m.
Office of Origin and Service Instructions.			Sent			Date	
			At	m.	Service.	From	
			To				
			By		(Signature of "Franking Officer.")	By	

TO O.C. NO 7 B.F.A.

Sender's Number	Day of Month	In reply to Number	AAA
83	9		

Two sections of your Unit from ROBECQ should be evacuated today and march tomorrow morning under your command via MT BER- NENCHON PONT LEVIS Square Q.32A LACORNET MALO LACROIX MARMUSE to L'EPINETTE arriving there by 9am and open there for reception of British Sick in Kunour Bde area of which will be communicated to you by O.C. No 113 F.A LACROIX MARMUSE

From A.D.M.S Lahore Divn
Place
Time

The above may be forwarded as now corrected. (Z)

Received at 12.20. Censor.   Signature of Addressor or person authorized to telegraph in his name

Colonel
A.D.M.S

"A" Form.   Army Form C. 2121.

MESSAGES AND SIGNALS.

Prefix	Code	m.	Words	Charge	This message is on a/c of:	Recd. at	m.
Office of Origin and Service Instructions			Sent		156	Date	
			At	m.	Service.	From	
Appendix			To			By	
			By		(Signature of "Franking Officer.")		

TO { OC Y B.F.A. at Zelobes Refilling Centre
     Sgr R 13 F.

Sender's Number	Day of Month	In reply to Number	AAA
F.24	11		

Send your bearer subdivisions and ambulance waggons to relieve those of 20 B.F.A. at Advanced Dressing Station S.8 line between a + b. (Dead Tree corner) this afternoon. On being relieved by Y B.F.A. waggons and bearer division of 20 B.F.A. will return to ZELOBES to rest. You will receive wounded tent division of your own ambulance

From
Place
Time

The above may be forwarded as now corrected.   (Z)

Censor.   Signature of Addressor or person authorised to telegraph in his name

*This line should be erased if not required.

Vol III appx- VI.

To Capt O'RIORDAN
         R.A.M.C.

The bearer sub division of C.T.D. Sections will proceed at 5-45 p.m. tonight, under your command, to Square S.8. line between a.16 ref. map BETHUNE 1-40000, & relieve bearer division of No 20, B.F.A. MEERUT DIVISION. The third ambulance will be sent after you on its return from MERVILLE

Z.J. Mellor. 1? Capt
               [illegible]
         for OC No 1.B.7.A.

11-3-15.
4-30 p.m.
R. 126.

"A" Form. Army Form C. 2121.

Volume III appen 7.

MESSAGES AND SIGNALS.

Prefix	Code	m.	Words	Charge	This message is on a/c of:	Recd. at	m.
Office of Origin and Service Instructions.			Sent			Date	
			At	m.	Service.	From	
			To				
			By		(Signature of "Franking Officer.")	By	

TO: OC Secs A.B. & 7 BFA
CALONNE

Sender's Number	Day of Month	In reply to Number	AAA
92	11		

The two Secs under your Command will march tomorrow morning to Square R.13.B. and rejoin the Head Quarters of your Unit via PARADIS Square R.13.C. arriving there by 7 a.m.

From: ADMS Lahore Divn
Place:
Time: 9.10 pm

The above may be forwarded as now corrected. (Z)

Jno Sloan
Lt Col
Colonel
ADMS

Censor. Signature of Addressor or person authorised to telegraph in his name

* This line should be erased if not required.

Vol iii appx VIII

MESSAGES AND SIGNALS.

"A" Form. Army Form C. 2121.

Prefix _____ Code _____ m. Words 30 Charge _____
Office of Origin and Service Instructions
Priority

Sent At _____ m.
To _____
By J Reid

This message is on a/c of:
_____ Service.
(Signature of "Franking Officer.")

Recd. at _____ m.
Date _____
From HC
By J Reid

TO Commdg 7 BHA

| Sender's Number | Day of Month | In reply to Number | AAA |
| 95 | 13th | | |

Send 2 bearer sub-divisions to assist evacuation of wounded of 8 [?] [?] [?] [?] location from Baker report Genl Reid.

From Place: 21st Hrs Lahore Divn 4.40 PM
Time

The above may be forwarded as now corrected. (Z)

Censor. Signature of Addressor or person authorised to telegraph in his name.

Vol iii Appx IX.

To:
Capt C.D.K. SEAVER
R.A.M.C.

Ref. A.D.M.S. No 95 dt 13-3-15.

(1) You will proceed with the Bearer sub division of A&B Sections to assist in evacuation of wounded of SIRHIND BRIGADE.

(2) Location of SIRHIND BRIGADE to be ascertained from Lahore H.Q. Report Centre.

(3) March out at 8-20 a.m.

7-20 a.m.
13-2-15.

T.J. Mitchell Capt.
R.A.M.C.
for O.C. No 7 B.F.A

121/5584

April 1915

General No 34

WAR DIARY
With Appendices
of
No. 7 British Field Ambulance Lahore
Division.
From 1st April 1915 to 30th April 1915

MK 6/7

Army Form C. 2118.

Page 1

WAR DIARY
or
INTELLIGENCE SUMMARY. No 7. B.F. AMBULANCE.
LAHORE DIVN.

Volume IV

(Erase heading not required.)

Instructions regarding War Diaries and Intelligence Summaries are contained in F. S. Regs., Part II, and the Staff Manual respectively. Title pages will be prepared in manuscript.

Hour, Date, Place.	Summary of Events and Information.	Remarks and references to Appendices.
1.4.15. VIEILLE CHAPELLE.	Sharpshaw Coy: - Admitted 4 wounded. Nothing special to note. Second Field Ambulance sent units to FEROZEPORE & SIRHIND Bde. Orders from A.D.M.S. LAHORE DIVN. for his Ambulance to collect sick and wounded from FEROZEPORE Bde. at night, also to collect sick of JULLUNDUR Bde. whose nearest F.A.	Sick & Wounded: Admitted 12, Transferred 10, Discharged 0, Died 1, Remaining 16. app: 12 attd.
2.4.15. VIEILLE CHAPELLE.	Genl. Sir J. WILLCOCKS visited Fd. Ambl. in the morning. 11 wounded admitted. 2 suspicious cases of Scarlet fever in Signal Coys. 3 A.B.C. men admitted to No. 11 F.A. suffering from mumps. Dull wet fine day.	Sick & Wounded: Admitted 29, Transferred 18, Discharged 0, Died 1, Remaining 26. S/Ab
3.4.15. VIEILLE CHAPELLE.	1 officer admitted shell wound (Fatal) 7 wounded. Some wounded admitted. Raining nearly whole day. Shrapnel wound G.S.W. Head. Nothing special to report. No. 11 relieving of A.B.C. + A.B.C. Servants.	Sick & Wounded: Admitted 10 off, 15 men, Transferred 10 off, 19 men, Discharged 0, Died 1, Remaining 9. S/Ab
4.4.15. VIEILLE CHAPELLE.	1 Officer admitted (Lt. Ambler) suffering from MEASLES. 5 A.B.C. sent to Fd. amb. suffering from MUMPS. 5 wounded admitted to troops - no serious cases. Rained all day on & off.	Sick & Wounded: Admitted 1 off, 20 men, Transferred 11, Discharged 2, Died 2, Remaining 25 men. S/Ab
5.4.15. VIEILLE CHAPELLE.	Rained all day. 2 officers with measles admitted. Acc. Sergt. TYNE (S.W.B.) 4 a.B.C. men with mumps. 3 cases of mumps in N.S.C. Nothing special to report.	Sick & Wounded: Admitted 3 off, 20 men, Transferred 2, Discharged 1, Died 1, Remaining (illegible). S/Ab

Army Form C. 2118.

WAR DIARY
or
INTELLIGENCE SUMMARY.
(Erase heading not required.)

Volume IV page 2.

N° vii British Field Ambulance
LAHORE Div?

Instructions regarding War Diaries and Intelligence Summaries are contained in F. S. Regs., Part II, and the Staff Manual respectively. Title pages will be prepared in manuscript.

Hour, Date, Place.	Summary of Events and Information.	Remarks and references to Appendices.
6.4.15. VIEILLE CHAPELLE	Fine sunny morning. Turned to rain in afternoon. Ferozepore Bde Hd.Qrs. near PONT DU HEM struck by shell in afternoon killing man & wounding 1 Officer (Maj. STEWART) & 1 Staff (Capt: (Cam. N.dr.s)) and 3 men. Dispatched motor Ambulance out at 4.45 p.m. & brought down 2 Fd Ambulance. All water (drinking) used in the 2d Ambulance to being treated with Bleaching Powder added to the water. The water carts - Travel latrines in use - Rubbish burnt in incinerators.	State of sick & wounded - Officers. Men Admitted 1 off. 23 men Wounded — 22 — Discharge — 2 — Remaining — 21 —
7.4.15 VIEILLE CHAPELLE	Fine with high wind. Bus shed in which 25 horses of Bn. were stabled came down this morning owing to the high wind - no horses seriously injured. Wounded in the A.F.I.S. Lahore Divn. 1 Off. admitted with wounds (Inftry) Admitted from a 2 admitted. Major O/Pa R.C. paid the afternoon. Right wounded admitted. Capt. Leroy Pinto R.N.O. admitted with wounds & transferred to LILLIERS. evidently contracted for the infected Villa - L'EPINETTE. O men of A.B.C. sent for duty. Lt. STRODE R.A.M.C. transferred to N° 3 B.F. Ambl.	State of sick & wounded: Admitted 1 off. 1 men — 38 Wounded — 16 Discharge — 2 Remaining 1 off. 42
8.4.15. VIEILLE CHAPELLE	Seven R.B.C. men sent for duty. One officer admitted with criticism - two wounded admitted. Cold dull windy day. Dispatched all Ambulance Wagons from the clearing stations. Nothing special to report.	State of sick & wounded Admitted 1 off. 23 men Wounded 1 — 32 — Discharge — 10 Remaining 1 off. 24
9.4.15. VIEILLE CHAPELLE	1st Bn. Manch. Regt. patients dispatched. Lt. ALLAM R.A.M.C. transferred to H.L. & Frantz for duty vice Lt. JEPSON Transferred sick. One officer - admitted from 4th Suffolk Regt. to Private - sent infection - Lt. JACKSON. Ambulance brought up to Regtl Aid Post. & arrived admitting base - 4th King (Liverpool) Regt. admitted 11 p.m. was reported dying on arrival from Cerebro Spinal Meningitis.	State of sick & wounded Admitted 1 off. 20 men Wounded — 16 — Discharge — 3 — Remaining 2 off. 27 —

Army Form C. 2118.

WAR DIARY
or
INTELLIGENCE SUMMARY.
(Erase heading not required.)

Vol: IV page 3.

N° VII British F.A. Ambulance
LAHORE Div:

Instructions regarding War Diaries and Intelligence Summaries are contained in F. S. Regs., Part II, and the Staff Manual respectively. Title pages will be prepared in manuscript.

Hour, Date, Place.	Summary of Events and Information.	Remarks and references to Appendices.
10.4.15. VIEILLE CHAPELLE.	Lt. JACKSON, Lt. KNAPP (Liverpool) Regt. transferred to 2nd OMAR Fd. Amb. (10.30am) hand over and Received information regarding Bearer cases which we had transferred to 9 Casualty Clearing Station which we placed one bicious case of Cerebro Spinal Meningitis, offic of A.D.M.S. LAHORE Div. Transferred to ESTAIRES. Capt. TURNER, 106 HAZARA Pioneers admitted G.S.W. HAND (L).	State of sick & wounded: — Admitted 1896 16 min 18 — Remaining 3 — 22 —
11.4.15. VIEILLE CHAPELLE.	One light morning — went out to see Old Posts (Regt.) Hd Qrs havana from relief. we are to collect casualties. Received orders from ADMS. LAHORE Div. regarding Collection of cases also from Regtl. aid Posts of the MEERUT Div. LAHORE — LAHORE & MEERUT Divs. sharing over, as the Divs. are now also composed by a portion of 8th Division (Army (2nd Bdy)). Appendix III attached. Admitted one previous case CEREBRO SPINAL MENINGITIS, removed from us at 10pm. 116	State of Sick & wounded: — Admitted 26 min Appendix III Discharge 3 — Remaining 20 — Appendix III attached.
12.4.15. VIEILLE CHAPELLE.	Had Richmony but Lt. JACKSON Hut and two tents erected CEREBRO-SPINAL MENINGITIS Patient (formal negative. two fields to but recently a confirmed by one Previous case of Cerebro Spinal Meningitis who to 4 London Regt: attached — VIEILLE CHAPELLE. Evacuations from ADMS LAHORE Div: that Bearer Divs. of this ambulance were to evacuate casualties on W. side of ESTAIRE — LA BASSE Road. Rendezvous at Cross roads S 2.00 1am. SP horse appeals to be more satisfactory. If all Regtl aid Posts were moved at the morning One district shewed magnis early 4 must now commenced done — safer than at night. Evacuations from ADMS. Div. to bearers to No XX B.F.A. Division, and march to New Wells. All remaining cases to be handed over to JO XX B.F.A. 116	State of sick wounded: — Admitted 16ff 25min General Do — Discharge d — Remaining 26ff 1816 — Appendix iv attached. Appendix V attached

Army Form C. 2118.

WAR DIARY
or
INTELLIGENCE SUMMARY.
(Erase heading not required.)

Vol. IV. Page 4

N° VII British Fd. Ambulance

LAHORE DIV.

Hour, Date, Place.	Summary of Events and Information.	Remarks and references to Appendices.
Rc 13.4.15. ROBECQ.	Left VIEILLE CHAPELLE at 11.30 a.m., on arrival of N° XX B.F.A. Marched via FOSSÉ Bridge – Rqc – R7D – L'ÉPINETTE – Q12C – CALONNE – and arrives ROBECQ 2.15 a.m. Excellent march, both men & transport going well. Handed over 5 cases to N° XX B.F.A. on our departure, including one case of sunstroke. CO'S Bde = PIMA MENINGITIS in the 4th London Regt. Received orders from A.D.M.S. for Capt: MITCHELL R.A.M.C. to take over charge of the Baths via Capt: BOYD IMS. (proceeding on leave on 16th inst:). Reported arrival here to A.D.M.S. 25th ABC left behind (vide list in Batho.	State of Unit: twenty-eight Admitted 0 Invalided 1 off, 22 men Transferred to XXX + XX 5 Remaining 1 Discharge 1 man
14.4.15. ROBECQ.	Billets – Rue de Bethune P29d – are Quart of followers in Barn & Wellsgood. Received orders for one Ass. Surgeon to report to Detached Section, LAHORE Div. Amm. Col. at CALONNE. Had all wagons + Ambulances washed + cleaned. Pulls drizzly day.	V.G.
15.4.15. ROBECQ.	Ass. Surgeon THYNE detailed for duty with detached Sect. Div. Am. Col. am. left this morning. Two men A.B.C. admitted to Hosp. suffering from trench feet. Visit from A.D.M.S., LAHORE Div. 2 I/C man of A.B.C. who was left behind at VIEILLE CHAPELLE for duty at the battle rejoined today.	V.G.
16.4.15. ROBECQ.	Senior Dental Surgeon DEWEY I.S.M.D. Lieut Lieutenant. Btne. visits Ambulance this afternoon – also a Senior Veterinary Surgeon (Lt. Col.) Dull, dryish day.	V.G.

Army Form C. 2118.

WAR DIARY
or
INTELLIGENCE SUMMARY.

(Erase heading not required.)

XXVII Portd Field Ambulance. LAHORE DIV?

VOL IV pages 5

Instructions regarding War Diaries and Intelligence Summaries are contained in F. S. Regs., Part II, and the Staff Manual respectively. Title pages will be prepared in manuscript.

Hour, Date, Place.	Summary of Events and Information.	Remarks and references to Appendices.
17.4.15. ROBECQ.	Commenced evening over the midden. The centre of the farm yard with earth in accordance with Lt. Col. Omay's orders. A.D.M.S. 1-4-15 a most flagitious & impracticable order to fulfil, in the midst or centre of this large sq. the men R.E.C. admitted Hospital. Having all ambulances & wheeled [transport?]. 1/6	
18.4.15. ROBECQ.	Orders received for Capt. MacArthur R.A.M.C. to report to O.C. V.B. de Ca.... R.F.A. for duty, as M.O. Vacancies exist. This leaves myself + one other M.O. for duty with the Ambulance. 1/6	
19.4.15. ROBECQ.	Two horses broke loose during night 18/19 & are still missing this morning. They have been in various raids & stables apparently made little or no effort to retain them. They were grazed on the C. one. But they were driven from there when he (master of them) galloped off. Report to A.D.M.S. Lahore Div. Sunday day. 1/6	
20.4.15. ROBECQ.	Horses not yet found. Bungle search was made all day yesterday. Report to O.C. L.F.D.T. SVS morning but fruitless. all fruitless. 1/6	
21.4.15. ROBECQ.	The two lost horses were found this morning with the 81st Bt. R.F.A. Received one horse from No.1 Cmd. Lahore Division to replace one lost by A.D.V.S. one [man?] admitted to Hospl. rep'g. Sect: Dull day with a little rain	
22.4.15. ROBECQ.	No 34499 Pt. SHAW J. A.S.C. awarded 7 days R.P. Punishment No 1 for "absent from 4.P.M. stable". Sent to A.P.M. Bri. to have punishment carried out. H. FINDLEY R.A.M.C. of 16th [unclear] ordered, but was late, undertaken from ABrive, ordered to	

Gulab Singh & Sons, Calcutta — No. 22 Army C—5/8/14–1,07,000.

Army Form C. 2118.

WAR DIARY
or
INTELLIGENCE SUMMARY.

(Erase heading not required.)

No vii British Field Ambulance "LAHORE Div." Vol IV Page 6

Instructions regarding War Diaries and Intelligence Summaries are contained in F. S. Regs., Part II, and the Staff Manual respectively. Title pages will be prepared in manuscript.

Hour, Date, Place.	Summary of Events and Information.	Remarks and references to Appendices.
22.4.15 (Cont) ROBECQ.	Relieve Capt. MACARTHUR as Medical charge of 5th Bde. R.F.A. He letter to return to this Ambulance (orders). A.D.M.S. visits this ambulance today.	
23.4.15 ROBECQ.	Fine day - Received orders at 5:30 pm for this Ambulance (Bde prepares) to move at short notice by train - all arrangements were made - waggons attacked + all personal warned and to have kits (Appendix attached) Capt MAC ARTHUR R.A.M.C. developes measles - views to A.D.M.S. Applic to O.C. LAHORE D.T. for another in am to replace BRENAN A.S.C. sent a Hosp. measles + invalided. NB.	Appendix vi (attached).
24.4.15 ROBECQ.	Capt. MAC ARTHUR R.A.M.C. admitted to Hpl with measles. 11.45 am recd: order from ADMS to be prepared to move at short notice - waggons to be packed (App: vii) 2.35 pm received orders to march, at starting point LE GRAND PACAUT 3.20pm) to KROIXTRAELE and South of MT DESCAT. (App xviii). Started at 2pm marching near No 112 IFA headqrs. Many stops on joined owing to congestion of troops. Went into billets at MT DESCAT. A team here. Trung strenous march, fine at first but heavy rain from 11 p.m.	App: vii (attached) App: viii (attached)
25.4.15 MT. DESCAT.	2.30 am. Recd orders to march to NUTMURTS N.E. of ORDERDOM from starting point at 10.40 am. Later received verbal orders to march at 11 pm. On arrival at WESTOUTRE Started ambulance and noted on to see ARMOUR OUDERDOM. Received from ADMS verbal orders to point bill	Appendix IX (attached)

Gulab Singh & Sons, Calcutta.—No. 22 Army C.—5.8.14—1,07,000.

Army Form C. 2118.

Vol. VI. P. 7
N° un Bntish Fd Amb.
LAHORE DIV.

WAR DIARY
or
INTELLIGENCE SUMMARY.
(Erase heading not required.)

Instructions regarding War Diaries and Intelligence Summaries are contained in F. S. Regs., Part II, and the Staff Manual respectively. Title pages will be prepared in manuscript.

Hour, Date, Place.	Summary of Events and Information.	Remarks and references to Appendices.
25.4.15. WESTOUTRE	1st night at WESTOUTRE. At 7.30pm. ASHore visited the Ambulances & informed me Field Ambulance might have to move at daybreak. Instructions were to await March from MT BISCAT to WESTOUTRE difficult owing to bumpy hilly road. Lt. Frankfort + men came along splendidly without a breakdown of any kind. Fine summer day.	
26.4.15. WESTOUTRE OUDERDOM	7.5 am. received orders from ASHore to march at 8am. to OUDERDOM and take over billets from N° 8 R.F.A. Open to receive Sick. Arrived OUDER. DOM 8.55 am. took over 15 sick, including 1 case measles. Capt. MITCHELL RAMC reported his arrival at 12 noon on return from leave. Took over temporarily duty = charge of Duties. Received orders from ASHore (from N°1's Field Ambulance) tents operating and utensils to be temporarily (from N°1's Field Ambulance) prepared for the reception of Patients — these were ready. Received orders from ASHore this P.M. to 1112 I.F.A. to hand over 15th. Latter all tents in charge of N° 112 I.F.A. This was done. In accordance with instructions received at 11.45 pm. six Ambulance Wagons were placed at the disposal of O.C. N°112 I.F.A. At 6 pm. Received orders reserving from ASHore for Capt. O'RIORDAN RAMC to proceed to VLAMERTINGHE for temporary duty with 1st Bn. of N°9 B.F.A.	after: × attaches JG

Army Form C. 2118.

WAR DIARY
or
INTELLIGENCE SUMMARY.
(Erase heading not required.)

Vol vi P.2.
No viii British Fd Ambl.
LAHORE Dn

Instructions regarding War Diaries and Intelligence Summaries are contained in F.S. Regs., Part II, and the Staff Manual respectively. Title pages will be prepared in manuscript.

Hour, Date, Place.	Summary of Events and Information.	Remarks and references to Appendices.
27.4.15 OUDERDOM.	Took over two large barns (by patients plaster. Received about 130 wounded during the day (Br. 50, Ind, 80) + wounded. Evacuated during afternoon & night. All serious wounds treated with Formaline dressing, then Pl. vessine. 1500 write ambulance serv. Ambulance wagons continued at 10 a.m. to bring cases from Royal As post. Buses ordered to return owing to shelling which was very fce. Sent them out again at 4 p.m. When they managed to reach the posts in a circuitous route — bring back 50 Br & Ind. patients at about 8.30 p.m. Capt. O'RIORDAN rejoined Unit at 7.30 am. At 10 a.m. 3 ambulances OC No viii B.F.A. at VLAMERTINGHE & wounded to remove 100 Rho pts. Near hospital nearby but none was found. As hospital arrangement for wounded. No 8 B.F.A. was handed over to at the time.	State Wounded wdg 12 noon 27. British Rec'd O.R. 26 Indians O.R. 57 State wdd British O.R. 14 14 Indians to O.R. 4
28.4.15 OUDERDOM.	Took over another room for patients, other row, with the tents bring wounded to 12 noon 28. accommodation for about 250 pts. Sent out Ambulance wagons at 11.30 am. to bring cases from Regt. Aid Post of 57th JEAN. Rec'd verbal orders from RAMC for Capt O'RIORDAN to proceed to ST JEAN with 15 stretcher squads at 5 p.m. to clear Regt Ai Post bring wounded in his Ambulances.	British O.R. 35 Indians O.R. 41

Army Form C. 2118.

WAR DIARY
or
INTELLIGENCE SUMMARY.
(Erase heading not required.)

Vol. VI. P.9
30 VII B... Fd. Amb.   LAHORE Div

Instructions regarding War Diaries and Intelligence Summaries are contained in F. S. Regs., Part II, and the Staff Manual respectively. Title pages will be prepared in manuscript.

Hour, Date, Place.	Summary of Events and Information.	Remarks and references to Appendices.
	At 5 pm received instructions for Capt. MITCHELL RAMC to report for duty temporarily with 30 VIII B.F.A. Lieuts J.T. GUNN and G.D. CAIRNS RAMC and Cpl Sergeant McGUIRE 19 M.D. reports for duty with Regiment 6 ABC men join for duty 1/6	Strength of personnel 5.12 noon BRoR 15 S.O.R. 1 ORS. 3
29.4.15 OUDERDOM	Capt MITCHELL RAMC. returned from Tambourg duty with 3108 B.F.A. At 10 am received 8 Indian Ambulance for work in connection with the Fd. Ambulance. At 12 noon 4 went out to collect casualties from attack. Dressing Stn: at ST JEAN also went out at 4 pm. Capt O'RIORDEN returns about 10 pm to report that his Dressing Stn has been shelled during the afternoon & to report that his wounded personnel has been wounded. At 8.5 pm received orders from A.D.M.S. to effect that JULLUNDUR + FEROZEPORE Bde. were being relieved tonight at 9 & tomorrow respectively. On completion of clearing Aid Posts Bearer Div. proceed. Motor Ambulance to return. (App: XI attached) At 12 mn. Lt. GUNN RAMC. proceed with 7 motor Ambul. to advance crossing VLAMERTINGHE – YPRES road to pick up stragglers & the Bedes coming out of trenches.	State of personnel 15.12 noon B.O. 3 ORS 37 B.O. 4 ORS 12 After XI attack

Army Form C. 2118.

WAR DIARY
or
INTELLIGENCE SUMMARY.
(Erase heading not required.)

Vol VI P1a

No 7 British Fd. Amb.
LAHORE Dn.

Instructions regarding War Diaries and Intelligence Summaries are contained in F. S. Regs., Part II, and the Staff Manual respectively. Title pages will be prepared in manuscript.

Hour, Date, Place.	Summary of Events and Information.	Remarks and references to Appendices.
30.4.15 OUDERDOM	10.30am recd orders from APM[?] Fld Servs to retain No 7 Brit. & No 113 I.F.A. Sirhind Bde Field Ambs. is remaining. The Reinforcing Pack No 7 B.F.A. & No 113 I.F.A. men to remain there until Bde. had left. Ambulance to march after escorts to rejoin Divn. — (Appx XII). At 12.20 Sent memo to Staff Captain SIRHIND Bde: asking him to inform me as early as possible whether the Bde. moved much later than he could take destruction or arrangements he still made for evacuation of casualties then being Unstragglers (Appx XIII). At 7.45 pm received orders to evacuate all sick of FEROZEPORE & JULLUNDUR Bdes. tonight & tomorrow morning from HUTMENTS on VLAMER-TINGHE OUDERDOM Road. (Appx XIV). Arrange for this unit to collect sick of JULLUNDUR Bde & for No 113 I.F.A. to collect sick of FEROZEPORE Bde. One case measles admitted 11.55 pm from 4th Suffolk Regt. JC Attune Lieut/Colonel O.C. No VII B.F.A.	Strength of unit: Officers/NCO's 12 each [?] British B.O. 3 O.R.B. 48 Appx XII attached. Appx XIII attached. Appx XIV attached.

Appx 1. Volume V   146
                                8-4-15

To The O.C. No 7 B.F.A.
         III I.F.A.

The following transport and personnel
of your Unit should rendezvous
at ROUGECROIX tonight and till
further orders at 7.30 p.m. and
collect sick and wounded from the
~~Sirhind~~ Ferozepore Bde Units, British
                Sirhind
Casualties to No 7 B.F.A. Indian to
No III I.F.A:—
   One Officer, 2 I.S.M.D, ten stretcher
parties & 3 ambulance wagons
   One I.S.M.D. from each Unit
should accompany the party from
the other unit — each party being
thus a mixed one. One I.S.M.D.
from each Unit to remain out till
daylight with two stretcher parties
and one wagon to bring in Casualties
occurring during the night.
Route ZELOBES-VIEILLECHAPELLE-LA-
COUTURE-CROIXBARBEE-ROUGECROIX-
M.21A-M.26A-M.20C-VIEILLECHAPELLE
                                ZELOBES

BM Gray Colt
Colonel MS
DMS Lahore Divn

Appx II. Volume IV

"A" Form.
MESSAGES AND SIGNALS.
Army Form C. 2121.

TO: O.C. No 111 Indian Field Amb:

Sender's Number: 150
Day of Month: 1st

Send motor ambulance daily at 9 a.m. to collect Indian sick of Jullundur Brigade from area No 3 VIEILLE CHAPELLE (inclusive) to Square Q.30 (inclusive) AAA British sick to NO 7 B.F.A. VIEILLE CHAPELLE Indian to NO 111 I.F.A. aaa Traffic routes on the map issued to you this morning being observed aaa addressed NO 111 IFA repeated NO 7 B.F.A. for action regarding collection of British sick of Jullundur Bde

From: ADMS Lahore Divn
Place:
Time:

Colonel

"A" Form.   Army Form C. 2121.

MESSAGES AND SIGNALS.   No. of Message_____

appendix III

TO { OC No 7 BFA

Sender's Number.	Day of Month.	In reply to Number	A A A
161	11		

Two battalions Dehra Dun Bde Tonight relief two battalions of 1st Devon in trenches E of LABASSEE Road AAA your Bearer Division to clear this area only AAA Despatch Bearers and waggons at midnight to rendezvous junction of roads square S.12.c via LACOUTURE and X.5 and collect casualties from aid posts round Windy Corner and in square S.4.A taking care not to block road S.2A – S.8A AAA One Pack Surgeon and three waggons should join No 111 I.F.A tonight to collect British casualties from front now held by Lahore Division AAA OC No 111 I.F.A. ordered to detail

"A" Form.   Army Form C. 2121.
MESSAGES AND SIGNALS.

Prefix	m.	Words	Charge	This message is on a/c	Recd. at	m.
Office of Origin and Service Instructions					Date	
		Sent		Service.	From	
		At	m.			
		To		app [illegible]	By	
		By		(Signature of "Franking Officer.")		

TO

| Sender's Number. | Day of Month. | In reply to Number | AAA |

Sub Asst Surgeon and two bearers to join your bearer party tonight for Indian casualties new front AAA night of 12/13 remainder Dehradun Bde and one battalion Garhwal Brigade take over line to 400 yards S.W. Post ARTHUR.

From ADMS Lahore Div
Place
Time 3-30 pm.

The above may be forwarded as now corrected.   (Z)

Censor.   Signature of Addressee or person authorised to telegraph in his name.

* This line should be erased if not required.

App IV Vol IV 172 13
O.C. No 7 B.F.A. 12-4-15

Tonight your Bearer Divn should evacuate casualties on West side of ESTAIRES-LABASSEE Road from Units of Garhwal Brigade. Rendezvous at Junction of roads S.2.c at 1 A.M.

Aid posts at WINDY Corner.

Detail personnel to accompany No 111 I.F.A. as last night.

[signature]
Colonel
A.D.M.S.

1¼/6

Appendix IV

Attn V Volume V 165
12-4-15.

The O.C. No 7 B.F.A.

Your Unit on relief tomorrow 13th April by No 20 B.F.A. at midday will march to ROBECQ and go into closed billets vacated by No 19 B.F.A. Route FOSSE-bridge - R.9.C - R.7.D. L'EPINETTE - Q.12.C - CALONNE.

Sick and wounded for evacuation in your Unit at time of relief to be handed over to No 20 B.F.A.

Arrival at ROBECQ to be reported to this office.

Refilling 13th as at present 14th and subsequent dates QUENTIN!

On move to ROBECQ motor Ambulance with your Unit to be sent to No 8 B.F.A. for duty.

Maloney M
Colonel I.M.S.
A.D.M.S. Lahore Divn.

JC6

Appendix V

Appendix VI.

"A" Form.
MESSAGES AND SIGNALS.

TO:
OC No 7 B.F.A. ROBECQ
OC No 8 B.F.A. CALONNE
OC No 111 B.F.A. ROBECQ

Sender's Number.	Day of Month	In reply to Number	
180	23		A A A

Your Unit to be prepared to move at short notice by train

From A.D.M.S. Lahore Divn
Place
Time

"A" Form.   Army Form C. 2121.
MESSAGES AND SIGNALS.   No. of Message

| Prefix | Code | m. | Words | Charge | This message is on a/c of: | Recd. at | 15604 | m. |
| Office of Origin and Service Instructions. | | | Sent At To By | m. | Y/C 24.V.15 Service. (Signature of "Franking Officer.") | Date From By | | |

TO { OC No 7 BEA ROBECQ

| Sender's Number. | Day of Month | In reply to Number | A A A |
| 184 | 24 | | |

Be prepared to move at
short notice AAA waggons to
be packed AAA evacuate sick
in unit AAA Further cases
of sickness to be sent
British to L'EPINETTE Indian
to PARADIS

Recd. 11 55 am 24/5

From ADMS Lahore Divn

Place

Time 10.25 am

Lt Col
for ADMS

Appendix VIII. "A" Form.

MESSAGES AND SIGNALS.

Army Form C. 2121.

No. of Message

TO: OC NO 7 BFA ... BECQ

Sender's Number.	Day of Month	In reply to Number	AAA
106	24		

Your Unit will march for KRUIXTRAELE and south of MT DESCAT starting point LE GRAND PACAUT for leading field ambulance 3.20 p.m. today AAA order of march in rear of 18th Bde RFA. NO 8 BFA. NO 113 JFA. NO 112 JFA. NO 7 BFA. NO 111 JFA. AAA motor ambulances to proceed in rear of Own Amn Column and should leave LE GRAND PACAUT at 4.15 p.m. and rejoin units at destination AAA Officers should be sent ahead to meet

From: 2.55 p.m.
Place: Rec'd
Time:

"A" Form.
MESSAGES AND SIGNALS.

Army Form C. 2121.

CRA for billetting purposes AAA No 8 and No 113 field ambulances to open on arrival and be prepared to take in sick AAA Report arrival to DMS at BOESCHEPE AAA reference HAZEBROUCK map 5A 1/100000 AAA Route VERTE RUE LA RUE DU BOIS VIEX BERQUIN STRAZEELE FLETRE

From ADMS Lahore Divn

ADMS

Appendix IX "A" Form. Vol V   Army Form C. 2121.
MESSAGES AND SIGNALS

TO: O.C. NO 7 BFA

Sender's Number: 192
Day of Month: 24

AAA

Your unit will march tomorrow to HUTMENTS N.E. of OUDERDOM field ambulances passing the starting point Road Junction just North of the R in MT KOKEREELE commencing 10-40 a.m. AAA order of march NO 8 BFA NO 113 S.F.A. NO 112 S.F.A. NO 7 BFA and NO 111 S.F.A. AAA The leading field ambulance NO 8 BFA following the 15th Lancers AAA Route HEKSKEM RENINGHELST Road along North bank of river RENINGHELST road junction quarter mile North of the U in OUDERDOM aaa Billeting

"A" Form.
MESSAGES AND SIGNALS.
Army Form C. 2121.

Prefix	Code	Words	Charge	This message is on a/c of:	Recd. at ... m.
Office of Origin and Service Instructions.		Sent At ... m. To By		...Service. (Signature of "Franking Officer.")	Date From By

TO

Sender's Number.	Day of Month	In reply to Number	A A A

Officer from each field ambulance to meet a DWL Staff officer at the commencement of the Hut at 8.30am AAA one section No 8 BFA and one section No 113 SFA to standfast till such moment to await further orders AAA reference map Hazebrouck 1/100000 AAA report to GODEWAERSVELDE till 8.30am 25th and after 11am at OUDERDOM AAA refilling point on 25th to FLETRE 8am AAA all empty supply wagons to be S of a line drawn E and W through LECOQ de PAILLE about one mile N of FLETRE at 9am AAA

From
Place
Time

The above may be forwarded as now corrected.   (Z)
Censor.   Signature of Addressor or person authorised to telegraph in his name.
* This line should be erased if not required.

"A" Form. Army Form C. 2121.
MESSAGES AND SIGNALS.

Supply wagons will approach FLETRE from the north and leave via METREN & of Fontaine HOUCK to cross roads half mile North-west of St JANS CAPPEL BERTHEN (MT KOKEREELE thence follow route of division north of MT ROKEREELE and N of RENINGHELST river. rendezvous for supply wagons road junction quarter mile W of the O of OUDERDOM AAA field ambulances belong to Divl Troops refilling group AAA Motor ambulances to visit areas of troops and collect all sick after 10 a.m

From: ADMS Lahore Divn
Time: 12 p.m.

Lt Colonel

"A" Form.   Army Form C. 2121.
MESSAGES AND SIGNALS.

Appendix X Part IV

TO: O.C. No 7 B.F.A.

Sender's Number: 200
Day of Month: 26
AAA

Your Unit should march at 8 AM to ODERDOM and take over from No 8 BFA all sick in that Unit opening for that purpose on site already occupied by No 8 BFA AAA Your horse ambulances this forenoon should collect British sick left by troops in billets on ODERDOM-VLAMER-TINGHE road about 1½ miles from ODERDOM. AAA Orders re evacuation will follow.

Rep. 7.5 am.

From: A.D.M.S. Lahore Divn
Time: 5 am

Colonel
ADMS

"A" Form.
MESSAGES AND SIGNALS.
Army Form C. 2121.

TO: OC No 7 BFA
OC No 113 J.F.A

Sender's Number: 209
Day of Month: 29

AAA

Fullerton and Fevershore Bdes moving to OODERDOM hut tonight marching from present position 9.p.m. and 10.40 p.m. respectively AAA Motor ambulances should be sent up from your unit to collect and clear all sick and wounded on move of the completion of this duty Brigades AAA on No 7 BFA Bearer Divn should be withdrawn AAA the bearer Divn of No 113 to continue to clear aid posts of Sirhind Bde till further orders AAA extra motor ambulances for

Received 8.5 p.m.

"A" Form.
MESSAGES AND SIGNALS.
Army Form C. 2121.

	Words	Charge	This message is on a...	Recd. at .... m.
Origin and Service Instructions.			.... Service.	Date ....
	Sent At .... m. To .... By		(Signature of "Franking Officer.")	From .... By ....

TO: afte A.P. Cont.

Sender's Number.	Day of Month	In reply to Number	AAA

The clearing if required to be obtained from O.C. No 8 B.F.A. and O.C. No 112 2.F.A. OUDERDOM

From: A.D.M.S Lahore Divn
Place:
Time: 6-15 pm.

The above may be forwarded as now corrected. (Z)

Lt Col
for A.D.M.S

(632) —McC. & Co. Ltd., London.— W 11400/2045. 100,000. 2/15. Forms C 2121/10.

Appendix XII. No 216
                 20-4-15

O.C. No 7 B.F.A.

You will act as S.M.O. of the
Troops left in the Trenches until
they rejoin the Divn.
 Your Unit and No 113 I.F.A.
will remain open until the
Sirhind Bde has left.
 The Bearer Divns are not to
be removed until the aid
posts are clear.
 Your Unit will march after
evacuation to rejoin the ~~Head~~
~~Quarters~~ Divn picking up
stragglers on the road.
 Advanced Lahore Divn, Sirhind
Bde, C.R.A., C.R.E. & O.C. 34th Pioneers
have been informed of these
arrangements.

                    W Murphy(?)
                    Colonel
                    A.D.M.S.

Appendix XIII "A" Form. 308
Army Form C. 2121.
MESSAGES AND SIGNALS.

TO: Staff Capt. S(RN)(A)D Bde — 12.30pm

Day of Month: 30 — AAA

Will you kindly inform me as early as possible the date and hour at which the Sirhind Bde. will move back. Will you also kindly inform me the destination & route to be followed as arrangements have to be made for evacuation of casualties as for ambulances to follow the Bde. to pick up stragglers.

J. A. Stirrey Lt Col. RAMC
S.M.O. Sirhind Bde.

1/5/15 Nothing known about move at present —

Place: Sirhind Brigade

(Z)

"A" Form. Army Form C. 2121.
MESSAGES AND SIGNALS.

Priority
(London)
(6 A.M.)

TO: O.C. NO 7 B.F.A. OUDERDOM.

Sender's Number: 217   Day of Month: 30   AAA

See Jullieure and Ferozepore Bdes retuned to hutments VLAMERTINGHE OUDERDOM roads collect sick of these Brigades tonight and tomorrow morning British Sick to No 7 B F A Indian Sick to No 113 I F A.

Recd 7.45 P

From: ADMS Lahore Division
Place:
Time: 7-15 PM

Colonel
ADMS

Dear Howie

You and Bradley
Have plenty of time available
for this - Good an Op & 5aV
to find out such stuff

Humphrey Doe

12/5799

May 1915

WAR DIARY

With Appendices.

OF

No 7. British Field Ambulance. — Lahore Div

From 1st May 1915 to 31st May 1915

WAR DIARY
or
INTELLIGENCE SUMMARY.

(Erase heading not required.)

Army Form C. 2118.

Vol. VI p. 1

XCviii British Field Ambulance

LAHORE Div.

Hour, Date, Place	Summary of Events and Information	Remarks and references to Appendices
1.5.15. OUDERDOM.	S/Lieut. R. HILTON - HUTCHINSON R.A.M.C. reported his arrival for first-form duty with this unit. One officer A.S.C. admitted with measles. At 10.15 p.m. received instructions from A.D.M.S. to send 3 horse Ambulances with an O/Oi. Surgeon to follow the JULLUNDUR & FEROZEPORE Bdes which marched to billets S. of BERTHEN – Ambulances to join 3rd viii B.F.A on completion of duty. HB	Strength (wounded + sick) to 12 noon – B.O. 1 – B.O.R. 23 15
2.5.15. OUDERDOM.	Motor Ambulance also cleaning the Regtl. Aid posts of SIRHIND Bde. at ST. JEAN. Nothing special to report – O/Oi. Surgeon CREASSIS 1 S.M.D. reports for duty with this ambulance from the Base. HB	State of wounded + Sick to 12 noon B.O. 7 1 B.O.R. 91 19 French 4
3.5.15. OUDERDOM.	Orders from A.D.M.S. (Ambulance became one field-ambulance and two motor Ambulances to march through at 9 p.m. to an rest of METEREN + S.W. of ST JANS CAPPEL, BERTHEN. The detached Park Ambulance to remain behind in OUDERDOM. (App.1 attached) Later, received verbal orders to follow. Full particulars were not known behind. SIRHIND Bde. Operation order No 36 of 3.5.15 received. Am. Survey orders of march + instructions regarding the march. Billeting centre to be a head and billets allotted :- FLETRE. Received verbal orders from Bde. Major that this Bde. would move from starting point at 8 p.m. + not 7.30 p.m. as stated in Operation order. Ambulances marched at 8.30 p.m. and arrived FLETRE at 4.30 a.m. 4.5.15. She marched halts on the road. Pro. Commr. who kept flying among the numerous R.e. Commn. Gave orders about 11 p.m. and continued until we arrived – on tillet.	Appx II attached State of wounded + sick to 12 noon B.O. 0 3 B.O.R. 23 9 Distance about 12 miles

Army Form C. 2118.

WAR DIARY
or
INTELLIGENCE SUMMARY.
(Erase heading not required.)

Vol. V page 2.
No 7 British F.A. Ambulance, Lahore Divn.

Hour, Date, Place	Summary of Events and Information	Remarks and references to Appendices
4.5.15. LINE OF MARCH	Received LAHORE DIVN: Operation order No 82 at 12.5 am. giving instructions regarding the march from billets near an previous order, to new area. Starting point to be FLÊTRE, and route followed FLÊTRE - STRAZEELE - MERVILLE. Ambulance to follow 2 I R W D Bde. and be billeted PARADIS area - (App x III)	App. III attached.
FLETRE	At 3.40 pm received orders amending operation order No 82, having Starting Point STRAZEELE, Para, Wheat point Ambulance Shed Pass 10.45 pm (App IV). Capt. MITCHELL went ahead in motor Ambulance to look for billets. Ambulance marched 10.15 pm from FLÊTRE & rest O/C the Bde and arrived in billeting area at 4.20 am 5/5. Weather fine. Men from Irish horse (god march along god road) did this men came along Irish horse (a good march along god road) about 12 mile. The ambulance marched splendidly no men fell out. The Regiment McRongada has sometimes numbers of stragglers which filled alone Ambulance wagonette - varying of Bagg. co. the Irish the stragglers has the R.H. — all men who has been picked up were portion of the wagon — Near billeting area	App: IV attached.
5.5.15. PARADIS	5 men of A.S.C. joined for duty. Billets very drive & intelligent - billed. Cab for officers. Sent 3 motor Ambulances to remove infectious cases from I.S.A. at GODEWAERSVELDE.	

WAR DIARY or INTELLIGENCE SUMMARY.

Army Form C. 2118.

Vol. V / p 3.
No VIII R.F.A. LAHORE DIVN.

Hour, Date, Place	Summary of Events and Information	Remarks and references to Appendices
5.5.15. PARADIS	Received orders 11.30 p.m. to send all motor Ambulances of No VIII Coverg. to AIRE immediately. Ambulances also started — no cases — still have 250 vols.	
6.5.15. PARADIS	At 10.30 a.m. received return from APMO to Capt. N. O'RIORDAN R.A.M.C. to report himself to OC No VIII R.F.A. (O'day) at CALONNE. Motor Ambulances No VIII Covg. vol/g AIRE at 8.45 a.m. At 12.30 p.m. received order from A.Dir.S. for unit to march tonight at 8 p.m. to R.3.B (near L'EPINETTE) forming an accommodation from Field Ambulances at present there. On arrival to prepare for reception of sick and wounded. (Appx. attached) Capt. MITCHELL proceeded to take over billets. On arrival at 8.10 p.m. we found Capt. KENNEDY I.M.S. who informed us that he had received instructions from the A.D.M.S. to take over part of the billets allotted to the Ambulance for No VIII R.F.A. the officer Comdg. Lt. King (Liverpool Regt.) informed me at the same time that no M.Ts. forms allotted to the unit had been allotted to his Regt. also. However our ambulances arrived. Reported arrival of unit to A.D.M.S. on the Farms which it was intended to use for patients had been allotted over to No VIII F.F.A. who requiring the accommodation from 250 to 150 patients. Hospital tents have been pitched in readiness for patients. Single of March 1 mile.	Appx. V (attached) State of Sick — O.R.R. 34. Doolegas 17.
7.5.15. L'EPINETTE	9.00 a.m. CAIRNS and GUNN R.A.M.C. named the area of Reg. Aid Posts of the LAHORE Divn. near CROIX BARBEE. Also showed them where the proposed establish a Divl. Advanced Dressing Station. Lt. A.E.S.P. PATTISON R.A.M.C. reported his arrival for duty with this unit	State of Sick — R.O. 1 B.O.R. 12 Wounded 26.

(73989) W4141—463. 400,000. 9/14. H.&J.Ltd. Forms/C. 2118/10.

Army Form C. 2118.

WAR DIARY
or
INTELLIGENCE SUMMARY.
(Erase heading not required.)

Vol. V. p. 4.

No VII British Field Ambulance
LAHORE DIV.

Instructions regarding War Diaries and Intelligence Summaries are contained in F.S. Regs., Part II and the Staff Manual respectively. Title pages will be prepared in manuscript.

Hour, Date, Place	Summary of Events and Information	Remarks and references to Appendices
7.5.15. L'EPINETTE	Capt. Tobin received orders from A.D.M.S. to send Motor Ambulance at once with this unit for duty with No. III B.F.A. - Also for Bearer Sub's to proceed of this unit to move to RUE DE POUCH so as to arrive there by 6 a.m. 8/5/15 be in reserve in case of necessity. (Appx: VI attached.) At 7.30 p.m. received orders cancelling above arrangements (Appx: VII attached.) J.G.	Appx VI attached Appx VII attached
8.5.15. L'EPINETTE.	Inspection by D.A.M.S. Indian Corps this morning — Under instructions from A.D.M.S. from No. VIII unit of Motor Ambulance were sent to No. 8 B.F.A. for temporary use - Under instructions from A.D.M.S. Capt. T.J. MITCHELL R.A.M.C. to be transferred to command No. 8 B.F.A. (temporarily). Under instructions from A.D.M.S. Lieut. CAIRNS to assume medical charge of Highland L.I., relieving Lieut. ALLAN, who on relief is to report to this unit for duty. Lieut. ALLAN R.A.M.C. reported his arrival for duty this evening. 7.30 p.m. received instructions ordered from A.D.M.S. Divisional Reserve Ambulance to be despatched Bearer Sub Unit (1 Officer, 2 Asst Surgs; 80 Bearers, 15 Stretchers), also to arrive at RUE DE POUCH by 6 a.m. 9.5.15 - Also to send the Motor Ambulance at present with this unit to report to No. 8 Brit FA J.G.	State of Pers. 8 B.F.A. 95 Horses — 7 B.O. 1 G.R.B. 8 Appx VIII
9.5.15. L'EPINETTE.	Bearer Sub. under Lt. Gunn, with 2 Asst Surgeons & 80 bearers started at 4.30 a.m. for RUE DE POUCH, according with above order. They returned away all day, and returned about 9.30 p.m. under orders of A.D.M.S. D.D.M.S. Indian Corps inspected the Field Ambulances the case of Ambulances admitted from 4th Londons etc. J.G.	Sick Nil - Admitted O.R. 17 To Ch. at Corp O.R. 3

(73989) W41141—463. 400,000. 9/14. H.&J.Ltd. Forms/C. 2118/10.

WAR DIARY or INTELLIGENCE SUMMARY.

Army Form C. 2118.

Vol. V Page 5.
N° vii British Field Ambulance
LAHORE Div¹

(Erase heading not required.)

Hour, Date, Place	Summary of Events and Information	Remarks and references to Appendices
10-5-15. L'EPINETTE.	9 prs womens transferred from N° 8 B.F.A. One bright warm day. Bearers went for Route march. Milking special to report.	Strength (Udr + vrnd):— Res: 3, S.B.R: 7, Drivers: 5, O.R.: 21
11.5.15. L'EPINETTE.	10 Bearers of A.B.C. rejoined for duty from Base. Six more Bearers returned sick from B.Sn.B. Relief (Parial) arrival of B.U.F. (Partial) arrival of the Ambulance established by N°8 B.F.A. This practically means that the Ambulance will be closed except for odd cases coming in. (App. IX attached.) Bearers went for Route march in Thurmez. No Cases numbers A.B.C.&c miles 116	Relief of sick: B.R. — 4; Res. — 7 (APP IX attached.)
12.5.15.	One bright day. Interval. Bearers went for Route march.	Sick Officer: O.R. miles
13.5.15. L'EPINETTE.	One Case of measles — A.S.C. personnel. — No case numbers A.B.C. personnel. Capt° J'RIORDAN R.A.M.C. rejoined for duty. Bearers continued as before. — A.B.C. out for a route march —	Strength Off. sick: B.S.R. — 10, Res — 2, Sick — 16
14.5.15.	Milking special to report. — Rained hard all day — A.B.C. went for Route march.	Sick — 16
15.5.15. L'EPINETTE.	10/am received orders from A.D.M.S. for Bearer Div° (N°vii Ambl.) to proceed to Rue de Portion + there await orders. Advanced Dressing Stn being formed by N°8 B.F.A & N° 112 I.F.A. N°vii Ambulance will then meet to report to N° 112 I.F.A today. (App X). Bright fineday. — Showed Operating Theatre + made ready to receive. N° of cases in hospital 4 (App ?). Forward N°8 B.F.A & N°112 I.F.A to come N°	App X attached. Strength Sick: B.S.R. — 4, Sick — 16

WAR DIARY or INTELLIGENCE SUMMARY.

(Erase heading not required.)

Army Form C. 2118.

Vol. I p. 6

No VIII British Fd. Ambl. LAHORE DIV.

Hour, Date, Place	Summary of Events and Information	Remarks and references to Appendices
16.5.15 L'EPINETTE	No A.B.C. men admitted with wounds. Bright, sunny day. At 1.29 p.m. received orders from A.D.M.S. to leave one section with half Bearer Divn. under Capt. O'RIORDAN in readiness to move with No VII F.A. to a destination which would be notified later. The Bearer personnel which is at present at the Rue du Porch to be recalled forthwith. (App XI). Issued orders to Capt. O'RIORDAN in accordance with the above (App XII) app XII attached. In accordance with instructions from A.D.M.S. sent stretchers to No VII F.A. + 12 to No 119 J.F.A. Lt. PATTISON detailed to accompany Capt. O'RIORDAN. Ambln. received latest information from B.P.O.M.O. that it was moving that the Sodn. Ambulance which is coming toward, was moving. JK	App XI attached (App XII) app XII attached Stretchers R.O. - B.O.R. 4
17.5.15 L'EPINETTE	19 Neer Coll men admitted for a week. At 8 a.g. received yesterday from Ordnance Stas. All one too small + useless for the heavy draught horses. Therein were great difficulty in obtaining harness + when it arrives it is unable to maintain. Some of the horses are NWR - too small to a mule. Rained practically all day - Heavy gale - first all day. Section Field Ambulance undertook to mend a still line. 6 p.m. 3 P.O. one hand Bag: Janice from No 8 R.F.A. Trg = New hours 2 P.O. one Temporary Horse - JK	
18.5.15 L'EPINETTE	2nd Gde W. S. Formahere from No 8 F.F.A. is being retired as a 2nd Gladesham home. Sale = days 2nd Gd WS arrived. Two A.B.C. and troops. Nebutalfm. JK	

Army Form C. 2118.

Vol.5 p.7
No VII B.F.A. LAHORE DIV"

WAR DIARY
or
INTELLIGENCE SUMMARY.
(Erase heading not required.)

Instructions regarding War Diaries and Intelligence Summaries are contained in F.S. Regs., Part II. and the Staff Manual respectively. Title pages will be prepared in manuscript.

Hour, Date, Place	Summary of Events and Information	Remarks and references to Appendices
19.5.15. L'EPINETTE.	Damp-mist all day. – no A.B.C. admitted with measles. 6.50 pm received mobilization orders for A.D.M.S. for Lt. PATTISON to b.b. on Med. Change fr? MANCHESTER Regt. vice Capt. BURNEY RAMC.	Sch. Stat. B.O. 1 B.o.R. 1
20.5.15. L'EPINETTE.	Lt. PATTISON reported this afternoon abt. 2.30 pm Pstep – A.Bg. man admitted to hospital. A.B.C. v A.R.C. had an arrival this morning and + an hour or so much later – this morning – Two heavy showers during – some evening dews.	1/6
21.5.15. L'EPINETTE.	One A.B.C. admitted with measles. One Pte. RAINS (Q.B. Sentry) granted for duty in place of one Murin Nicely admitted to hosp. wounded at YPRES.	Still fine B.o.R. 3 1/6
22.5.15. L'EPINETTE.	Two O.O. Surgeons + 3 (Meneno (A.S.C. v A.M.C.)) Proceeded this morning to LAHORE Div? Advanced Dressing Station to clean v prepare the place for cases – Spent all while Capt. MITCHELL to supervise the work & not the above there. O.C. has had over 30 L cases of measles amongst the Mhowa Main which had been changed + the 2nd one division taken – also on O.C. Surgeon R.P. ELLOY I.S.M.D. has been awarded the B.C.M.	Still fine B.o.R. 3 1/6
23.5.15. L'EPINETTE.	Orders from A.D.M.S. for Lt. ALLAN F.F.B. on Med. Charge of 4 Jumbal Regt to Asst. McGUIRE to assume charge of 84: Bd. R.F.A. Bde disbanded at 11 am. Capt. MITCHELL reports his arrival forthwith with tomorrow from temp. form. duty with No. 8 B.F.A. A.B.C. +A.S.C. drill + parade round day. 1/6 Fine bright day.	Still fine B.O. B.o.R. 1

WAR DIARY or INTELLIGENCE SUMMARY.

(Erase heading not required.)

Army Form C. 2118.

Vol V P8
XVII B.F.A.
LAHORE DIV

Hour, Date, Place	Summary of Events and Information	Remarks and references to Appendices
24.5.15. L'EPINETTE	Nothing special to note. Chakdi Sab. Jullundur Bde: A/80 & A/MC personnel route-marched & drilled.	State of trick — B.O. 1 R.O.R. 10
25.5.15. L'EPINETTE	Beautiful day — Nothing special to report. A/10 + A/30 drill & route march with Transport & in full marching order. L.t. Curran made inspection from A/30. (Proceeded tomorrow Marchais 18 Bde: R.F.A.	State of trick — B.O. 1 R.O.R. 4.
26.5.15. L'EPINETTE	Nothing special — Fine summer day — 30 Lancers working trenches advances for followers — 37 arrived today.	Invisible being State trick — B.O. 1 R.O.R. 10
27.5.15. L'EPINETTE	General interfiring MANOR reported his departure for duty with some other division. Indian workmen. Fine from A/20. A very great inconvenience for the Ambulance, as no one will ? must available speak French. A request for another interpreter was forwarded thru A/30 this day. madage mumps — A.D.O	State of trick — B.O. 1 R.O.R. 6.
28.5.15. L'EPINETTE	Cold dull day. 1 case German measles — 4 S. Lancs — One Holdsworth Ak? sent hospital with Bronchitis. Sutlej Bde relieved Ferozepore Jullundur Bde.	Still sick — B.O. 1 R.O.R. 52
29.5.15. L'EPINETTE	Nothing to report. B/Amb visits the Ambulance in my absence. Warm bright day.	Our trick — B.O. 1 R.O.R. 6.
30.5.15. L'EPINETTE	Nothing special to report. Sun. March day. At 5.15 p.m. received orders to move forthwith to LAGORGUE to report to Asst Director Medical Services Meerut Division at CHATEAU LE COMTE when he arrived at 7.30 p.m. Forced to Moderns A/mb + will arrive the A.R.D I.M.T reported the arriving for duty.	State of trick B.O. 1 R.O.R. 6 Rept 11. (Apt XIII No. 662)

WAR DIARY
or
INTELLIGENCE SUMMARY.
(Erase heading not required.)

Army Form C. 2118

VOL. V p 9

No VII B.F.A. LAHORE DIV.

Hour, Date, Place	Summary of Events and Information	Remarks and references to Appendices
31.5.15. LA GORGUE.	The reconnaissance of the château is very limited until at least approximately 8.0 p.m. + 5.0 a.m. — Seem trying to get possession of the Stables above side the château - who there will be held (Room allotments for Patients) is possible - The W. Riding Fd. Ambulance reports have area altogether. 9.30 p.m. received orders to take on the Lahore Ground Hospital the Guildur Rd. + also take on the Rn't. D'Coursez Zm. & of North LA BASSÉE ROAD (South of RUE CHAPELLE) (appdx iv). Instruct M.O., staff Sergt, 4 NCOs, 10 A.B.C. + 1 Imber Orus — The M.O. + A.O. Surgn to return the remainder staying out at the D'Coursez Zm. with others N. Hutchinson out with Bearer Party made instructions Capt. Capt. O'Riordan. Travels Ambulance joined from Rd. no VII BFA.	Opp - X Wallets/

J. C. Stone.
Lieut: to Colonel Runner,
OC No VII B.F. Ambulance.

"A" Form.
MESSAGES AND SIGNALS.
Army Form C. 2121.

Prefix	Code	m.	Words	Charge	This message is on a/c of:	Recd. at _____ m.
Office of Origin and Service Instructions.			Sent		_____ Service.	Date _____
			At _____ m.			From _____
			To _____			
			By _____		(Signature of "Franking Officer.")	By _____

TO	O.C.	B.F.A.		

Sender's Number.	Day of Month	In reply to Number		AAA
224	3rd			

Your unit less one cavalry subdivision and two motor ambulances will march tonight at 7-30 to area just NORTH of METEREN and South West of FLETRE ST. JANS CAPPEL BERTHEN both exclusive and East of the and MONT DES CATS road aaa Follow in rear of SIRHIND BRIGADE aaa Send an officer to SIRHIND BRIGADE HDQRS who will arrange billeting aaa Section left at OUDERDOM will remain open to take in British and Indian Artillery units

From ARMD
Place Lahore Div
Time

Appendix II vol V

OPERATION ORDER No.36 Copy No. 10

by

Br.General W.G.WALKER,V.C.,C.B., Commanding Sirhind Brigade, d/-3/5/15.

1. The SIRHIND Brigade and attached troops named below will march to New billeting area North of METEREN tonight as follows, via WESTROUTE - MONT NOIR - LA MANCHE.

2. The head of the Column will pass the Starting Point, the Farm on the South of the OUDERDOM road, about 200 yards S.W. of the 4th King's present hutments at 7-30 p.m.

ORDER of MARCH.

20th Coy, S & M.) Will join the Head of the Column at road junct-
21st Coy, S & M.) ion at OUDERDOM, Sq.G 30 C 9.5.

1st H.L.I.
1/4th G.R.
1/1st G.R.
15th Sikhs.
4th King's.
34th Pioneers.
Supply Section, SIRHIND Bde.
No.7 British F.A.(less one Section).
No.113 Indian F.A.

3. O.C., 20th Coy, S & M. will arrange to drop men to block each side road, he will also arrange to have an officer or N.C.O. in rear of the Column to collect these men.

4. Billeting Officers have gone out and will meet their units at cross roads S.W. of LA MANCHE.

5. Baggage Sections now at BOESCHEPE have been directed to rejoin their units tomorrow morning.

6. Reports to Head of Column.

Ridgeway
Captain.
Brigade Major, Sirhind Brigade.

Copy No.1 to 20th Coy, S & M.
 2   21st Coy, S & M.
 3   1st H.L.I.
 4   1/4th G.R.
 5   1/1st G.R.
 6   15th Sikhs.
 7   4th King's.
 8   34th Pioneers.
 9   No.4 Coy, Train.
10   No.7 B.F.A.
11   No.113 I.F.A.   Issued to Signal Section at 4-45 p.m.

"A" Form. Army Form C. 2121.

MESSAGES AND SIGNALS.

Prefix	Code	m.	Words	Charge	This message is on a/c of:	Recd. at 1421 m.
Office of Origin and Service Instructions			Sent At ___ m. To By		Service. (Signature of "Franking Officer.")	Date From By

TO: ~~Lahore Div~~ C.R.A. — A.D.M.S. — 2/7 Cy S&M3
34th Pioneers — C.R.E. — No 7 B.F.A. — S.S. D... Train
2/1 Cy S&M — A.A.S.&M.S — No 113 I.F.A.

Sender's Number	Day of Month	In reply to Number	AAA
G-569	3rd		

Operation order 82 AAA Reference HAZEBROUCK map sheet 5-A aaa The Lahore Division will march in two columns on night 4th-5th aaa Right column starting point FLETRE route FLETRE - STRAZEELE - MERVILLE aaa 18th Field Artillery Brigade eight p.m. to billets on ST. VENANT - GUARDBECQUE road aaa Sirhind Brigade 8-20 p.m to CALONNE Area aaa 7th B.F.A. less one section and 113th I.F.A. to follow Sirhind Bde to MERVILLE and thence to PARADIS Area aaa Left Column starting point road junction half mile South East of METEREN route NOOTEBOOM DOULIEU ESTAIRES aaa 5th 11th 43rd Bdes in succession under orders of C.R.A. 8-15 p.m to area RIEZ VINAGE and LE CORNET MALO aaa 34th Pioneers 9-15 p.m 20th and 21st

From		
Place		
Time		

The above may be forwarded as now corrected. (Z)

Censor. Signature of Addressee or person authorised to telegraph in his name.

* This line should be erased if not required.

"A" Form.
MESSAGES AND SIGNALS.
Army Form C. 2121.

| TO | 2 |

companies sappers & miners 9-20 p m to their old billets in the front line area aaa Divisional Headquarters march tomorrow to ESTAIRES

From: Lahore Div
Time: 8.5 pm

Appendix IV

"A" Form.
MESSAGES AND SIGNALS.
Army Form C. 2121.
No. of Message 27

Prefix	Code	Words	Charge	This message is on a/c of:	Recd. at .... m.
	Priority				Date
		Sent At .... m.		Service.	From
		To			
		By		(Signature of "Franking Officer.")	By

TO: Accident Train C.R.A. — 20th Coy S&M — A&QMG
Indian Corps C.R.E. (2nd Div) — 34th Coy S&M — 113 I.F.A.
2nd Army — Sirhind Bde — ADMS (Yells grew) 7 B.F.A.
4th Corps — 34th Pioneers

Sender's Number.	Day of Month	In reply to Number	A A A
G-576	4th		

First Army orders all moves tonight to take place by STRAZEELE road aaa Amendment to Operation Order 82 as follows aaa Starting point STRAZEELE aaa Lahore Divl. Artillery under orders from C.R.A 8-30pm aaa 20 & 21st Companies S & Miners 9-50pm aaa 34th Pioneers 10pm aaa Sirhind Brigade 10-5pm aaa 7th B.F.A. and 113th I.F.A 10-45pm aaa Acknowledge aaa Added all concerned as shown above repeated Indian Corps 4th Corps and 2nd Army

From: Lahore Divn
Place:
Time: 12.15 pm

"A" Form. Army Form C. 2121.
MESSAGES AND SIGNALS.

TO: O.C. No 7 BFA Q.18A.

Sender's Number: 239
Day of Month: 6
AAA

Your Unit will march tonight at 8 p.m. to R.13B via Q 24 C R 13 D and take over accommodation at present held by Field Amb meerut Divn AAA on arrival open and prepare for reception of sick and wounded AAA Two horse amb waggons to be sent to Head Qrs Ferozepore Bde at time settled in consultation with Ferozepore Bde to collect sick ascribed here AAA British to No 7 BFA Indian to No 113 IFA at factory Q.18d 10.6 AAA Bearers and Ambulance waggons to be held

"A" Form.   Army Form C. 2121.

MESSAGES AND SIGNALS.

Prefix	Code	m.	Words	Charge		This message is on a/c of:		Recd. at .... m.
Office of Origin and Service Instructions.			Sent At ..... m. To ..... By			.... Service. (Signature of "Franking Officer.")		Date ..... From ..... By .....

TO

Sender's Number.	Day of Month	In reply to Number	**A A A**

in readiness to move on short notice after arrival at new position AAA Report arrival immediately to this office

Rec 12.30 pm

From ADMS Lahore Div
Place
Time 11-20 am

The above may be forwarded as now corrected.   (Z)

Censor.   Signature of Addressor or person authorised to telegraph in his name.
Colonel

"A" Form.
Army Form C. 2121.
MESSAGES AND SIGNALS.

TO: OC No 7 B.F.A. OC No 8 B.F.A.
OC No 112 S.F.A. OC No 113 S.F.A.

Sender's Number: 256
Day of Month: 7

AAA

A combined advanced dressing station will be formed tonight at point M 27 D 2.2 by No 8 B.F.A. and No 112 S.F.A. AAA The full Bearer Division personnel from each of Units will be despatched to reach above point by midnight AAA Extra supply of bandages and dressings to be sent AAA No 112 S.F.A. will send 4 motor ambulance wagons making up his present number by the VAUXHALL Car from No 7 B.F.A. AAA No 8 B.F.A. will send three motor ambulances AAA Aid posts of Jullunder Brigade to be

"A" Form.
MESSAGES AND SIGNALS.
Army Form C. 2121.

cleared at midnight as already ordered and Bearer divisions to remain at Dressing Station till further orders AAA Bearer division personnel of No 7 B.F.A. and No 113 I.F.A. to move up in reserve to RUE de POUCH at 6 a.m. 8-5-15 and await orders AAA a dug out or protected house to being prepared at site of advanced dressing station AAA British wounded to NO 8 B.F.A. overflow to NO 7 B.F.A. Indian wounded to NO 112 I.F.A. overflow to NO 113 I.F.A. AAA Route to be strictly adhered to according to traffic map already issued to you.

From ADMS Lahore Divn
Place
Time 3 pm

"A" Form.
MESSAGES AND SIGNALS.
Army Form C. 2121.

Prefix	Code		Words	Charge	This message is on a/c of:	Recd. at .... m.
Office of Origin and Service Instructions.					Service.	Date ....
		Sent				From ....
		At .... m.				
		To			(Signature of "Franking Officer.")	By ....
		By				

TO — OC NO 7 BFA   OC NO 8 BFA
OC NO 112 IFA   OC NO 113 IFA

Sender's Number.	Day of Month	In reply to Number	
258	7		A A A

The orders issued in my 256 of date regarding formation of combined dressing station by Nos 8 BFA and No 112 IFA at point M27D 2.2 and for heavy divn personnel of No 7 BFA and No 113 IFA to move up in reserve to Rue du Paich are cancelled AAA. The orders issued in my 253 dated 7th May 15 to OC No 8 BFA and No 112 IFA for clearing the front tonight stand good.

Recd 7.30 pm

From ADMS Lahore Divn
Place
Time 6.30 pm

Colonel
ADMS

"A" Form. MESSAGES AND SIGNALS. Army Form C. 2121.

TO: OC. No 7 B.F.A. OC. No 8 B.F.A. OC. No 112 1 F.A. OC. No 113 J.F.A. DDMS J.C.

Sender's Number: 262 **Day of Month:** 8 **AAA**

A combined Advanced Dressing Station will be formed tonight at point M.27 D.1.1 by No 8 BFA and No 112 J.F.A. AAA The full bearer personnel from each of these units will be despatched to reach above point by midnight AAA They will bivouac for the night in the field 150 yards North of above points Motor ambulances to be parked behind house at M 27 D 1.1. AAA Hospl shelter trenches are on South side of road at above point

"A" Form.
MESSAGES AND SIGNALS.
Army Form C. 2121.

and floor of these should be covered as far as possible with straw AAA Extra supply of bandages dressings and blankets should be sent with Bearer Divn AAA No 112 GFA will send four motor Amb wagons making up his numbers / by Vauxhall car from No 7 B.F.A. AAA No 8 BFA will send 8 motor ambs at present with his Unit AAA Aid posts of Inkerman Bde will be cleared at midnight as usual and Bearer Divns to remain at Dressing Stns till further orders AAA

"A" Form.
MESSAGES AND SIGNALS.
Army Form C. 2121.

Bearer dvin personnel of No 7 B.F.A. and No 113 I.F.A. to move up in reserve to RUE de PONCH at 6 a.m. 9-5-15 to await orders AAA ~~over~~ ~~from~~ ~~British to~~ ~~No 7~~ ~~B.F.A.~~ British wounded to No 8 B.F.A. overflow to No 7 B.F.A. Indian wounded to No 112 I.F.A. overflow to No 113 I.F.A. AAA Route to be strictly adhered to according to Traffic map already issued to you AAA Reports to A.D.M.S at ESTAIRES

From: ADMS Lahore Dvn
Time: 6.30 pm.

"A" Form.   Army Form C. 2121.
MESSAGES AND SIGNALS.

TO: OC No 8 BFA OC No 112 IFA
    OC No 7 BFA OC No 113 IFA

Sender's Number: 268   Day of Month: 11   AAA

All sick of No 8 Brit and No 112 IFA Collection to be arranged for Sirhind Bde tomorrow morning and till further orders in area CROIX MARMUSE and for Ferozepore Bde area RIEZ BAILLEUL AAA Jullundur Bde and one Battn Ferozepore Bde remain in trenches AAA attention is drawn to my No 38/2 dated 7th May AAA addressed No 8 BFA and No 112 IFA copy to No 7 BFA and No 113 IFA

From: ADMS Lahore Div
Time: 2-40 pm

"A" Form.
MESSAGES AND SIGNALS.
Army Form C. 2121.

Appy

TO No 7 BFA No 8 BFA No 112 2FA No 113 2FA

Sender's Number	Day of Month	In reply to Number	
271	15		A A A

A combined Groupment Evacuation Scheme will be formed tonight by No 2/10 to be by No 2 BFA and No 112 2FA AAA The full scheme of these units with cars east of No 112 2FA will be despatched to work above point at 7.30pm AAA Two motor ambulances from each of these units to accompany bearer divns remaining motor ambulances will be held in reserve to move if called for from above Stn AAA Until further orders

From
Place
Time

The above may be forwarded as now corrected. (Z)
Censor. Signature of Addressor or person authorised to telegraph in his name.

"A" Form.
MESSAGES AND SIGNALS.
Army Form C. 2121.

| Prefix | Code | Words | Charge | This message is on a/c of: | Recd. at ... m. |
| Office of Origin and Service Instructions. | | Sent At ... m. To By | | ... Service. (Signature of "Franking Officer.") | Date From By |

TO

| Sender's Number. | Day of Month | In reply to Number | A A A |

wounded will be collected from Jullun
Bde AAA bearer divisions to send
No 7 BFA and No 113 FA to meet
ambulance at Rue de Pomey by
9.30 pm. AAA one day rations to
be carried by all AAA British
sick to No 2 BFA Indians to
No 113 FA - overflow to No 7 British
FA and No 113 FA respectively
aaa Route to be strictly adhered to
according to table no. A.1 v. 5
Cars 4734 . AAA Report to
ADMS Estaires

Read 8 pm

From ADMS Lahore Divn
Place
Time 7 pm

The above may be forwarded as now corrected. (Z)

Censor. Signature of Addressor or person authorised to telegraph in his name.

* This line should be erased if not required.

"A" Form.
MESSAGES AND SIGNALS.

Army Form C. 2121.
No. of Message

| Prefix | Code | Words | Charge | This message is on a/c of: | Rec'd. at .... m. |
| Office of Origin and Service Instructions. | Sent At .... m. To By | | | Service. (Signature of "Franking Officer.") | Date .... From By |

| TO | No 7 BFA R 13.B | |

| Sender's Number. | Day of Month | In reply to Number | |
| 274 | 16 | | A A A |

Have one Section and half bearer division which should atonce be recalled from RUE du PONCH ready to move atonce under Cap O'RIORDAN with NO III 2 F.A. AAA destination follows

Rec'd 1.29 pm

From A.D.M.S. Lahore Div
Place
Time 12·15 pm

Sgd Sloan Lt Col

Capt. O'RIORDEN
R.A.M.C.

You will be ready to proceed in Command of one Section + half the Bearer Division of this Ambulance with 30th I.F.A., to a destination which will be notified later.

1.40 pm
16.5.15.

H. A. Stone
Lt.Col. R.a.m.c.

APP XII   VOL V

Appendix XIII Volume V

MESSAGES AND SIGNALS.
Army Form C. 2121.

TO: NO 7 BFA
NO 112 I.F.A.

Sender's Number	Day of Month	In reply to Number	AAA
313	30		

Your Unit should march forthwith via L'EPINNET bridge north of LESTREM to LAGOURGUE opening there for reception of sick and wounded aaa report arrival to this office aaa Bearers and waggons of no 112 I.F.A rendezvous tonight as usual

5.15pm

From ADMS Lahore Div
Place
Time 4.30 pm

for ADMS Lt Col

"A" Form. — MESSAGES AND SIGNALS.
Army Form C. 2121.

TO: OC No 7 BFA

Sender's Number: 322
Day of Month: 31st
AAA

Your Bearer Deen to clear Sick and wounded of Inf[antry] Bde tonight aaa Rendezvous at Advanced dressing station which should be taken over forthwith from OC No 8 BFA at 7.30pm RAA OC No 8 BFA ordered to send you two motor amb wagons this afternoon RAA Send one Asst Surgeon with motor ambulance tonight to dressing station ST VAAST to take over British wounded of Brigade on right from Bearer Divn No 112 IFA aaa OC No 112 IFA will take to detail one 1 SMD motor ambulances to take

"A" Form.   MESSAGES AND SIGNALS.   Army Form C. 2121.

Prefix	Code	m.	Words	Charge			Recd. at	m.
Office of Origin and Service Instructions.			Sent		This message is on a/c of:		Date	
			At	m.		Service.	From	
			To					
			By		(Signature of "Franking Officer")		By	

TO

| Sender's Number | Day of Month | In reply to Number | AAA |

Once Indian women of Jullundur Bde from you bearer men aaa British sick to No 7 to E A Indian to No 112 I.F.A AAA sick of Sahna Bde area L'EPINETTE to be collected daily by you

From: ADMS Lahore Division
Place:
Time: 2-50 pm

The above may be forwarded as now corrected.   (Z)

Censor.   Signature of Addressor or person authorised to telegraph in his name

Colonel
ADMS

Serial No. 34.

121/8128

WAR DIARY
OF

No 7. British Field Ambulance, Lahore Division.

From 1st June 1915 TO 30th June 1915.

June 1/5

Army Form C. 2118.

WAR DIARY
or
INTELLIGENCE SUMMARY.
(Erase heading not required.)

No VII BRITISH FIELD AMBULANCE LAHORE DIVN

VOLUME VI page 1.

Instructions regarding War Diaries and Intelligence Summaries are contained in F.S. Regs., Part II. and the Staff Manual respectively. Title pages will be prepared in manuscript.

Hour, Date, Place	Summary of Events and Information	Remarks and references to Appendices
1.6.15. LA GORGUE	One Motor Ambulance sent for duty from 3ᵒ via B.F.A. Went out to inspect our Advanced Dressing Station - All clean & working well. See last night 9 x the sick, bearers, and dressers out some steady post title stretcher Regtl. Aid Post on the LA BASSEE Road cases brought in and inspected. Cases to the advanced dressing station stretcher. Sabs one infected stretcher. Carried into Regtl Aid Post - Lt. C.L.PACKMAN R.A.M.C (Temp) joins for duty.	Staff Sick + Wounded:— B.O. 1 O.R.B. 28 6
2.6.15. LA GORGUE	Lt. R.H. HUTCHINSON RAMC repelled his departure this afternoon Lt. R.M ALLAN RAMC comp. charge of "Wins"(Liverpool) Regt. Asst Surg Surrey I.S.M.D. relieved Asst Surg WINDSOR at Advanced Dressing Stn.	Staff Sick + Wounded:— B.O. 1 O.R.B. 31. 7
3.6.15. LA GORGUE	Pte. STEVENSON Worcester Regt. died. Half the morning into Burial - Committee Service. Pte admitted with lethal sores. Was transferred from Nᵒ8 B.F.A by No5 Fld Ambulance attached to this Ambulance to ARQUES to our Eye Specialist.	Staff Sick + Wounded:— B.O. 2 O.R.B. 28 12
4.6.15. LA GORGUE	Pte. PHILLIPS, 4Suffolks, just left the nursery for bombardiers Band — casualty less. Report Lt.Col. NIMMO's name has been submitted Promoted 3oxxviii Field Ambulance. One A.S.C. driver admitted with measles.	Staff Sick + Wounded:— B.O. 2 O.R.B. 15. 8
5.6.15. LA GORGUE	SIRHIND Bde. relieves FEREZEPORE Bde. Trenches Tonight. Nothing special to report — Advanced dressing Station personnel being changed tomorrow. One officer to be ABC at Advanced Dressing Stn.	Staff Sick + Wounded:— B.O. 1 O.R.B. 26 4

(9 29 6) W 4141—463 100,000 9/14 H W V   Forms/C. 2118/10

WAR DIARY or INTELLIGENCE SUMMARY.

Army Form C. 2118.

Vol. VI. P. 2.

No VIII British Field Ambulance, LAHORE DIV.

(Erase heading not required.)

Instructions regarding War Diaries and Intelligence Summaries are contained in F. S. Regs., Part II. and the Staff Manual respectively. Title pages will be prepared in manuscript.

Hour, Date, Place	Summary of Events and Information	Remarks and references to Appendices
6.6.15 LA GORGUE	Proms of Advanced dressing Station changed. Kho orderly ABC &NC dfc. Weight Rans Since 31.5.15. One Sergeant discharged from A.B Duo:- All Motor Ambulances running well.	Stab: Sick + Wounded B.O. — ORB. 19 4.
7.6.15 LA GORGUE	Motor Ambulance sent for inspection by India Expt. Ordnce near MERVILLE. Orders received by Lt.Col. HIME R.A.M.C. to report to the A.D.M.S. IN DIV (Indian) and to command No XXVIII Field Ambulance Robert Ambulance located at NAM. No VII B.F.A. also handed over to Capt. MITCHELL R.A.M.C. 1/6	8 (lb.) Reft trouble B.O. 1 ORB. 22 12.
8.6.15 LA GORGUE	Took over command of unit at 10am. H BLACK HIME R.A.M.C. left at 11am to command No 28 F.A. 4th Groad Surg. C.H. WINDSOR relieved 4 Goord Surg SWEENEY as dressing Station. A.D.M.S. rec'd visit at 10:30 am. the D.D.M.S. at 3:15 pm. Hospital closed at 3.30 pm by No 2 M.A.C. Weather bright & warm. Thunder storm during the afternoon. f.f Mitchell Capt R.A.M.C.	Stab: of Sick & wounded B.O. 1 2. ORB. 22 8 30
9-6-15 LA GORGUE	In case Pte HENDERSON 1st H.L.I. accidental wound of left foot. Seen by A.D.M.S. L/C GOULDEN H 1st MANCH. Reg. died in hospital from wounds received in action. Collection of Sick evacuated as usual. Sick collected from 4th LONDON REG. & CONNAUGHT RANGERS at 9.30 am. Sick & wounded collected from 4th SUFFOLKS, 4th KINGS LIVERPOOL REG, 1st H.L.I. & 1st MANCHESTER REG at 9.30 pm. Weather dull & warm. A.D.M.S. paid unit at 10:30 am. & 3:30 pm. f.f.m.	Stab: of Sick & Wounded Ae = 6 B.O. 6 ORB. 20 1 21

WAR DIARY
or
INTELLIGENCE SUMMARY.
(Erase heading not required.)

Army Form C. 2118.

VOL VI page 3

No 7 B.F.A. LAHORE DIVISION

Instructions regarding War Diaries and Intelligence Summaries are contained in F.S. Regs., Part II. and the Staff Manual respectively. Title pages will be prepared in manuscript.

Hour, Date, Place	Summary of Events and Information	Remarks and references to Appendices
LA GORGUE 10-6-15.	Collection of Sick Personnel as usual. 1st C.P. moved into La Gorgue. A.D.M.S. visited the unit. Visited advanced dressing Station Pool Park. 1st Local Super Sanitary Det out to advanced dressing Station to relieve 4th local Super WINDSOR. Nothing important arose. Weather warm. Fine. Jgh.	State of Sick Personnel Sick BO 3 bd 3 ORB 39 16 55-
LA GORGUE 11-6-15.	Two Surgeons passed the unit A.D.M.S. visited the unit at 10-15 am. 7 sick + sgs cases inspected. Nothing unusual. Weather warm. Fine. 1 Duk. Jgh.	BO 1 2 ORB 22 1 23
LA GORGUE 12.6.15.	A.D.M.S. visited unit at 10. Man exploded 3 b.H. cases y on hand case. Wound accidental caused by VERY PISTOL. Officer case be forwarded. Eye case defective vision sent by motor car to ARQUES. Two cases died of wounds received in action. 12-14 received ords from A.D.M.S. that FEROZEPORE Bde. was to relieve JULLUNDER Bde. tonight. JULLUNDER Bde. to be distributed 1st MANCHESTERS } LA GORGUE 59th RIFLES 47th SIKHS } RIEZ BAILLEUL 40th PATHANS } BOUT DEVILLE and SUFFOLKS } L'EPINETTE Casualties the collected accordingly Appendix No 1 attached. Weather Dull warm. Jgh.	BO Ad loss 1 -1 ORB 36 10-36 Appendix No 1. attached

Army Form C. 2118.

WAR DIARY
or
INTELLIGENCE SUMMARY.
(Erase heading not required.)

VOL VI Page 4.
No 4 B.F.A. LAHORE DIVISION

Instructions regarding War Diaries and Intelligence Summaries are contained in F.S. Regs., Part II. and the Staff Manual respectively. Title pages will be prepared in manuscript.

Hour, Date, Place	Summary of Events and Information	Remarks and references to Appendices
LA GORGUE 13-6-15.	D.D.M.S. visited Hospital at 10.15 am. A.D.M.S. visited at 10.30 am. Inspected one Syp. case one case Gangrenous self inflicted wound. Two gangrenous transferred one to No 5 S.F.A. two to No 111 I.F.A. Each wounded collected as usual. Weather bright & warm. Afn.	Stat. of Sick Wounded. R.O. 1 2 ORB 19 1 20
LA GORGUE 14-6-15.	A.D.M.S. visited evening at 10.30 am. Inspected R.13X cases of 4th London Reg. Each wounded collected at Bght. Beaver S. Edwaren at Dressing station relieved weather bright & warm. Afn.	R.O. 1 ORB 29. 9 38
LA GORGUE 15-6-15.	A.D.M.S. visited evening at 10.15am an. inspected Syp. Hull. Cases. 11-15 am. 4 cases Sych-ture Poison and is not bright evol. fit the unit Yall. Officers to be treated. D.G. Stationary Hospital ARQUES. Received wire that D.G.A.M.S. did not come. 4-15 pm. Received send orders to send out ½ Beares Division to ST VAAST Dressing Stn. at 8½.m.1. called each wounded with Beares Division 13 No 112 I.F.A from B/RHIND Bgd. AREA. ½ Beares Division under an officer to M2Y D Dressing Station at 5 pm the old posts on the ESTAIRES LA BASSÉE Road to be closed 2 motor ambulances to ST VAAST Dressing Station 1.25 M2YD Beares. Station. Reports at 9pm bright weather Victoria 16.2 attached 6am. 12 Noon 19 pm. also send S.A.D.M.S. Appendices No. 2 attached	B.O. 2 1 3 ORB 33 36 69 Appendices 77 attached

Forms/C. 2118/10

Army Form C. 2118.

WAR DIARY
or
INTELLIGENCE SUMMARY.
(Erase heading not required.)

VOL VI PAGE 5-
No. Y B.F.A. LAHORE DIVISION

Hour, Date, Place	Summary of Events and Information	Remarks and references to Appendices
LA GORGUE 15-6-15	Orders issued to LIEUT C L SPACKMAN RAMC 133rd Field Ambce Guy. ELLIOT at 4-45 p.m. Orders attached. Hols Officer No 344. 5 p.m. Lieut N F WARWICK RAMC reported for temporary duty 6-30 p.m. Inspected 50th Dressing Station. Wounded Convoyed to Army Sanitation Reserve Section in cars 8-45 p.m. No call attd. an Lostin Field Hospital. Apx.	Appendices III & IV attached
LA GORGUE 16-6-15	A.D.M.S. Visited cases at 10-30 am. Inspected Eye - sick & Indigestion wounded cases. No 2 M.B.C. closed sick parade at 11 am. 11-45 am received instructions by wire from A.D.M.S. Lahor Division to reduce Personnel at Dressing Stations. 5 wounded cases during normal condition. Hols Officer No V attached. Extra personnel marched at 12-6 p.m. 1-12-10 p.m. Hols Officer. No call attached. Sick wounded at Light Escrits. As usual at Light Hosp. Fyld Amcs. Capt Guys WINDSOR Y SWEENEY to return each other at different stations. Lghn 48 hours duty.	Stats & Sick Thomas as B.O. 1 ORB 32 2nd 1 Y 39. Appendix No V attached
LA GORGUE 17-6-15	A.D.M.S. Inspected Unit at 11-30 am. Inspected Eye Nose cases. 9 NBC reported for duty with the unit. Subaltern of Bearer Division was charged at the Dressing Station. 7 wounded cases attacked on account. Wounds arm Trigd. Lghn.	BO 3 Vol 3 ORB 15- 10 25

WAR DIARY
or
INTELLIGENCE SUMMARY.
(Erase heading not required.)

Army Form C. 2118.

Vol VI Page 6
No 7 BFA LAHORE DIVISION

Hour, Date, Place	Summary of Events and Information	Remarks and references to Appendices
LA GORGUE 18-6-15	A.D.M.S. visited unit at 11.30 am. Inspected by hand case. 6 pm inspected Brewery Station - local collection of Sick & wounded. Weather bright & warm.	State of Sick & wounded list BO nil ORB 18 10 28
LA GORGUE 19-6-15	A.D.M.S. visited unit at 10.30 am. Inspected Sick Mental case. Evacuation of all cases today to civil commenced today. Sick & wounded evacuated as usual. Sent Sick & wounded from VIII Division & 5th Cav Bde to civil hospital. One case died from wounds received in action. Weather bright & warm.	State of Sick & wounded list BO nil ORB 12 12 - 24
LA GORGUE 20-6-15	A.D.M.S. visited unit at 10.30 am. 1 pm received information by wire that JULLUNDUR Bde. relieves SIRHIND Bde tonight. SIRHIND Bde. to occupy billeting area of SIRHIND Bde. Collection of casualties the same as for JULLUNDUR Bde. Offensive No VII attacked. Received instruction from ADMS re hand cases. All cases will be seen by the ADMS but only Surgeons cases will be reported to the A.D.C. to be Station in duplicate will only be made out for Surgeons cases. 6 pm DGMS visited the unit. 9.30 pm Receiving Station. Sick & wounded received. One case died from wounds received in action. Weather bright & warm.	BO 1 nil ORB 25 - 10 35 Appendix No VII attached

Army Form C. 2118.

VOL VI
PAGE 4
No 7 BFA LAHORE DIVISION

WAR DIARY
or
INTELLIGENCE SUMMARY.
(Erase heading not required.)

Instructions regarding War Diaries and Intelligence Summaries are contained in F.S. Regs., Part II. and the Staff Manual respectively. Title pages will be prepared in manuscript.

Hour, Date, Place	Summary of Events and Information	Remarks and references to Appendices
LA GORGUE. 21-6-15.	A.D.M.S. visited unit at 11 a.m. Sick & evacuated collected as usual. Weather bright & warm. JPR	Sick & Evac. wounded & killed BO 1 1 OR 3 26 15 41
LA GORGUE 22-6-15.	A.D.M.S. finished visit at 11 a.m. 9 wounded Dressing Station at 12.30 p.m. Called on M.O. i/c 5 Brigade RFA re cases of Albuminuria. Report on cases of Albuminuria sent in. R.A.D.M.S. Bearer Subdivision personnel changed at dinner. Weather bright & very hot wet. JPR	BO. 1 OR 3 16 9 23—
LA GORGUE 23-6-15.	A.D.M.S. visited the unit at 11 a.m. Capt W.H. O'RIORDAN R.A.M.C. reported from leave early this morning. Lieut R.M. ALLAN R.A.M.C. evacuated on area occupied by 5.R. Bty. RFA re cases of Albuminuria. Samples of brass 1oaks bought back. These were taken to the Chemical Analyst at G.H.Q. Received instructions by wire from the A.D.M.S. that JULLUNDUR BRIG. would be relieved by troops of MEERUT DIVISION. He accept the evacuation of their casualties bright. Received Officers No VII attached. Weather bright but cold at night. One officer died during night 23rd 24th of wounds received in action. JPR	BO 2 1 3 OR 3 18 5— 23 Appendix No VII attached

Forms/C. 2118/10

Army Form C. 2118.

VOL VI PAGE 8
No 7 B.F.A. LAHORE DIVISION

WAR DIARY
or
INTELLIGENCE SUMMARY.
(Erase heading not required.)

Instructions regarding War Diaries and Intelligence Summaries are contained in F.S. Regs., Part II. and the Staff Manual respectively. Title pages will be prepared in manuscript.

Hour, Date, Place	Summary of Events and Information	Remarks and references to Appendices
LA GORGUE 24-6-15	Lieut R.M. ALLAN R.A.M.C. collected samples of Bus. vomit. from supply used by 11th Bgde. R.F.A. These were forwarded to Chemical Analyst at G.H.Q. Received orders from A.D.M.S. at 3-30 pm that JULLUNDUR Bgde. was to take over ford of 25th & 24th Brigade on 6/7 & FEROZPORE Brigade. C/ MAST. dressing station to be located ½ m from a combined dressing station of M.29.D. Bearer parties to be rendezvous at M.29.D. before 10pm - on arrival there Relief to be arranged by B.O. F.A.S. 5-30 p.m. 6/7 of MAST moved by 6 pm dressing station ref DC No 112.E.3. 6/7 MAST arrived by 6-15 pm Appendix VIII collected after 10 pm Lieut F. BURTON is Self-wounded Sherwood For. dead & wounds received in action	State of Sick Wounded etc B.O. nil nil G.R.3 24 2 26 Appendix VIII attached
LA GORGUE 25-6-15	A.D.M.S. held until at 10.45 am handed over and Orders from JULLUNDUR Bgde. extends to two small valleys from 25th Brigade as far N as M.24.C ½. GIRRARD Sny to placing a British Batt as reserve to JULLUNDUR Bgde and an Indian Batt as reserve to FEROZPORE Bgde. Also regimental Aid Held Appendix IX attached with of Brigades British attacked Spn arranged with or No 112 I.F.A. that bearer Division of No 7 I.F.A. would clear JULLUNDUR Bgde No 112 I.F.A. bearer Division would clear FEROZPORE Bgde	Appendix IX attached

Forms/C. 2118/10

Army Form C. 2118.

VOL VI
PAGE 9
No 4 B.F.A. LAHORE DIVISION

WAR DIARY
or
INTELLIGENCE SUMMARY.
(Erase heading not required.)

Instructions regarding War Diaries and Intelligence Summaries are contained in F.S. Regs., Part II. and the Staff Manual respectively. Title pages will be prepared in manuscript.

Hour, Date, Place	Summary of Events and Information	Remarks and references to Appendices
LA GORGUE 25-6-15	MOs of regiments were instructed by ADMS to send a guide to dressing station at M2YD to show bearer parties their aid posts. They failed to do this. Officers to have collected from No 4 B F A aid posts and goto as follows. ① 4th SUFFOLKS M16D26 ② 59th RIFLES M23 a 4.4 ③ 40th PATHANS } M20 C 7.4 ④ 47th SIKHS } ⑤ 1st MANCHESTERS - Aid post not discovered. Red Hunza aid cleared from 1,2,3,4, aid posts. 3rd Cargo Coast Sergt CUMMINS 15 MD attached No 6 BFA attached to hospital suffering from an overdose of morphia taken with intent to commit suicide Rank Pte. No 8854 8 felled	State of Sick Wounded etc BO nil OR 13 24 2 - 26
LA GORGUE 28-6-15	ADMS visited unit at 10-30am. He was informed that No Guides had been sent to dressing station M2YD to persons bearers to gde sketches bearers to the aid posts. The late Commander Lieut Gen Sir C J WILLCOCKS inspected the F.A. at 1-30pm.	State of Sick Wounded etc BO 1 nil OR8 33 5 -

(9 29 6) W 4141—463 100,000 9/14 H W V   Forms/C. 2118/10

Army Form C. 2118.

VOL VI
Page 10
No Y.B.F.A. LAHORE DIVISION

WAR DIARY
or
INTELLIGENCE SUMMARY.
(Erase heading not required.)

Instructions regarding War Diaries and Intelligence Summaries are contained in F.S. Regs., Part II. and the Staff Manual respectively. Title pages will be prepared in manuscript.

Hour, Date, Place	Summary of Events and Information	Remarks and references to Appendices
LA GORGUE 26-6-15	Sick removed collected from Gnd Posts. Weather damp with bright intervals. 9/h	
LA GORGUE 27-6-15	ADMS. Visited unit at 10-30 am. & inspected 3 cases of Dental Cases. Two men suspicious hand removed. Received Orders to send one Officer - one Asst Surgeon +4 A.B.C. Crew & to 5 MASONS - 6 tool parad. & detachments to Go. The party waited until 4-20 pm no demon chalan took place. Sick & wounded collected as usual. Weather damp with bright intervals. The existing with Lieut Colon Thursday 7/h Asst Surg CUMMINS & admit in hospital placed under aural by OC No 8 RFA	Sick & Sick wounded sent
		B Officers 1 hd 1
		ORB 46 16 62
		BO 1 2 3
		ORB 27 4 33
		Appendix No X attached
LA GORGUE 28-6-15	10 am GOC LAHORE DIVISION Y.A.D.M.S inspected the unit. 11-20 am Received orders from ADMS re readjusting of lines held by LAHORE DIVISION. Bade affaire No X. 1-30 pm unit inspected by D.O.M.S & rehearsalation of chalan Funl. Two new motor Cars replaced two inefficiens taken away by No 1 M.A.C. Two lorries joined the unit. Sick & wounded collected from area held by JULLUNDUR Brigade. Weather damp with bright intervals. No men died in hospital. Sick & Wounded removed to field Brigade. 9/h	

Forms/C. 2118/10

Army Form C. 2118.

Vol VI   Page 11
No Y.B.F.A. LAHORE DIVISION

WAR DIARY
or
INTELLIGENCE SUMMARY.
(Erase heading not required.)

Instructions regarding War Diaries and Intelligence Summaries are contained in F. S. Regs., Part II. and the Staff Manual respectively. Title pages will be prepared in manuscript.

Hour, Date, Place	Summary of Events and Information	Remarks and references to Appendices
LA GORGUE 29.6.15.	A.D.M.S. visited unit at 10 a.m. Inspected 2 lock cases. Some also accidental wound left hand. Case not to be evacuated. Two A.B.C. Bearers joined unit - one officer, one Assistant Surgeon, four Army Bearer Corps men, afterwards gas demonstration. Weather damp.	State of sick & wounded B.O - 1 } B.O 2 D.R.13 - 29 } O.R.13 4
LA GORGUE 30.6.15	CAPT T. J. MITCHELL R.A.M.C. proceeded on one weeks leave to England. A.D.M.S. inspected one case accidental wound left hand. 2/Sikh Cases. Hand case not to be evacuated. Moving station inspected. One pts invalid. Sick & wounded evacuated by us at 9 pm. Four serious cases trench & mouth mortar admitted. W.R. O'Riordan Capt. R.A.M.C. Weather dull & damp.	State of sick & wounded B.O - 1 } B.O - 1 O.R.B - 29 } O.R.B - 14

W.R. O'Riordan
Capt R.A.M.C.
for O.C. No. 4. B.F.A.

"A" Form.   Army Form C. 2121.
MESSAGES AND SIGNALS.   No. of Message_____

Prefix___ Code___ m.	Words	Charge	This message is on a/c of:	Recd. at___ m.
Office of Origin and Service Instructions.	Sent			Date___
	At___ m.		___Service.	From___
	To___			
	By___		(Signature of "Franking Officer")	By___

TO { NO 7 BFA
     NO 112 JFA

| Sender's Number | Day of Month | In reply to Number | |
| 337 | 12 | | AAA |

Ferozepore Bde relieves Jullundur Bde tonight aaa Jullundur Bde on relief distributed as follows:-

1st Manchesters }
59th Rifles   } LA GOORGIE

47th Sikhs   } RIEZ BAILLEUL
40th Pathans   } BOUT-DEVILLE and
Suffolks   } L'EPINETTE

Please arrange collection of casualties accordingly.

From: ADMS Lahore Divn
Place:
Time: 10-45 am

Recd 12.15 pm.

The above may be forwarded as now corrected. (Z)

Censor.   Signature of Addressor or person authorised to telegraph in his name

Lt Col

* This line should be erased if not required.

"A" Form.   Army Form C. 2121.

MESSAGES AND SIGNALS.   No. of Message _____

Prefix ____ Code ____ m.   Words | Charge
Office of Origin and Service Instructions.   This message is on a/c of: Recd. at ____ m.
                                                                                 Date ____
~~Secret~~   Sent   From ____
                            At ____ m.   Service.
                            To ____
                            By ____   (Signature of "Franking Officer")   By ____

TO { O.C. N° 112 IFA

Sender's Number: 329   Day of Month: 15   In reply to Number: AAA

Full Bearer Division N° 112 IFA with two officers & one half Bearer Division N° 7 BFA will rendezvous at 6 pm tonight at ST VAAST dressing station and collect wounded from area occupied by SIRHIND Bde AAA full water cart from N° 112 IFA to accompany Bearer Division AAA Motor ambulance waggons should not go forward till 6-30 pm AAA 4 motor ambulance waggons of N° 8 BFA are placed at disposal of OC N° 112 IFA who will not send any more waggons forward than are necessary for evacuation of cases from dressing station AAA one half Bearer Division N° 7 BFA under an officer will rendezvous at N 27 B dressing station at

From ____
Place ____
Time ____

The above may be forwarded as now corrected.   (Z)

                             Censor.   Signature of Addressor or person authorised to telegraph in his name
* This line should be erased if not required.

"A" Form.   Army Form C. 2121.

MESSAGES AND SIGNALS.

			Day of Month	In reply to Number	
	Sender's Number		15		AAA

6 pm I clear aid posts on ESTAIRES LA BASSEE road AAA Full water cart of No 7 B+a to accompany this part AAA OC No 7 B+a will send two motor Ambulance wagons to STVAAST + two to M27D AAA British wounded to No 7 B.F.A. Indian to No 112 F.A. AAA The usual 6am noon + 9pm wires rendered during operations will be sent to ADMS commencing 9pm tonight AAA Reports to ADMS at ESTAIRES AAA. OC No 112 FA will detail a sub-assistant surgeon + one motor Ambulance to take over Indian wounded from M27D dressing station

From: ADMS
Place: ESTAIRES
Time: 3-15 pm

Appendix III

2.

To Lieut C.L SPACKMAN
          R.A.M.C.

(1) ½ bearer Division under your command will march out at 5 p.m tonight to reach Dressing Station at 6 p.m. – Dressing Station at M 27 D.

(2) Composition of ½ Bearer Division

    16 bearers
    1 motor
    1 water Cart full.

The remainder of the ½ bearer Division is already at the Dressing Station

(3) The aid posts on ESTAIRES – LA BASSEE ROAD to be cleared immediately on arrival at Dressing Station.

(4) One Sub assist Surgeon & one motor Car will be detailed by O.C. No 112 I.F.A. to clear Indian S&W from Dressing Station M 27 D.

(5) British S&W to No 7 B.F.A.

(6) Reports to No 7 B.F.A.

4-45 p.m.
15/6/15.

T J Mitchell Capt
        RAMC
O.C. No 7 B.F.A.

Appendix IV

To 3rd Class Assist Surg ELLY

½ Bearer Division composed as under will march out tonight under your command at 5 pm. Report to the M.O. I/c No 112 IFA at O. VAAST Dressing Station tonight at 6 pm.
Wounded to be collected from Sirhind Pole area

  40 Bearers
  10 Stretchers
  1 Cook
  1 W.S
  1 Bhistie
  1 Sweeper
  2 Mule Cars

Your tonk O. & M. to be evacuated to No 7 BFA
Reports to No 7 BFA

     Blackhall Capt.
4-45 pm   Raine
15/6/15   OC No 7 BFA

"A" Form. Army Form C. 2121.

MESSAGES AND SIGNALS.

Prefix	Code	m.	Words	Charge	This message is on a/c of:	Recd. at ___ m.
Office of Origin and Service Instructions.			Sent			Date ___
			At ___ m.		___ Service	From ___
			To ___		(Signature of "Franking Officer")	By ___
			By ___			

TO { No 7 BFA
     No 112 JFA

Sender's Number	Day of Month	In reply to Number	AAA
340	16		

Personnel at advanced dressing stations may now be reduced to number under normal conditions

From   ADMS Lahore Div
Place
Time   10.30 am

Recd 11.45 am

(Z)

Lt Colonel
ADMS

"A" Form.   Army Form C. 2121.
MESSAGES AND SIGNALS.   No. of Message_____

Prefix	Co... m.	Words	Charge	This message is on a/c of:	Recd. at_____ m.
Office of Origin and Service Instructions.		Sent			Date_____
		At_____ m.		_____Service.	From_____
		To_____			
		By_____		(Signature of "Franking Officer")	By_____

TO { NO 7 B.F.A.
     No 112 I.F.A.

| Sender's Number | Day of Month | In reply to Number | AAA |
| 347 | 20 | | |

Jullundur Bde relieves Sirhind Bde
tonight aaa Sirhind Brigade will
take over the billetting area
of the Jullundur Bde and
will place one British and
one Indian battalion at LAGORGUE
aaa Please arrange collection
of casualties accordingly

From   ADMS Lahore Div
Place
Time   10-25 AM

The above may be forwarded as now corrected.   (Z)

Censor.   Signature of Addressor or person authorised to telegraph in his name
                                                                      Lt Colonel
                                                                      for ADMS

Recd at 1 PM

"A" Form. Army Form C. 2121.

MESSAGES AND SIGNALS.

TO — O.C. No 112 I.F.A.

Sender's Number: 346
Day of Month: 23

Jullundur Brigade being relieved tonight by troops Meerut Division aaa Please arrange to evacuate their casualties tonight aaa Details of Units will be communicated later aaa Addressed No 112 I.F.A. repeated No 7 B.F.A.

From: ADMS Lahore
Time: 5 pm.
Recd 5.46 pm.

Lt Colonel
for ADMS

"A" Form.   Army Form C. 2121.

MESSAGES AND SIGNALS.

TO: OC NO 7 BFA
OC NO 112 JFA

Sender's Number: 848
Day of Month: 24
AAA

Jullundur Bde tonight takes over front of 24th Bde on left of Ferozepore Bde AAA ST VAAST dressing station should be vacated forthwith and a combined dressing station formed at Green barn M27D AAA Bearers and waggons should not rendezvous at dressing station before 10 pm to avoid blocking of roads on movement of troops tonight AAA Dressing station party as heretofore with one motor ambulance waggon to be always on duty reliefs being arranged between OCs Field Ambulances concerned AAA Position of Regimental

"A" Form.
Army Form C. 2121.

MESSAGES AND SIGNALS.

No. of Message _____

Prefix	Code	m.	Words	Charge	This message is on a/c of:	Recd. at _____ m.
Office of Origin and Service Instructions.			Sent			Date _____
			At _____ m.		_____ Service.	From _____
			To _____			
			By _____		(Signature of "Franking Officer")	By _____

TO {

Sender's Number	Day of Month	In reply to Number	AAA

| aid | posts | as | notified today |
| by | OC | 26th | Field Ambulances |

From ADMS Lahore Div
Place
Time 3-15 pm

Recd 3.30 pm

The above may be forwarded as now corrected. (Z)

Censor.   Signature of Addressor or person authorised to telegraph in his name

* This line should be erased if not required.

"A" Form. Army Form C. 2121.
MESSAGES AND SIGNALS.

TO: O.C. No 7 B.F.A.
O.C. No 112 J.F.A.

Sender's Number: 352
Day of Month: 25

AAA

Jullundur Brigade tonight extends its front and takes over line from 25th Brigade as far N as M24c 3/2. AAA Sirhind Bde is placing a British battalion as reserve to Jullundur Bde and an Indian battalion as reserve to Ferozepore Bde to be billetted under orders of Brigades to which attached

From: A.D.M.S Lahore Divn
Time: 10.36 am
Recd 11 am

Colonel

"A" Form.
MESSAGES AND SIGNALS.
Army Form C. 2121.

TO	O.C. No 7 B.F.A.
	O.C. No 112 S.F.A.

Sender's Number	Day of Month	In reply to Number	AAA
360	28		

Front held by Lahore Divn to be readjusted tonight AAA Right of line LABASSEE road inclusive left as at present aaa Ferozepore Bde South of LABASSEE road will be relieved tonight by Meerut Divn North of road by Sirhind Bde AAA Ferozepore Bde will detail one British Regt to PONT du HEM at disposal Jullunder Bde and one Indian Regt to BOUT DEVILLE at disposal of Sirhind Bde AAA 15th Lancers to place 120 rifles at disposal of Sirhind Bde from tomorrow AAA No 7 B.F.A will collect casualties

"A" Form.
MESSAGES AND SIGNALS.
Army Form C. 2121.

from	Left	Section	No 112	SFA
from	Right	Section	AAA	Each
Bearer	Division	to	have	as
usual	representatives	and		officers
from	Bearer	division	of	the
other	section	of	the	line

From: ADMS Lahore Bde

Recd 11.30 am

to Colonel D McKiev

July 15

121/1802

Serial No. 34.

WAR DIARY
with appendices.

OF

No. 7 British Field Ambulance

FROM 1st July 1915 TO 31st July 1915

Lahore Divn

WAR DIARY or INTELLIGENCE SUMMARY.

Army Form C. 2118.

VOLUME 4. page 1.

No. 7. BRITISH FIELD AMBULANCE. LAHORE DIVISION.

(Erase heading not required.)

Hour, Date, Place	Summary of Events and Information	Remarks and references to Appendices
1.4.15 LA GORGUE	A.D.M.S. Lahore Division visited hospital 10.30 a.m. One patient died in hospital from wounds received in action. One severe lung case remaining. A. & B. and Advanced dressing station visited at 9.30 p.m. Sick & wounded collected and advanced & evacuated to Tent Division. No serious cases admitted. Weather dull - with bright intervals. W.R. O'Riordan Capt R.A.M.C	State of Sick & wounded B.P. nil ⎫ nil ⎬ O.R.B 31 ⎭ 9
2.4.15 LA GORGUE	A.D.M.S Lahore Division visited hospital 10.15 a.m. One accidental wound of hand inspected by A.D.M.S not suspicious. Personnel of unit - letters for route march daily. Serious lung case remaining - one at 4.15 evacuated. Weather - bright & warm. WR	State of Sick ⎫ wounded B.O - 1 ⎬ nil O.R.B - 18 ⎭ 11
3.4.15 LA GORGUE	A.D.M.S Lahore Division visited hospital - inspected two Cavalry defective vision one dental case - four cases of defective vision sent Argus for examination by Eye specialist - by bus of the A.D.M.S - A.B.C & A.H.C personnel changes of Advanced dressing station 8.30 p.m. One serious head case remaining. Weather bright - very warm. WR	State of Sick ⎫ wounded B.O - 1 ⎬ nil & nil O.R.B - 40 ⎭ 2
4.4.15 LA GORGUE	A.D.M.S Lahore Division visited hospital 10.45 a.m. inspected one accidental Hand case. Two motor Ambulances sent to unit - in place of two returned. One serious chest case admitted to hospital - serious head case remaining. 004 p.m 3rd unit - evacuated - aid post cleared of sick & wounded 9.30 p.m. Weather - bright - very warm. WR	State of Sick & wounded B.O - nil ⎫ nil O.R.B - 24 ⎬ 12

Army Form C. 2118.

WAR DIARY
or
INTELLIGENCE SUMMARY.
(Erase heading not required.)

VOLUME 7. page 2.

No 4. BRITISH FIELD AMBULANCE LAHORE DIVISION.

Instructions regarding War Diaries and Intelligence Summaries are contained in F.S. Regs., Part II. and the Staff Manual respectively. Title pages will be prepared in manuscript.

Hour, Date, Place	Summary of Events and Information	Remarks and references to Appendices
5-4-15 LA GORGUE.	A.D.M.S LAHORE DIVISION visited hospital & inspected an accidental foot case. Asst. Surgeon K.P. Roy 9 S.M.P presented with D.C.M ribbon by G.O.C Lahore Division. One abdominal case, one case of measles admitted to hospital – three patients includ. Army Labour Corps sent to Civil Hospital BETHUNE. Advanced Dressing Station & aux post visited and evacuated of sick and wounded 9 p.m. Weather – bright – warm.	State of Sick & Wounded B.O – nil O.R.B – 29 } nil } 6.
6-4-15 LA GORGUE.	3rd Class Asst. Surgeon G.B. GIBBON I.S.M reported for duty on transfer from MEERUT Division. A.D.M S LAHORE DIVISION visited hospital 10.45 a.m. inspected one eye case. 11.15 a.m orders received from A.D.M.S that FEROZEPORE Bde relieves JULLUNDUR Bde to-night – in the Trenches and to arrange for the collection of sick and wounded accordingly. Advanced Dressing Station at M2 n D 5/2 ref BETHUNE MAP 1-40,000. Appendices Nos 1 + 2 attached. One abdominal case died in Hospital. Dressing station and out post cleared 9.30 p.m. Weather – bright – warm.	State of Sick B.O – 2 O.R.B – 38 } wounded } 1. } 9. Appendices Nos 1 + 2.
7-4-15 LA GORGUE.	A.D.M.S visited hospital 10.30 a.m. one accidental foot case inspected by A.D.M.S. to be evacuated – Advanced dressing station and out posts of left section of line visited by m.at 9.30 p.m. Sick and wounded evacuated. Weather – stormy – slight rain.	State of Sick B.O nil O.R.B 16. } wounded } nil } 4

Army Form C. 2118.

WAR DIARY
or
INTELLIGENCE SUMMARY.
(Erase heading not required.)

VOL 4 Page 3.
No 7 B.F.A. LAHORE DIVISION.

Instructions regarding War Diaries and Intelligence Summaries are contained in F.S. Regs., Part II and the Staff Manual respectively. Title pages will be prepared in manuscript.

Hour, Date, Place	Summary of Events and Information	Remarks and references to Appendices
LA GORGUE 8-7-15-	Returned from leave 10th. 4-7-15. ADMS would unit at Ham. Inspected two men who had broken their glasses. 11.30 am lectured Coons on Neil Davidson in H.L.I. re reported discoveries. Wrote Eye cases out to ARQUES. No 4 STATIONARY HOSP. No 2 MRC Cleared cases at 2.30pm. Aid posts cleared at 7.30pm. Weather bright but cold. 7pm.	State of Sick Throughout B.O. 1 OR.3 26 5- 31
LA GORGUE 9-7-15:	One case died in Hospital at 4.15am ADMS visited unit at 10.15am. Sick wounded attended as escort at night from Aid Posts Relieving Station. Weather tenant clear.	BO Lt 61 OR.3 16 6 22
LA GORGUE 10-7-15-	One case admitted in hospital from Dressing Station 5.30am HOHTS visited unit at 10.15 am. Inspected 4 York Coys. Received Circulars to Section Officer Forwarded from Army Corps for Inspection of HL1 re cases [?] by LAHORE DIVISION from ADMS relieved attached as an Officer Rate 9-30 pm Returned to unit lent Inspected Dressing Station [?] could Supply the Compy's lostages 3rd Class roads Suffered the Company lostages Hospital ships moving road road 8 hrs and healing Good	BO Lt 64 OR.3 23 2 33 Appendices 3 attached
LA GORGUE 11-7-15-	Orders received at 7.30 am marked Sect of 13- 3/4 SEAFORTHS Here offensive IV ADMS would unit at 11.15 am inspected one tested case Replies to have Cases Sick forwarded attached as escort Bright clear 7pm	BO Lt 61 OR.3 24 9 33 Appendices 8 attached

Army Form C. 2118.

Vol 1 Page 4
No W.5.4 LAHORE DIVISION

WAR DIARY
or
INTELLIGENCE SUMMARY.
(Erase heading not required.)

Hour, Date, Place	Summary of Events and Information	Remarks and references to Appendices
LA GORGUE 12-7-15	A.D.M.S. visited unit at 11 am. ambulance & Hqrs Casso Black Horse and 129 Hants Field H.E. JASON at 12.30 pm. No war died in hospital from wounds received in action. Sick evacuated collected as horse weather bright & warm. head R.M. ALLAN R.A.M.C. Lieut on one weeks leave 7/h.	Sick Rich Evacuated. B.O. 2 - 2 O.R.R. 31 6 - 31
LA GORGUE 13-7-15	A.D.M.S. visited unit at 10 am. inspected 3 bell tents from ESTAMINET wood by 73 Bde R.F.A. then present at ARMENTIERES where supplies be removed. Samples collected for by central laboratory G.H.Q as ordered too. for fuller was discovered in the samples to investigate the cause of abnormality - Received Secret orders at 5.30 pm re proposed attack into Germany & attacked Sick forwarded collected as usual at right Limakie reported hun. sit. for dressing station. aut. told. 7/h.	B.O. hd 1 - O.R.B 31 2 33 Appendix I attached
LA GORGUE 14-7-15	A.D.M.S. visited final at want evacuated 2 hold cases 2 pm Been collected on 13-7-14 seul to central laboratory 5 hr. Inspected 1a FINQUE with D.A.D.M.S. re Sets for a dressing Station ref: not BETHUNE - 1.0.000 Sick Evacuated collected as usual - one having 6 duty on leave - one man died from wounds Received in action weather broken dull a Damp 7/h. JULLUNDUR Brig relieves SIRHIND Bde tonight vide Appendix VI attached	B.O. Issued 1 - O.R.B 38 3 - 41 Appendix VI attached

WAR DIARY
or
INTELLIGENCE SUMMARY.
(Erase heading not required.)

Army Form C. 211

VOL 4
Page 5
LAHORE DIVISION

No Y B F A

Hour, Date, Place	Summary of Events and Information	Remarks and references to Appendices
LA GORGUE 15-7-15	10 am ADMS. Visited unit. Two field 2 bull cases. 11-30 am Received orders from ADMS - No 1/2 BFA relieved by No 5 BFA. Batted Sect of Scotland Rifle. Sick collected by No Y BFA - No 1 BFA to continue charging sick cases in up to 6 pm front. Usual Afficules VTT avrailed. Sick tournaded collected as usual. Weather bright hot.	Sick & Sick Wounded total BO 3 - 1 - 4 ORS 33 - 8 - 41 Afficules VTT attached
LA GORGUE 16-7-15	ADMS visited unit at 11-10 pm. Inspected two bill cases. One man brought into Hospital dead — due to drowning. Sick Wounded collected as usual. Weather steady. Staff Sert C B SPACKMAN RAMC detailed as No 1st MANCHESTER REF under instructions from ADMS	BO 3 1 4 ORB 21 5 - 26
LA GORGUE 17-4-15:	ADMS visited unit at 10 AM. inspected 2 bull cases. Sick Wounded collected as usual. Weather cool & sunny. JF	BO 3 hl 3 ORB 21 10 31
LA GORGUE 18-7-15	ADMS visited unit at 10 am inspected no sick cases. one both. case. Sick Wounded collected as usual. Driver K 4504 No Y899 42 KEIR W. Y No 7426 Pte ROBINSON J Sect 6 to 1st MANCHESTER RAMC formerly admitted to Hospital at 510 pm reauslio light Received orders Now to collect Sick Wounded of Taylor VA 3 & K.D.Gs at LA GORGUE base Affendices VTT attached.	BO 1 1 hl 1 OR 3 31 4 35 Afficules VIII attached
LA GORGUE 19-7-15:	ADMS visited unit at 10-15 am inspected two eye cases & two bone cases two eye cases and to ARQUES. Sick Wounded collected as usual. Weather by W Rain. JF.	BO 2 2 4 ORR 17 4 21

Army Form C. 2118.

WAR DIARY
or
INTELLIGENCE SUMMARY.
(Erase heading not required.)

Instructions regarding War Diaries and Intelligence Summaries are contained in F.S. Regs., Part II. and the Staff Manual respectively. Title pages will be prepared in manuscript.

VOL 4 PAGE 6
No Y.B.5.A   LAHORE DIVISION

Hour, Date, Place	Summary of Events and Information	Remarks and references to Appendices
LA GORGUE 20-7-15.	A.D.M.S. visited unit at 10 am inspected their bell tents and R.N. ALLAN R.A.M.C. returned from leave. Jar morning duty. W.O. P. Walls went to England. No 2 M.A.C. cleared unit at 9-15 am. 9.30 pm Ord Posts cleared of Sick Personnel. Weather Bright there 7/m	Stab B Sick I wounded BO 1 M 1 ORB 30 3 33
LA GORGUE 21-7-15.	A.D.M.S. visited unit at 11-30 am inspected 4 bell tents. Sick personnel cleared from SIRHIND Brigade in the morning & from Ord Posts of FEROZEPORE at Night. Weather Bright there	B.O. M - ORB 26 5- 31
LA GORGUE 22-7-15.	A.D.M.S. visited unit at 10 am inspected all Bycars. 11-15 am Received Secret orders from A.D.M.S. Vid LAHORE Div. area to take up line on Night 22/23 July from LA BASSEE Road inclusive to FAUQUISSART AUBERS Road inclusive. No LAHORE FRONT the SOUTHERN Sector. JULLUNDUR BRIGADE LA BASSEE Road inclusive to POLVIN TRENCH Northern Sector - SIRHIND Brigade POLVIN TRENCH Inclusive to No 68 B.S. including TX attached. BRITISH Sick Personnel - Several sectors received late. FEROZEPORE Brigade will be relieved Bright by SIRHIND Brigade - including Aine of FEROZEPORE Brigade supply LA GORGUE - Estaires - Lisbourg Sick also collected daily by No Y.B.5.A	Appendix IX attached Appendix X attached

Forms/C. 2118/10

WAR DIARY or INTELLIGENCE SUMMARY.

(Erase heading not required.)

Army Form C. 211

VOL 4 PAGE 4

No 7 R.F.A. LAHORE DIVISION

Hour, Date, Place	Summary of Events and Information	Remarks and references to Appendices
LA GORGUE 22-7-15-	4 pm. Received instructions from ADMS to detail Lieut R.M.ALLAN R.A.M.C for duty with 11th Bugade R.F.A vice Lieut SINCLAIR R.A.M.C sick 7.15pm received instructions from H.D.M.S to back 12 horses with Divisional Vetmals to be kept in Reserve as Brigade Closes. Div H.Q. horses admitted to No 112 I.F.A. Pte GILROY's Hearing acuity did return from leave - reported to A.D.M.S Been about meals resulting from Pte Perrin trouble bright both jaws at intervals. No 2 M.A.C. situated west 1.7m 4pm	State of Sick Personnel R.O. 1 4 3 40 O.R's all 40
LA GORGUE 23-7-15	A.D.M.S. visited unit at 10am finished back 12 Sgt cases. Sick collected at 10 am 2nd / 4th BLACK WATCH. 4th LONDON Reg 1 C.R's 7pm received instructions Bristol Sick R/173 by R.E. Pte GILROY'S returned from leave - absence due to attack on his wife at Crania. Sent back by No 2 M.A.C at 2pm trouble bright both jaws at intervals. 4pm	R.O. 1 O.R's 12
LA GORGUE 24-7-15	A.D.M.S visited unit at 10-15 am. Evacuated one both cases Two Eye cases. Sick Sgt Patel. BETHUNE Little difference in adminims of cases from Labour Corps & Canal Hospital. BETHUNE. Sick collected as usual trouble bright both jaws at intervals. 4pm	R.O. 2 O.R's 26

WAR DIARY or INTELLIGENCE SUMMARY.

(Erase heading not required.)

Army Form C. 2118

VOL Y PAGE 8
No Y R.F.A. LAHORE DIVISION

Hour, Date, Place	Summary of Events and Information	Remarks and references to Appendices
LA GORGUE 25-7-15	Sick collected as usual - Inspected Recreation Rooms in afternoon with a view to converting Hospital. Sketches being made. Weather bright. JfL	Sick attack returned 1 B.O. 2 ORO 24
LA GORGUE 26-7-15	A.D.M.S. visited unit at 10.15 am. Inspected 5 seek cases. 4 3 Sept cases. Sick collected from FEROZEPORE Brigade as usual - 5 Eye cases sent to Eye specialist at ARQUES. Dis. Assistant Surgeon detailed to his duties. Sick (x) No 1 Siege Battery R.E. Weather dull. JfL	B.O. 1 ORB 25 no sessions held in Hospital were taken for research a note
LA GORGUE 27-7-15	A.D.M.S. visited the unit and inspected 4 sick cases at 10.15 am. He also inspected invalid Officers for Board Survey. Stores - Sick collected as usual - Weather bright. Cooler evening. JfL Reconnoitred and sent — R M ALLAN RAMC No 13 FA to SCMH No Aulchery Camp No? nr inquiry. 61 PARADISE L. on NF attached No13 FA to SCMH. N.O 2748 Pte PARADISE L. NF attached No13 FA to SCMH. IND 3080 HAVILDAR NIKKA No24 FA No 34 FA to IDSM Kala Honi No 28/7-15 - all 27-7-15-	B.O. 2 CR 26 3
LA GORGUE 28-7-15	A.D.M.S. visited the unit and inspected 10 sick cases at 11-am. 1 NCO & other ranks from A.D.M.S. Seek collected as usual. Weather bright. JfL	B.O. 4 FRB 35
LA GORGUE 29-7-15	Special Medical Board at 11 am. 13 NCOs Examined for Physical fitness for Commissions in the Regular Army. A.D.M.S. visited unit at 12.30 pm. One motor cyclist with motor cycle injured the unit. Sick collected as usual Weather bright. JfL	B.O. 3 ORB 18 1

WAR DIARY
or
INTELLIGENCE SUMMARY
(Erase heading not required.)

of No. 7 B F A
LAHORE DIVISION
VOL 7 PAGE 9

Army Form C. 2118

Instructions regarding War Diaries and Intelligence Summaries are contained in F.S. Regs., Part II. and the Staff Manual respectively. Title Pages will be prepared in manuscript.

Place	Date	Hour	Summary of Events and Information	Remarks and references to Appendices
LA GORGUE	30/7/15	10 am	ADMS inspected units from the Division T Sec received from Left Cases	Sick admitted BO. 2
		11 am	1st Class Good Surg. J D THOMAS joined the unit	ORB 14
		12.20 pm	Hosted Divisional workshop unit. No teams for Sick. Surgical Stores	
		5.15 pm	Hosted various bottles to see Bugonels built a new decontaminating Hospital Bag cultivation Sick collected during the day from FEROZEPORE BRIGADE. Weather still warm	
LA GORGUE	31/7/15	10 am	ADMS visited unit. Inspected Sick cases. 4 cases of sick inflicted injuries remaining in Hospital. 3 cases to decided should be transferred. REECE, ROBINSON, KERR, O'BRIEN, SALTER	Sick BO. 2 ORB 18
		10.30 am	No. 130 IFA secured 1 car for be examined stated in FA Bentings ankle feather lobar— under instructions from NAMS.	
		11 am	Sick collected from FEROZEPORE BRIGADE	
		1 pm	Received instructions from ADMS to collect Sick on 1st Aug of 1/14 SEAFORTHS from LA GORGUE	Appendix II attached
		8 pm	Received orders from ADMS to take a Brenen Sick transferred of the 21st BRIGADE. Collected by No. 112 IFA. Vide appendix IV attached	

Lt. Archibald Gill
RAMC
O C No 7 BFA
LAHORE DIVISION.

"A" Form.
MESSAGES AND SIGNALS.
Army Form C. 2121.

Appendix No 1

TO: No 7 B.F.A.
No 112 I.F.A.

Sender's Number: 365
Day of Month: 6

A A A

Ferozepore Bde relieves Jullundur Bde tonight in trenches AAA Jullundur Brigade is detailing one Indian Battalion in reserve to Sirhind Bde to be billetted in BOUT DEVILLE and a British battalion in reserve to Ferozepore Brigade to be billetted in PONT du HEM aaa Please arrange for collection of sick and wounded accordingly aaa No 7 B.F.A to clear left section No 112 I.F.A to clear right section as before

11.15am

From: ADMS Lahore Divn
Lt Col

"A" Form.
MESSAGES AND SIGNALS.
Army Form C. 2121.

Appx 2
Appendix No 2

TO: Ferozepore Brigade

Sender's Number: 366
Day of Month: 6
AAA

Advance Dressing Station at M 27 D 5/2 Bearers and wagons rendezvous there at 9.30 p.m nightly AAA If any change in aid posts this should be notified to dressing station as early as possible

Copy for information to:-
OC. No 7 B.F.A
OC. No 112 2.F.A

From: Medical Lahore Divn
Place:
Time: 10·55 am

Lt Col

APPENDIX 3 - Volume 7   Copy

Copy of a circular Memorandum No 29/48 dated Head Quarters Lahore Divn 9th July from A.D.M.S. Lahore Divn.

The following methods of evacuation of wounded from the front is circulated for the information of O's C and M.O's in charge of units:-

1. A permanent dressing station for both British and Indian troops is established at M 27 D 5/2 with personnel and motor transport on duty day and night

2. Walking cases sick or wounded may be directed to the dressing station by units at any time and these will be retained there till an opportunity offers to have them transported to the Field ambulances

3. Lying down cases sick or wounded may in cases of urgency be sent at any time to the Dressing Station and be immediately sent from there to the Field ambulances, but if cases are not urgent or if they are numerous they should be kept at the Regimental Aid posts till called for by Bearer Divisions

4. Regimental aid posts are visited nightly between the hours of 9 and 10 P.M by Bearer Divisions and as these positions are constantly changing Medical officers of units will immediately they have occupied an aid post send an exact description of its position to the Asst Surgn in charge of the Dressing station who will keep in the Dressing Station a spot map of all aid posts up to date with names of units occupying them

5. One stretcher squad of Army Bearer Corps will be allotted to remain at each regimental aid post for removal to the Dressing station of urgent cases mentioned in para 3, reliefs being carried out by Officers commanding Field ambulances concerned.

6. The Dressing station is being put on to telephonic communication with Brigade Head Quarters and in cases of urgency bearers or motor ambulance transport can be obtained immediately

A wheeled stretcher carriage is also available at the dressing station.

True Copy   sd B.B. Grayfoot
Capt Rame   Colonel
O.C. No. 7 British Field Ambulance   A.D.M.S. Lahore Divn

"A" Form.   Army Form C. 2121.

MESSAGES AND SIGNALS.

TO: NO 7 B.F.A. ~~Jullundur Bde~~
     NO 112 S.F.A.

Sender's Number: 357
Day of Month: 11
AAA

47th Sikh transferred to Meerut Divn 1st Serfoth and 4th Serfoths joins Jullundur Bde NFA arrange collection of sick accordingly and addressed No 7 BFA No 112 S.F.A. repeated Jullundur Bde

From Place: Meerut Lahore Divn Jullundur

Time: 9-15 a.m.

The above may be forwarded as now corrected. 9.30 am

Secret Appx V   No 371
                    13-7-15
O.C. No 7 B.F.A.
O.C. No 112 d.F.A.   Appendix V

The following moves will take place on the dates specified; arrangements for collection of sick should be made accordingly:—

July 13th – 40th Pathans to join Dehra Dun Bde. 57th Rifles to join Bareilly Bde.
2nd Royal High and 1/4th Royal High on relief from trenches during night 13th/14th join Ferozepore Bde who will arrange billets in present area

July 14th – 59th Rifles to join Dehra Dun Bde. 129th Baluchis to join Bareilly Bde

July 15th – 89th Punjabis will join Bareilly Bde, 15th Sikhs, 1/1st and 1/4th Gurkha Rifles will join Garhwal Bde.
2nd Leicesters & 1/3rd Londons join Sirhind Brigade who
                                  will

will arrange billets in the reserve
Bde area.

\[signature\]
Colonel
A.D.U.S Lahore Divn

"A" Form.   Army Form C. 2121.
MESSAGES AND SIGNALS.   No. of Message...........

| TO | NO 7 B.F.A. |
| | NO 112 I.F.A. |

| Sender's Number. | Day of Month. | In reply to Number | AAA |
| 373 | 14 | | |

Jullundur Brigade relieves Sirhind Brigade tonight aaa British Units Sirhind Bde to LAGORGUE and L'EPINETTE on relief aaa arrange collection of sick and wounded accordingly aaa No 7 BFA to clear left Section No 112 IFA to clear right Section as before

From   ADMS Lahore Div
Place
Time   11.30 am.

12 pm.

"A" Form.
Army Form C. 2121.
MESSAGES AND SIGNALS. No. of Message..........

Prefix	Code	Words	Charge	This message is on a/c of:	Recd. at ...... m.
Office of Origin and Service Instructions.		Sent At VII m. To By		Service. (Signature of "Franking Officer.")	Date...... From...... By......

TO { O.C. No 7 B.F.A.
     " No 8 B.F.A.
     " No 112 F.F.A.

Sender's Number	Day of Month	In reply to Number	AAA
374	13		

O.C. No 8 B.F.A. will take over tonight the duty of clearing the sick and wounded from the right sub section AAA Position of all aid posts to be obtained from O.C. No 112 F.F.A. AAA Personnel and equipment of No 112 F.F.A. at dressing station will be returned to the F.A. on relief by O.C. No 8 F.A. AAA British sick to be collected under arrangements of O.C. No 7 B.F.A. who will also continue to clear the left sub section of the front

From
Place
Time

The above may be forwarded as now corrected. (Z)
Censor. Signature of Addressee or person authorised to telegraph in his name.
*This line should be erased if not required.

"A" Form. Army Form C. 2121.
MESSAGES AND SIGNALS. No. of Message..........

Prefix......Code........m. Office of Origin and Service Instructions.	Words	Charge	This message is on a/c of: ....Service. (Signature of "Franking Officer.")	Recd. at.........m. Date........ From........ By........
	Sent At.......m. To.... By....			

TO {

*	Sender's Number.	Day of Month.	In reply to Number	A A A
	time	AAA	OC	No 112	2.F.A.
	will	arrange	for	Collection and
	treatment	of	Casualties of
	15th	Lancers	84th	Pioneers Sappers
	and	Miners	his	Troop and
	also	will	take	over	any
	Indian	details	collected	by	No 7
	and	8 B.F.As	from	front line
	AAA	NO 112	2FA	will	also
	detail	a	Sub	asst	Surgeon
	to	See	morning	sick	of
	Field	Troop	R.E.	at LA MARAIS
	Farm	in	relief	of	Asst
	Surg	of	No 8	B.F.A.

From ... A.D.M.S. ...
Place
Time 10.45 am
The above may be forwarded as now corrected. (Z)
  11.15 am
Censor. Signature of Addressor or person authorised to telegraph in his name.
* This line should be erased if not required.

"A" Form.
MESSAGES AND SIGNALS.
Army Form C. 2121.

TO: No 7 B F A

Sender's Number: 376
Day of Month: 18
AAA

Arrange to collect daily sick and wounded digging party Kings Dragoon Guards (1st Indian Cavly Divn) at LAGORGUE

From: ADMS Lahore Divn

"A" Form.
MESSAGES AND SIGNALS.
Army Form C. 2121.

TO
- O.C. NO 8 B.F.A
- O.C. NO 112 I.F.A
- O.C. No 7 B.F.A.

Sender's Number: **380**
Day of Month: **22**
AAA

On the night 22nd/23rd July Lahore Divn will take up line from LABASSEE road inclusive to the FAUQUISSART AUBERS road inclusive AAA The Lahore front will be as follows AAA Southern Section Jullundur Bde LABASSEE road inclusive to GOLVIN TRENCH inclusive AAA Northern Section Sirhind Bde GOLVIN trench exclusive to FAUQUISSART-AUBERS road AAA The Advanced dressing station at Green Barn will be in charge of Bearer Division of No 8 B.F.A. AAA NO 112 I.F.A. will establish an Advanced Dressing Station at LA FLINQUE in square M.10.C 3/6 AAA mixed bearer

"A" Form. Army Form C. 2121.

MESSAGES AND SIGNALS.

divisions	will	be	formed	at		
these	dressing	Stations	the	necessary		
bearers	and	Establishment	to	be		
detailed	by	O.C.s	No 8 B.F.A	and		
112 I.F.A.	AAA	one	Asst	Surgeon		
from	No 8	B.F.A.	to	join	the	
Bearer	Divn	of	No 112	I.F.A.	and	
one Sub	Asst	Surgeon	from	No 112		
I.F.A.	to join	the	Bearer	Divn	of No 8	
B.F.A.	AAA	The	mixed	bearer	divn	
of No 8	B.F.A	will clear	the	Southern		
section	and the	mixed	bearer	division		
of No 112	I.F.A.	will clear	the	Northern		
section	AAA	One	Motor	Ambulance		
will	be	present	at each	advanced		
dressing	station	respectively	from	No 8		
B.F.A	and	No 112	I.F.A	AAA	one	

"A" Form.
MESSAGES AND SIGNALS.
Army Form C. 2121.

			AAA
wheeled	stretcher to		be
kept at	each	dressing station	
AAA Rendezvous	for bearers		
and waggons 7.30	p.m.	daily	
AAA. British	sick and	wounded	
To No 8 B.F.A	Indians to No 112 I.F.A		

From A.D.M.S Lahore Div'n
Place
Time 7.30 a.m.

Colonel

"A" Form. Army Form C. 2121.
MESSAGES AND SIGNALS.

TO O.C. No 7 B.F.A.

Sender's Number.	Day of Month.	In reply to Number	AAA
381	22		

Ferozepore Brigade will be relieved from the trenches by the Sirhind Brigade tonight AAA Billeting areas of Ferozepore Bde roughly LAGORGUE, Eastern end ESTAIRES-LEDRUMEZ AAA arrange for collection of sick daily aaa addressed NO 7 BFA copy to NO 8 BFA.

From: ADMS Lahore Division
Time: 9.30 am

Colonel
ADMS

Appendix II
Volume 7

"A" Form.
MESSAGES AND SIGNALS.
Army Form C. 2121.

Apr 11.

TO: O.C. No 112 JFA

Sender's Number: 396
Day of Month: 31st

AAA

Please take over Dressing Station at St VAAST tomorrow morning at 10 am and arrange to collect from front of 21st Bde tomorrow night AAA Sick and wounded to No 7 BFA LAGORGUE AAA Front extends from LABASSEE Road to BOND St Communication trench a distance of about 700 yards AAA The above is in addition to collection of Lahore Divn Casualties aaa addressed ~~to~~ No 112 JFA copy to No 7 BFA

From: ADMS Lahore Divn
Place: Lui Doan
Time: 7.45 pm

Rec'd 8 pm

Lt Col
for ADMS

Serial No. 34.

121/6958

Aug '15

WAR DIARY
with appendices.

OF

No. 1 British Field Ambulance.

FROM 1st August 1915 TO 31st August 1915

Army Form C. 2118

WAR DIARY
or
INTELLIGENCE SUMMARY
(Erase heading not required.)

No 7 B.F.A. LAHORE DIVISION
VOLUME 8 page 1

Instructions regarding War Diaries and Intelligence Summaries are contained in F.S. Regs., Part II. and the Staff Manual respectively. Title Pages will be prepared in manuscript.

Place	Date	Hour	Summary of Events and Information	Remarks and references to Appendices
LA GORGUE	1-8-15	10.15 a.m	A.D.M.S. visited the unit	
		11 A.M	Received orders from A.D.M.S. that LAHORE DIVISION line is to form SPAN POST LANE M.36.D to BOND STREET TRENCH in S.10.A in two sections the dividing line being OXFORD STREET TRENCH at S.5.C. The Northern section to be held by FEROZEPORE BRIGADE – this section to be closed supplied by No 8 B.F.A. & thereafter by No 7 B.F.A. No 7 B.F.A. to take over dressing station at M.21.D. at 10 am 2-8-15.	Vide Appendix (1 attached)
		4 p.m	Lieut. R M ALLAN rejoined No 7 B.F.A. for duty	
		9 p.m	Capt. H L GARSON detailed to accompany Bearer Division of No 8 B.F.A. then proceeding to Aid Posts.	Stab & Staff Nominal Roll No 1 ORR 11 3
			4th class Corpl Serj S.S. GAYNOR I.S.M.D. posted for temporary duty. Vealth Bryd Hosm	
			J.J. Mitchell Capt R.A.M.C. OC No 7 B.F.A.	
LA GORGUE	2-8-15	9.15	4th class Corpl Serj J E SWEENEY I.S.M.D. on one weeks leave to ENGLAND Bearer Subdivision marched out to take over dressing Station at M.21.D. composed as under Capt H L GARSON R.A.M.C. 2 Indoor Surgeons – 1 British Nursing Orderly. A.H.C. Jones A.B.C. 33 Stockline 12. Equipment. The section has been detailed to remain at M.21.D.	
		11.30	Capt H L GARSON R.A.M.C. reported that dressing station has been taken over & section 3A and parts had been obtained from FEROZEPORE BRIGADE HEADQUARTERS.	
		12 noon	A.D.M.S visited the unit	
		3.30 pm	Received instructions from A.D.M.S. that the following troops of 19th Division would arrive in Lahore area & be posted as follows – Seek to be collected by No 7 B.F.A.	

Army Form C. 2118

No 7 RFA LAHORE DIVISION
VOLUME 8
Page 2

WAR DIARY
or
INTELLIGENCE SUMMARY
(Erase heading not required.)

Instructions regarding War Diaries and Intelligence Summaries are contained in F. S. Regs., Part II. and the Staff Manual respectively. Title Pages will be prepared in manuscript.

Place	Date	Hour	Summary of Events and Information	Remarks and references to Appendices
			SIRHIND BRIGADE HQrs M&D	See official reports
			1 Coy S.W.B. PIONEERS	BO No -
			4th Batt N LANCASHIRE REGT	ORB 14 -
			1 Platoon CYCLIST COY	
			MMG Section	to arrive 3-8-15
			FEROZEPORE BRIGADE	
			4th Batt R LANCASTER REGT	
			1 Platoon CYCLIST COY	
			Dressing Station & aid posts cleared by Bearer Division at 9.30 pm. Weather bright & warm. JJh.	
LA GORGUE 3-8-15	3-8-15	10-15 am	Case of Senuida admitted.	BO 1
		11-30 am	A.D.M.S. visited unit. Sirhind & Ferozepore Brigades report that regiments of 17th Division have not arrived.	ORB 20 3
		6 pm	Inspected Dressing Station.	
		9 pm	Sick & wounded collected from Aid Posts. Portion of Aid Posts taken on Spot that attached Side offensive & attached. Weather bright & warm. JJh	
LA GORGUE 4-8-15	4-8-15	10-30 am	A.D.M.S. visited unit. Returned in action. One hussar orderly on leave. One man sent to Furnes.	BO - 1
		9 pm	Sick & wounded collected as usual. Weather bright & warm. JJh	ORB 15-5

Army Form C. 2118

WAR DIARY
or
INTELLIGENCE SUMMARY
(Erase heading not required.)

No 7 B.F.A. LAHORE DIVISION
VOL. 8   PAGE 3

Instructions regarding War Diaries and Intelligence Summaries are contained in F. S. Regs., Part II. and the Staff Manual respectively. Title Pages will be prepared in manuscript.

Place	Date	Hour	Summary of Events and Information	Remarks and references to Appendices
LA GORGUE	5-8-15	9:30 am	O.C. & 3 officers from 57th F.A. arrived for 24 hours course of instruction.	Sketch of S.V.W. B.O. 1 — O.R.B. 17
		11 am	A.D.M.S. paid usual twice daily visit to sick convoy two Enteric cases — one severe injury solved the Enteric cases	
		5:14 pm	D.A.D.M.S. gave his usual instructions to clear up Kings Liverpool Aid post	
		5:30 pm	Inspected Dressing Station accompanied by O.C. & 3 officers of 57th F.A.	
		9 pm	Aid Posts cleared — bearer subdivision accompanied by O.C. & 3 officers of 57th F.A.	
			Weather bright humid [sig]	
LA GORGUE	6-8-15	9:30 am	O.C. & 3 officers from No 57 F.A. departed — O.C. & 3 officers from No 58 F.A. arrived for 24 hours course of instruction.	Sketch of S.V.W. B.O. ll ll O.R.B. 16 8
		10:15 am	A.D.M.S. visited the unit two fresh Enteric cases	
		11:30 am	Inspected Dressing Station accompanied by O.C. & 3 officers from No 58 F.A.	
		12:30 pm	Lieut E MAPOTHER R.A.M.C. (T.C.) reported his arrival for duty.	
		8:30 pm	Aid Posts cleared — O.C. & officers from No 58 F.A. accompanied Bearer subdivision	
			Weather dull with rain [sig]	
LA GORGUE	7-8-15	9:30 am	O.C. & 3 officers from No 59 F.A. arrived for 24 hours course of instruction O.C. & officers from No 58 F.A. departed	
		10:15 am	A.D.M.S. inspected unit	

Army Form C. 2118

WAR DIARY
or
INTELLIGENCE SUMMARY
(Erase heading not required.)

No 7 B.F.A.
LAHORE DIVISION
Vol 8   Page 4

Place	Date	Hour	Summary of Events and Information	Remarks and references to Appendices
LA GORGUE	7-8-15	2.30pm	Lieut R M ALLAN R.A.M.C took the offices of No 39 F.A around Dressing Stations.	Stab of S.T.W
		3.30pm	The Coys Commander Lieut General Sir JAMES WILLCOCKS inspected unit	B.O - 1
		5-30pm	Aid posts cleared. Collected officers recovering cases the Rams. Sub abnormal	O.R.3 13 - 3
			4th Class Asocl Surgeon C H WINDSOR I.S.M.D transferred sick to C.C.S.	
			Weather dull. JRA	
LA GORGUE	8-8-15	10am	OC 1 officer from No 39 F.A departed. 40 MG visited unit	Stab of S.T.W
		5pm	Received orders that JULLUNDUR BRIGADE relieves SIRHIND Bde in the trenches tonight.	B.O -
		8.30pm	Sick forwarded the collected. accordingly. Appendix III attached.	ORS 14 3
			Aid posts cleared by Bearer Subdivision. 40th PATHANS ¼ 1st SUFFOLKS have relieved	
		9pm	1st KINGS - LIVERPOOLS ¼ 4th ? Posts of Aid Posts noted in Spt hosp. Appendix III	Appendix III attached
			Proposed plan for forward habitues sent in to A.D.M.S.	
			Weather bright. JRA	
LA GORGUE	9-8-15.	7am	Two Epps Cases sent to ARQUES & No 4 Stationary Hospital	Stab of S.T.W
		10am	A.D.M.S. visited unit. Inspected me suspicious hand case - Case to be evacuated owing	B.O be N
			to severely frozen wound	O.R.3 2 Y
		8-10pm	Inspected Dressing Station & visited Aid Posts. Personnel at Dressing Station changed	
			4th Asocl Surg J E SWEENEY I.S.M.D. ¼ one Motor Ambulance Driver returned from	
			Seven days leave. Weather dull - raining & very warm JRA	
LA GORGUE	10-8-15.	11am	A.D.M.S. visited Hospital - Lecture to Section M.M.G. or first aid given by Capt W.V.	Stab of S.T.W
		2pm	O'RIORDAN. R.A.M.C.	B.O W A2
		3pm	F.A cleared by No 2 M.A.C Lecture to Section M.M.G on first aid given by Capt GIRSON	O.R.3 14 1
		5-sept	lecture to Section M.M.G on first aid given by Revd R M ALLAN R.A.M.C. R.A.M.C	
			Sick forwarded cleared from Aid Posts. Weather dull but fair, warm. JRA	

1875 Wt. W593/826 1,000,000 4/15 J.B.C. & A. A.D.S.S./Forms/C. 2118.

Army Form C. 2118

No 7 B.F.A
LAHORE DIVISION
Vol 8 Page 5

WAR DIARY
or
INTELLIGENCE SUMMARY
(Erase heading not required.)

Instructions regarding War Diaries and Intelligence Summaries are contained in F. S. Regs., Part II. and the Staff Manual respectively. Title Pages will be prepared in manuscript.

Place	Date	Hour	Summary of Events and Information	Remarks and references to Appendices
LA GORGUE	11.8.15	11.30am	A.D.M.S visited the unit Inspected our both case officer	
		1 pm	Received evacuations from A.D.M.S Estaburst. Sent hospital stores as under.	BO 1 1
			JULLUNDUR Bde 5- horses FEROZEPORE Bde 3 horses Shoe DEPOT FOSSE 4 horses.	ORR 17 4
		8.30 pm	Inspected Dressing Station. Visited Red posts. And posts cleaned Personnel changed weather warm	
LA GORGUE	12.8.15	9 am	Issued duties of Class clerkship as above	
		11 am	A.D.M.S visited the unit. BHUTIA ordered west of A.B.C from No 1131 F.A. Arrived for a course of 3 days instruct on at Aid Posts & Dressing Station	BO - 1 ORR 10 5-
		8.30 pm	Aid posts cleared. weather close. Wind 7ph.	
LA GORGUE	12.8.15	9 am	4th Good Sup. S.S. GAYNOR I.S.M.D sent & P.1 H.L.I to duty and instructions from A.D.M.S. 3rd Class C.B. GIBSON I.S.M.D joined and from 1/3 H.L.I	Bdll 275 7M 20 - 1 ORR 10 5-
		2.15pm	Received orders from A.D.M.S that on withdrawal of Bearer Division from Dressing Station M 27 D. had was to be evacuated tobred cases awaiting investigation trivial cases to be transferred to No 8 B.F.A. Closed billets at Sq R 13 B take over 3 farms from O.C No 20 B.F.A Copy of orders sent to O.C. No 8 B.F.A received & offended to Bearer Division recalled following station handed over to No 8 N.F.A weather Bright	
		4 pm	No 2 M.A.C evacuated unit Staff cases except Staff cases Reserve cases awaiting investigation 7ph	

WAR DIARY or **INTELLIGENCE SUMMARY**
(Erase heading not required.)

Army Form C. 2118

No Y B.F.A LAHORE DIVISION
VOL 8 Page 6.

Place	Date	Hour	Summary of Events and Information	Remarks and references to Appendices
LA GORGUE	14-8-15	9.30am	4 Sick 1 3 wounded transferred to No 8 B.F.A Hospital	
		10am	Handed over billets B.O.C. No 20 B.F.A	
		11am	Unit marched to R.136.	
		2pm	Unit arrived & billeted in these farms at R.14.b. L'EPINETTE – ADMS notified	
		3-15pm	Weather bright 7/h	
L'EPINETTE	15-8-15	10-30am	A.D.M.S. conferred with O 1st H.L.I. 1/4 Kings Liverpool Reg.	
		11am	Attended Court of Enquiry at No 6 B.F.A on Pte BURKE C.R.	
		2-30pm	Attended usual 2 officers' lecture by Bacteriological Commission	
			Weather showery 7/h	
L'EPINETTE	16-8-15	12-noon	Board, President A.D.M.S., held at No 118.F.A	
			Weather wet & showery 7/h	
L'EPINETTE	17-8-15	11am	Lieut A.B.C. Wee joined the unit – Weather showery 7/h	
L'EPINETTE	18-8-15	10am	Medical Board – examining candidates – physical fitness for Regular Commission	
			Training of unit commenced. Physical exercise – 8 to 9am	
			Route march 11-30 am	
			Drill 5 pm	
			Fatigue work – repairs etc	
		11-30am	Lieut E MAPOTHER R.A.M.C. attached to 114 Brigade R.F.A for temporary duty. Weather thundery 7wet 7/h

1875 Wt. W593/826 1,000,000 4/15 J.B.C. & A. A.D.S.S./Forms/C. 2118.

Army Form C. 2118

WAR DIARY
or
INTELLIGENCE SUMMARY
(Erase heading not required.)

No 7. B.F.A.
LAHORE DIVISION
Vol 5. Page 7

Instructions regarding War Diaries and Intelligence Summaries are contained in F. S. Regs., Part II. and the Staff Manual respectively. Title Pages will be prepared in manuscript.

Place	Date	Hour	Summary of Events and Information	Remarks and references to Appendices
L'EPINETTE	19-8-15		Training continues – nothing to note – weather bright no rain. JHR	
L'EPINETTE	20-8-15		Training continues – nothing to note – weather bright no rain. JHR	
L'EPINETTE	21-8-15		Training continues – nothing to note. Weather cloudy rainy. JHR	
L'EPINETTE	22-8-15		Training continues – nothing to note. Weather bright. JHR	
L'EPINETTE	23-8-15		Training continues – nothing to note. Weather bright. JHR	
L'EPINETTE	24-8-15	11am	Medical board. Physical fitness of candidates for regular commissions. Training continues one extra hour. Shells but cooled. Weather bright warm. JHR	
		2 pm	Lieut R M ALLAN RAMC detailed for temporary duty with Connaught Rangers under evacuation from A.D.M.S. Capt H L GARSON RAMC & 3rd Class Coool Surgeon E J CREAIS I.S.M.D. on 7 days leave to ENGLAND. 3 A H C Recovered and sick 6. JHR	
			No 111 / F A. JHR	
L'EPINETTE	25-8-15		Training continues – weather fine. JHR	
L'EPINETTE	26-8-15		Training continues – Lieut E MAPOTHER RAMC reported the unit. Weather very warm bright. JHR	
L'EPINETTE	27-8-15		Training continues – nothing of note. Weather very warm bright. JHR	

1875 Wt. W593/826 1,000,000 4/15 J.B.C. & A. A.D.S.S./Forms/C. 2118.

WAR DIARY
or
INTELLIGENCE SUMMARY

(Erase heading not required.)

Army Form C. 2118

No 7. B.F.A.
LAHORE DIVISION
Vol 8 Page 8

Place	Date	Hour	Summary of Events and Information	Remarks and references to Appendices
L'EPINETTE	28.5.15		Out moving orders on one weeks leave. Training continues - weather bright warm. yfh	
L'EPINETTE	29.5.15		Lieut R M ALLAN reported sick from temporary duty with CONNAUGHT RANGERS. Civil Surgeon 3rd class C R GIBBON I.S.M.D detailed by A.D.M.S. to relieve Civil Surgeon in Sub. medical charge 1st Manchester Reg. 4th class Civil Surgeon A.R. D'ABREU I.S.M.D joined unit from MANCHESTER REG. Civil Surg. C B GIBBON. weather, hot. yfh. Report on patient history schedule forwarded to A.D.M.S.	
L'EPINETTE	30.5.15	9.30am	Lieut R M ALLAN R.A.M.C. detailed for temporary duty with L.D.T until instructions from A.D.M.S. Report on return of Slews for use required during month sent to A.D.M.S.	
		10.40am	Lieut E MAPOTHER R.A.M.C. detailed for temporary duty with 1st MANCHESTER REG until instructions from A.D.M.S. One A+C joined the unit from No 8 B.F.A - training continues - weather bright yfh	
L'EPINETTE	31.5.15	11.30am	Field Ambulance opened for the reception of Sick of SIRHIND Brigade. Had afternoon Capt H L GARSON R.A.M.C. 1st Civil Surgeon returned off leave - weather bright. Training of unit continues yfh	Appendix VI attached

Y Mitchell Capt
R.A.M.C
O.C. No 7 B.F.A
LAHORE DIVISION

"A" Form.
MESSAGES AND SIGNALS.
Army Form C. 2121.

TO:
- OC. No 7 B.F.A
- OC. No 8 B.F.A.
- OC. No 112 D.F.A

Sender's Number: 397
Day of Month: 1st
AAA

Sirhind Bde relieves 21st Bde in trenches tonight AAA Front extends from LABASSEE road to BOND street communication trench about 700 yards in extent aaa Lahore divn will then hold a line from sign post Lane M35D to Bond Street trench in S10A in two sections the dividing line being Oxford street trench at S.5.C Northern held by Ferozepor Bde and Southern by Sirhind Bde AAA The northern section will be cleared tonight by No 8 BFA and thereafter by No 7 B.F.A who will

"A" Form.
MESSAGES AND SIGNALS.

Army Form C. 2121.

Prefix	Code	m.	Words	Charge	This message is on a/c of:	Recd. at _____ m.
Office of Origin and Service Instructions			Sent At _____ m. To By		Service. (Signature of "Franking Officer.")	Date _____ From _____ By _____

TO {

Sender's Number	Day of Month	In reply to Number	AAA

take over the dressing station at M27D at 10 a.m. second August AAA Southern Section to be cleared to ST VAAST Dressing Station by NO 112 2.F.A.

From ADMS Lahore Div'n
Place
Time 11-40 am

Colonel

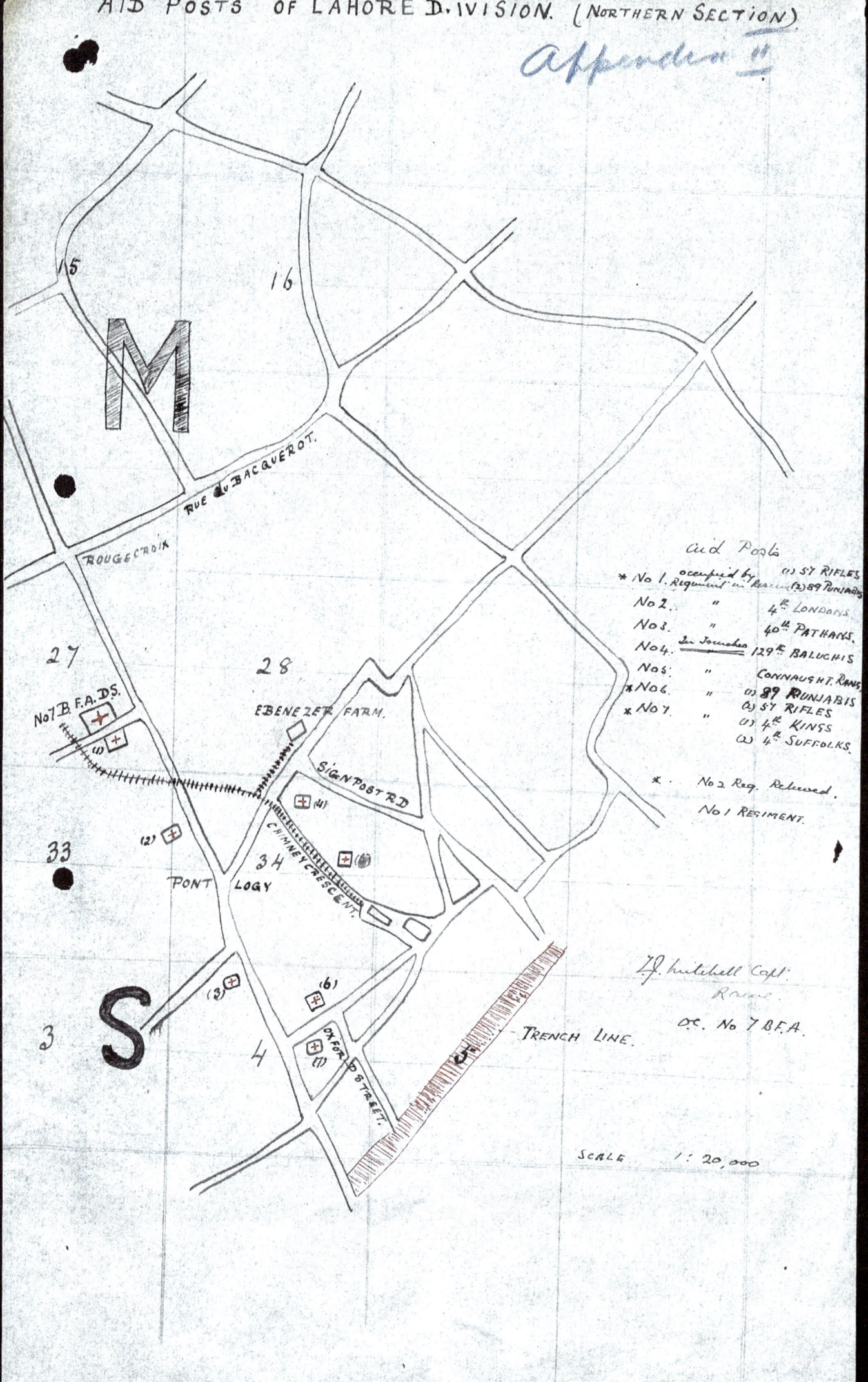

"A" Form.　　　　　　　　　　Army Form C. 2121.
MESSAGES AND SIGNALS.

TO: OC NO 7 B.F.A.
    OC NO 112 I.F.A.

Sender's Number: 13　　Day of Month: 8　　　　　　　　AAA

Jullundur Bde reliefs Sirhind Bde in trenches tonight AAA attached troops of 19th Divn remain in present billets AAA Please arrange collection of sick and wounded accordingly.

Copy for information to
OC No 8 BFA
OC No 111 IFA.

To Capt. O'Riordan
This affects the 4th King's Regt only. Tell Garson to get into touch with the Regiment relieving 4th Kings.

"A" Form.
MESSAGES AND SIGNALS.

Army Form C. 2121.

TO: OC No 7 B.F.A.

Sender's Number: 117
Day of Month: 13

AAA

On withdrawl of your Bearer Division from dressing station at M27D your Unit should be evacuated and closed AAA Cases in your Unit being held back for investigation and cases likely to be fit to return to duty should be transferred to NO 8 BFA VIEILLECHAPELLE with a statement for information of OC No 8 BFA AAA Your Unit will march tomorrow at 2 pm to closed billets at Sq R13B taking over 3 farms from OC. NO 20 B.F.A. aaa Route LESTREM - R9C - R13B aaa Refilling point unchanged aaa Report arrival to this office aaa addressed NO 7 BFA repeated NO 8 BFA

From: ADMS Lahore Division
Time: 10.15 am

Lt Colonel
for ADMS

"A" Form.
MESSAGES AND SIGNALS.

Army Form C. 2121.

TO: O.C. No 8 B.F.A.

Sender's Number: 15
Day of Month: 3
AAA

Your Unit will take over from tonight the collection of sick and wounded of the section of Lahore Divn front, extending from signpost lane on the left to the ESTAIRES LABASSEE road on the right AAA Troops holding the front are Ferozepore Bde and one battalion Jullundur Bde AAA The dressing station at M27D should be taken over at once from O.C. No 7 B.F.A. who will inform you of the position of all regtl aid posts with which you are to keep touch AAA British casualties to No 8 B.F.A Indian to No 111 I.F.A ZELOBES AAA Collection of sick from reserve

"A" Form.
MESSAGES AND SIGNALS.
Army Form C. 2121.

Bde still to be carried out by you as heretofore AAA Report to this office when dressing station taken over by you AAA addressed No 8 BFA repeated No 7 BFA.

From ADMS Lahore Div

Time 10.15 am

Lt Colonel
for ADMS

"A" Form.
MESSAGES AND SIGNALS.
Army Form C. 2121.

Approved V1

TO: OC No 7 BFA

Sender's Number: 4031
Day of Month: 26

AAA

Your Unit should open for collection and reception of sick of Sirhind Brigade from morning 31st August AAA Area of Brigade CALONNE.

Copy forwarded for information to OC No 8 BFA

From: ADMS Lahore Division
Place:
Time: 12.30 pm

Rcd. 2 pm

Lt Colonel

121/7286
Serial No. 34

121/7286

WAR DIARY
OF

No 7 British Field Ambulance

From 1st September 1915 To 30th September 1915

Sept. 1915

Army Form C. 2118

No. 7 B.F.A.
LAHORE DIVISION
I F F A
VOL 9 Page 1

WAR DIARY
or
INTELLIGENCE SUMMARY
(Erase heading not required.)

Instructions regarding War Diaries and Intelligence Summaries are contained in F. S. Regs., Part II. and the Staff Manual respectively. Title Pages will be prepared in manuscript.

Place	Date	Hour	Summary of Events and Information	Remarks and references to Appendices
L'EPINETTE	1-9-15	10 a.m.	Sick collected from SIRHIND BRIGADE - Evening of unit uncertain - weather cloudy	State of Sick B.O. ORB 1
L'EPINETTE	2-9-15	10.30 a.m.	Sick collected from SIRHIND BRIGADE.	State of Sick
		11.30 a.m.	Received orders from A.D.M.S. to detail 1st Class Cord. Sergt. J.O. THOMAS R.A.M.C. for Sub. medical charge of 1st MANCHESTER REGt. - Weather Cloudy - nothing Erotic. JM	R.O. Nil ORB 6
L'EPINETTE	3-9-15	10.15 a.m.	A.D.M.S. inspected two bath cases	State of Sick R.O. —
		11.30 a.m.	Received orders from A.D.M.S. that No. 7 B.F.A. would close hole otherwise I attached Weather rainy - cloudy tested. JM	ORB 2 appx 1 attached State of Sick B.O. ORB 1
L'EPINETTE	4-9-15		Nothing to note - own unit engaged with ordinary barrack general. JM	State of Sick B.O. ORB 1
L'EPINETTE	5-9-15	—	Transport Serjeant on leave one week to England. Nothing Erotic. Weather close & rainy. JM	
L'EPINETTE	6-9-15		One Nursing orderly on leave - one week to England. Training of unit continued. Bogsey wagons etc being painted. JM	
L'EPINETTE	7-9-15	10.30 p.m.	Training of unit continued Lieut. E. MAPOTHER R.A.M.C. reported unit on completion of temporary duty with 1st MANCHESTER REGIMENT. Weather fine. Warm. JM	
L'EPINETTE	8-9-15		Lieut. R.M. ALLAN R.A.M.C. reported unit on completion of temporary duty with L.D.T. Weather rain and fine - Training of unit continues. JM	

WAR DIARY or **INTELLIGENCE SUMMARY**

Army Form C. 2118

No. 4 B.F.A. LAHORE DIVISION
Vol 9 Page 2 / E.F.A

Place	Date	Hour	Summary of Events and Information	Remarks and references to Appendices
L'EPINETTE	9-9-15		Nothing to note. Training of unit continues – weather bright & warm 7/h	
L'EPINETTE	10-9-15	10-45am	Training of unit continues. ADMS visited the unit. weather bright & warm 7/h	
L'EPINETTE	11-9-15		Training of unit continues. weather bright & warm 7/h	
L'EPINETTE	12-9-15		Training of unit continues. weather bright & warm - 7/h	
L'EPINETTE	13-9-15		"	
L'EPINETTE	14-9-15	6-30am	One motor ambulance wagon detailed by A.D.M.S. to take Eye cases to ARQUES	
L'EPINETTE	15-9-15	11 am	Board – Examining candidates. Physical fitness for commission in the Regular army.	
		11-30am	Lecture to Assistant Surgeons by Capt. R.M. ALLAN R.A.M.C. "Regimental Medical Work". Training of unit continues - weather bright 7/h	
L'EPINETTE	16-9-15		One A.S.C. driver on 7 day's leave. Training of unit continues. weather bright 7/h	
L'EPINETTE	17-9-15		Training of unit continues – weather bright 7/h	

WAR DIARY
or
INTELLIGENCE SUMMARY
(Erase heading not required.)

Army Form C. 2118

Page 3.

Place	Date	Hour	Summary of Events and Information	Remarks and references to Appendices
L'EPINETTE	18.9.15	11 am	One hundred & sixty on seven days leave to England.	
			Lieut E. MAPOTHER R.A.M.C detailed by A.D.M.S. for temporary duty with 88th	
		12.30pm	D.D.M.S. inspected unit. Evening of usual continues – weather bright. JMcD	
L'EPINETTE	19.9.15		Morning of usual continues – weather bright. Wire fire broke out in iron stack at BOUTS FARM – Lieut called out to assist in	
		6 pm	putting fire out. JMcD	
L'EPINETTE	20.9.15	7.30pm	Claim for damages against No 7 R.F.A. made by Proprietor – Investigation held MAIRE – LESTREM present. Weather bright & fine. Evening of usual continues. JMcD	
L'EPINETTE	21.9.15	11.30am	Report of investigation sent to A.D.M.S.	
		4 pm	Unit inspected – all kit examined – find field dressings – Gas helmets – Emergency rations examined. Weather bright & fine. JMcD	
L'EPINETTE	22.9.15	10 am	Verbal orders issued for following personnel to hold themselves in readiness to move out on reinft of Div. (all) H L GARSON R.A.M.C. Capt R.M. ALLAN R.A.M.C. 4 anaest Surgeons. 4 Nursing Orderlies. 80 A.B.C. with 20 stretchers	
		3 pm	Unit packed loading transport wagons. Weather bright & warm. JMcD	

No 7 B.F.A
or
LAHORE DIVISION
L.F.F.A
Vol 9. Page 4

Army Form C. 2118

WAR DIARY
or
INTELLIGENCE SUMMARY
(Erase heading not required.)

Instructions regarding War Diaries and Intelligence Summaries are contained in F. S. Regs., Part II. and the Staff Manual respectively. Title Pages will be prepared in manuscript.

Place	Date	Hour	Summary of Events and Information	Remarks and references to Appendices
L'EPINETTE	23-9-15	11 am	Unit practiced loading transport wagons	
		4.15 pm	Received Local Medical Operation Order No 46 by A.D.M.S. LAHORE DIVISION - note Appendix III attached	Appendices I & II attached
		8 pm	Issued Field Ambulance Order No 1. note Appendix III attached. Weather warm bright with rain at intervals. JfM	
L'EPINETTE	24-9-15	8-30 am	Received picked Detachment of Draughman's 1st Army Operation No 12 marked Urgent Report. Detachment was detailed in Field Ambulance Orde No 1. marched out.	
		11 am	Three bicyclists transferred to No 8 R.F.A for temporary duty. Horses GASH & ASC failed to return from leave. Weather dull stormy. JfM	
L'EPINETTE	25-9-15	8 am	Hospital open for Sick. 1 Officer & 10 men transferred from No 8 R.F.A.	Daily State Sick
		10 am	Chance of Driver GASH A ASC reported to A.D.M.S	
		11-30 am	Driver GASH reported his arrival. delay due to military reasons at BOULOGNE. This was reported to the A.D.M.S.	O.R.B. 11
		10 pm	One case self-inflicted wound thood admitted from No 1 Sect. L.D.A.C. Weather dull with heavy rain. JfM	
L'EPINETTE	26-9-15	10-30 am	Horse Ambulance sent to No 8 R.F.A to take Sick	Daily State
		1 pm	Six missing O duty Pte WALKER returned from leave. Weather dull with bright intervals JfM	O.R.B.
L'EPINETTE	27-9-15	8-30 pm	Attachment arrived back at billets, from No 8 R.F.A note Appendix IV attached TV also heavy rain. JfM	Daily State Sick O.R.B. 12 Appx IV attached

1875 Wt. W593/826 1,000,000 4/15 J.B.C. & A. A.D.S.S./Forms/C. 2118.

WAR DIARY or INTELLIGENCE SUMMARY

Army Form C. 2118

No Y B.F.A.
LAHORE DIVISION
Vol 9 Page 5

Place	Date	Hour	Summary of Events and Information	Remarks and references to Appendices
LEPINETTE	26.28	8.30am	Capt W.H. O'RIORDAN R.A.M.C. detailed by A.D.M.S. LAHORE DIVISION for duty at 9 am. 8.30 M.S. Indian Corps. Capt O'RIORDAN detailed	Stole Official Sect
		11 am	Court of Inquiry assembled to enquire into fire at BOUTS FARM. Personnel of No Y B.F.A. present as witnesses.	B.O. 1 O.R.O. 21
		1 pm	Received instructions from A.D.M.S. LAHORE DIVISION to send 3 large motor cars at once, with two days rations for the drivers, to ZELOBES, to form part of a M.A.C. proceeding to BETHUNE under Capt BOYD I.M.S. Vide appendix V attached. Cars despatched to ZELOBES.	appx V attached
		1.15 pm 1.35 pm	Received orders from A.D.M.S. LAHORE DIVISION to have one section of the Field Ambulance ready to march at once from a mixed Field Ambulance will two sections of No 113 I.F.A under the command of G.O.C. No 113 I.F.A. for duty with SIRHIND BRIGADE attached to 19th DIVISION. Vide appendix VI attached. One section ready to move out at once.	appx VI attached
		2 pm	Orders for three motor Ambul. proceeding to BETHUNE cancelled by A.D.M.S. LAHORE DIV. Vide appendix VII	appx VII attached
		2.35 pm	Motor Cyclist despatched to BETHUNE with order for return of motor ambulances.	
		3 pm	Received order from A.D.M.S. detailing two sections to be prepared to march out to join No 113 I.F.A as a mixed Field ambulance. Vide appendix VIII	appx VIII attached
		5.15 pm	Received order from A.D.M.S. for two sections to march No 113 I.F.A. to LESLOBES spur of with R.20 & Y.R.21 d to ESSARS X 25.A. ref. BETHUNE hoof 1:40.000. Vide appendix IX. The mixed Field Ambulance formed	appx IX attached

Army Form C. 21

No. 7 B.F.A.
LAHORE DIVISION.
Vol. 9 Page 6

WAR DIARY
or
INTELLIGENCE SUMMARY
(Erase heading not required.)

Instructions regarding War Diaries and Intelligence Summaries are contained in F.S. Regs., Part II. and the Staff Manual respectively. Title Pages will be prepared in manuscript.

Place	Date	Hour	Summary of Events and Information	Remarks and references to Appendices
L'EPINETTE	28.9.15	5.40pm	Sections of No 7 B.F.A. to be rationed by FEROZEPORE BRIGADE. Issued Field Ambulance Ordrs No 2. detailing C1D Sections to move off at one hour to with No 113 I.F.A. at LESLOBES. note appendix X.	Appx X attached
		5.40pm	C1D Sections complete under Capt. H L GARSON R.A.M.C. marched out.	
		6.20pm	Two motor ambulances left to join No 7 Field Ambulance at ESSARS X 25 A.	
		8 pm	4th Class Asst Surg. H. G. FUREY I.S.M.D. joined for duty. Weather dull. Very wet. JM.	
L'EPINETTE	29.9.15	9.30am	Lieut E. MAROTHER R.A.M.C. reported the unit under instructions from A.D.M.S. LAHORE DIVN.	Staff Officer B.O.1. ORB 5.
		2 pm	Received ordrs from A.D.M.S. LAHORE DIVISION that British S & K of Division would be admitted to No 8 B.F.A. until further notice.	
		6 pm	Visited C1D Sections at ESSARS X 25 A. Weather dull. cold. wet. JM.	
L'EPINETTE	30.9.15		C1D Sections still detached forming part of a mixed Field Ambulance under the command of O.C. No 113 I.F.A. Weather bright during early part of the day - wet + cold at night. JM.	

J. Mitchell Capt.
R.A.M.C.
O.C No 7 B.F.A
LAHORE DIVISION
I.E.F.A

"A" Form.
MESSAGES AND SIGNALS.
Army Form C. 2121.

TO	O.C. No 8 B.F.A.	11-30 am
	O.C. No 111 I.F.A.	3-9-15

Sender's Number: 462 Day of Month: 3rd   AAA

Sirhind Bde having moved into billeting area vacated by Jullunder Bde the ~~British Indian~~ sick of the Bde should be collected by your third from tomorrow 4th Sept ~~night~~ F.A. No 7 B.F.A. will close and No 112 I.F.A. will only take in hand wounds transferred from No 111 I.F.A. aaa addressed No 8 B.F.A. and No 111 I.F.A. repeated No 7 B.F.A. and No 112 I.F.A.

From: ADMS Lahore Divn
Place:
Time: 10. a.m.

Lt Colonel

Appendix 2.

```
xxxxxxxxxx
x SECRET. x                                             Copy No. 1.
xxxxxxxxxx
              MEDICAL OPERATION ORDERS NO. 48.
                              by

        Colonel B.B.Grayfoot, I.M.S., A.D.M.S., Lahore Division.

    Reference maps 1:40,000
              BELGIUM AND FRANCE - SHEET 36.
              FRANCE.            - SHEET 36A.         23rd September, 1915.
```

1. **INTENTION.**

    During the forthcoming operations the duties assigned to the Lahore Division will be :-
    (1). To cover the flank of Meerut Division.
    (2). To take advantage of any weakening on the part of the enemy and to push forward to establish a line on E. of BOIS DU BIEZ and eventually turn the defences of LA-BASSEE from the North.

    The objective of Ferozepore Brigade will be the road through S. 16. d. to LA TOURELLE cross roads, and that of Jullundur Brigade the East face of the BOIS DU BIEZ.

    Jullundur Brigade extends to its left during the night 23rd/24th to SUNKEN Road exclusive in relief of portion of Dehra Dun Brigade.

    Sirhind Brigade on the night 24th/25th will occupy the trenches between CROIX BARBEE and ROUGE CROIX.

2. **FIELD AMBULANCES.**

    Open for wounded :-
       No. 8 British Field Ambulance - VIEILLE CHAPPELLE.
       No. 111 Indian Field Ambulance - ZELOBES.
    Open for sick :-
       No. 7 British Field Ambulance - L'EPINETTE.
       No. 112 Indian Field Ambulance - CROIX MARMUSE.
    To be ready to move at short notice, either evacuating sick or leaving personnel behind to look after them till evacuated.
    In reserve :-
       No. 113 Indian Field Ambulance - PACAUT
       Ready to move at one hour's notice.

3. **DRESSING STATIONS.**

    For left section :-
    GREEN BARN M.27.d.5.7. under Officer Comndg, No. 8 B.F.A.
    For right section :-
    ST.VAAST, under Officer Commanding, No. 111 I.F.A.

    S.8.b.5.0. Collecting Station for extreme right under O.C., No. 111 I.F.A., casualties from this to ST.VAAST via footpath from S.8.b.8.8.

4. **EVACUATION from AID POSTS and TRENCHES to DRESSING STATIONS.**

    Communication trenches as under have been allotted for rearward traffic including evacuation of wounded from the trenches :-
    Northern section ... ... EUSTON ROAD.
    Southern section ... ... ORCHARD COMMUNICATION TRENCH.
                                    PALL MALL.
    LA BASSEE TRENCH)
    EDWARD ROAD   ) may be used both ways.
        Ingoing trenches :-
    Northern section ... ... BALUCHI ROAD.
                                    PONT LOGY STREET.
    Southern section ... ... LANSDOWN COMMUNICATION
         COCKSPUR STREET. EMBANKMENT.
                                                        (Full -

2.

Full use is to be made of tram lines for evacuation of wounded, especially at night.
Notice boards issued to O.C., No.8 B.F.A. and O.C., No.111 I.F.A. to be erected and controls posted at positions already specified, to direct walking cases to Dressing Stations.

5. EVACUATION FROM DRESSING STATIONS TO FIELD AMBS.
For the conveyance of walking cases horse ambulance wagons will rendezvous about 11.20.a.m.c. and such cases will be despatched in parties in charge of some responsible person to the rendezvous for transport to Field Ambulances.
British and Indian casualties to be sent in defferent wagons.
Sick similarly are to be sent in different wagons to wounded.
Horsed Ambulance wagons will be allotted as shown under (6) for this purpose.
Motor Ambulance wagons will normally be used for lying down or severe sitting up cases.
Traffic routes for vehicles as in maps already issued.

6. ALLOTMENT OF PERSONNEL TRANSPORT ETC.
The following personnel and transport will be allotted for temporary duty forthwith, as shown below:-

From No.7 B.F.A. to No. 8 B.F.A.
R.A.M.C.Officers   2.   Assistant Surgeons   4.
Nursing Orderlies   4.   A.B.Corps 100 (with 20 stretchers)
Motor Ambulances   4.   Horsed Ambulances   1.

From No.112 I.F.A. to No.111 I.F.A.
I.M.S. Officers   2.   Sub-assistant Surgeons 4.
Ward Orderlies   3.   A.B.Corps 100 (with 20 stretchers)
Motor Ambulances   4.

From No.112 I.F.A. to No. 8 B.F.A.
Horsed Ambulance   1.

From No.113 I.F.A. to No. 111 I.F.A.
I.M.S.Officer   1.   Assistant Surgeon   1.
Bhutia Bearers 100 (with 20 stretchers)
Motor Ambulances   2.   Motor Ambulances (to No.8 B.F.A.) 2.
Horsed Ambulances (to No.111 I.F.A.) 2.

The personnel allotted to O.C., No.111 I.F.A. from No. 113 I. F.A. to be used at his own discretion with due regard to the probability of a large number of wounded from the extreme right finding their way out of the trenches towards CHOCOLAT MENIER Corner via CADBURY TRENCH.
In the event of an advance all detached personnel and transport will immediately rejoin its permanent unit.

7. DISTRIBUTION OF PERSONNEL AND TRANSPORT.
Only such personnel and transport as is actually required is to be at the dressing stations or otherwise distributed in front and the remainder held in reserve at the Headquarters of No.8 B.F.A. and No. 111. I.F.A. ready for immediate use, touch being kept with O's C., of dressing stations by means of motor cycles.

8. SANITARY SECTION.
Officer Commanding Sanitary Section will be attached for duty with No. 112 I.F.A. from 6 p.m. 24th instant. He will detail one R.A.M.C. orderly for telephone duty at GREEN BARN and at ST.VAAST, 4 sweepers each to No. 8 B.F.A. and No.111 I.F.A. and two sweepers each to GREEN BARN and ST.VAAST.

(9) GERMAN -

3.

9. GERMAN PRISONERS.
Officers Commanding Field Ambulances will take steps to carefully examine all wounded prisoners for the presence of infectious disease. All such cases should be isolated and the A.D.M.S., immediately informed. No prisoners are to be evacuated until they have been interrogated and all papers found in their possession are to be taken charge of and handed over to the Staff Officer carrying out the interrogation.

10. RATIONS.
All detached personnel and animals will continue to be rationed by their permanent units.

11. REPORTS.
Reports to A.D.M.S., at LESTREM.

Copy No. 1. to No. 7 B.F.A.
" 2. to No. 8 B.F.A.
" 3. to No. 111 I.F.A.
" 4. to No. 112 I.F.A.
" 5. to No. 113 I.F.A.
" 6. to D.D.M.S., Indian Corps.
" 7. to A.D.M.S., Meerut Division.
" 8. to A.A. & Q.M.G.
Copies No. 9, 10, 11 & 12 - File and War Diary.

Lieut.-Col., R.A.M.C.
for Assistant Director of
Medical Services,
Lahore Division.

Issued to Signals at 5 pm

Received 7.15 pm
23/9/1915

Appendix III

Field ambulance order no 1.

To Capt H L GARSON RAMC

(1) A detachment as under will parade in full marching kit at 10-30 am on 24-9-15 under your command

    Capt R M ALLAN R.A.M.C.
    E J CREAIS
    K P ELLOY   } Asst. Surgeons
    A R D'ABREU
    J E SWEENEY
    Pte GILFOY
    Pte WHITTLES   } Nursing Orderlies
    Pte SELL
    Pte DEVENPORT

100 ABC with 20 Stretchers, 4 MOTOR AMBULANCE WAGONS & 1 horse wagon

(2) March to No 8 BFA at 11 am & report the arrival of the detachment to the OC No 8 BFA for temporary duty.

(3) The detachment will take rations for the 25th Sept 1915. Rations for the succeeding days will be sent from No 7 BFA.

(4) Every man must have a first field dressing & two smoke helmets.

                T.J. Mitchell Capt
                RAMC

8 pm
23/9/15 Copy No 1 to Capt ALGARSON OC No 7 BFA
                RAMC
      No 2 to WAR DIARY

"A" Form.   Army Form C. 2121.
MESSAGES AND SIGNALS.

Prefix	Code	m.	Words	Charge	This message is on a/	Recd. at	m.
Office of Origin and Service Instructions			Sent At	m.	Service.	Date	
			To		W	From	
			By		(Signature of "Franking Officer.")	By	

TO { OC. 108 BFA   OC No 113 JFA
     OC No 7 BFA

Sender's Number	Day of Month	In reply to Number	
485	27		A A A

All personnel and transport attached temporarily to your unit should rejoin their parent Units forthwith with the exception of personnel from No 113 JFA attached to No 111 JFA which will remain for the present with No 111 JFA AAA orders issued regarding readiness to move at short notice temply in abeyance.

Copy for information to OC No 7 BFA
                        OC No 113 JFA
                        OC FA Workshop
                                    Unit.

From   ADMS L Div
Place
Time   12.45 pm

The above may be forwarded as now corrected. (Z)
                                    Censor.   Signature of Addressee or person authorised to telegraph in his name.
                                                for ADMS

Recd. 1.15 pm.

"A" Form.   Army Form C. 2121.
MESSAGES AND SIGNALS.   No. of Message

| Prefix | Code | m. | Words | Charge | *This message is on a/c | Recd. at | m. |
| Office of Origin and Service Instructions | | | Sent At 1 pm m. To By | | Service. (Signature of "Franking Officer.") | Date From By | |

TO { O.C. No 112 J.F.A.

| Sender's Number | Day of Month | In reply to Number | |
| 24/105 | 28 | | AAA |

Please detail Cap BOYD I.M.S. to proceed to Seminary STVAAST BETHUNE to assist entraining wounded aaa Ten motor ambulances to accompany him two days rations to be taken aaa Detail of cars to assemble atonce at ZELOBES

112 J F A	3 Cars	
7 B F A	3 "	
113 J.F.A.	2 "	} Large cars
111 J F A	1 Car	
8 B F A	1 "	

Captain Boyd to report departure to this office through O.C. no 111 J.F.A.

From
Place
Time 12-10 pm.

"A" Form. Army Form C. 2121.

MESSAGES AND SIGNALS.

Prefix	Code	m.	Words	Charge	This message is on a[...]	Recd. at	m.
Office of Origin and Service Instructions			Sent			Date	
			At ____ m.		Service.	From	
			To		Appendix VI		
			By		(Signature of "Franking Officer.")	By	

TO { OC No 113 JFA
     OC No 7 BFA ✓

| Sender's Number | Day of Month | In reply to Number | AAA |
| 457 | 28 | | |

Please be ready to march atonce with two sections of your Field ambces one sec No 7 BFA for duty with Sikhim Bde to be attached 19th Divn aaa The mixed unit to be under your command aaa your four motor ambulances to accompany the mixed unit Ford car being returned to you atonce aaa addressed No 113 J.F.A. repeated No 7 BFA one car being detailed from No 8 BFA to replace your damaged car which should go atonce to works unit—

From ADMS Lahore Divn
Place
Time 12.45 pm

Mowbray? Lt
Colonel

*113 JFA

"A" Form.　　　　　　　　　　　　　　　　Army Form C. 2121.

MESSAGES AND SIGNALS.

Prefix	Code	Words	Charge	This message is on a/c of	Recd. at
Office of Origin and Service Instructions		Sent At m. To By		Service. (Signature of "Franking Officer.")	Date From By

Wright

TO { O.C. No 112 JFA   O C No 73 F A
       O.C. No 111 J.F.A

Sender's Number	Day of Month	In reply to Number	
24/109	28		AAA

Please cancel my 24/105 of date regarding motor ambulances to proceed to Bethune for entraining wounded

From ADMS Lahore Divn
Place
Time 2-25 pm

The above may be forwarded as now corrected.　　(Z)

Censor.　　Signature of Addressee or person authorised to telegraph in his name.

2.53 pm.

MESSAGES AND SIGNALS.

Army Form C. 2121.

TO {
O.C. No 7 B.F.A.
O.C. No 113 I.F.A. Appendix VIII
}

Sender's Number: 491
Day of Month: 28
AAA

My 487 of date for
"one section No 7 BFA" read
"two sections No 7 BFA"

From: Adm S Larac Div
Time: 2-45 pm

3.0 pm

Army Form C. 2121.

MESSAGES AND SIGNALS.

Prefix	Code	Words	Charge	This message is on a/c of:	Recd. at
Office of Origin and Service Instructions		Sent At ... m. To By		Service. (Signature of "Franking Officer.")	Date From By

TO { OC NO 7 B.F.A.
     OC NO 113 I.F.A.

Sender's Number	Day of Month	In reply to Number	
493	28/9		AAA

In continuation of my 487 of date the mixed field ambulance will march atonce to ESSARS X25A. aaa secs NO 113 I.F.A via PARADIS and LESLOBES Secs NO 7 B.F.A. via Cross Roads R20C – R21C.D LESLOBES where units will join up and proceed via LOCON ~~X~~ W30C AAA Motor ambulance wagons which will be sent on will be five large with Ford car at present with NO 113 I.F.A. aaa Horse ambulances to be left behind aaa report arrival to ADMS 19th DIVN LOCON aaa Rations

From
Place
Time

The above may be forwarded as now corrected.   (Z)

Censor. Signature of Addressor or person authorised to telegraph in his name.

* This line should be erased if not required.

MESSAGES AND SIGNALS. Army Form C. 2121.

No 113 R 15/c Ferozepore	to J.F.A. 10.4 Bde	be drawn from Secs as	for Secs No 7	Secs Bde BFA before

From ADMS Lahore Divn
Time 4.15 pm

Copy no 2   Appendix 10.

Field Ambulance Order No 2

by
Capt. L. J. Mitchell R.A.M.C.
O.C. No 7 B.F. Ambulance

To   O.C. "C & D" Sections No 7 B.F.A.

(1) Two Sections "C" and "D" under your command will march at once to ESSARS X 25 A via Cross roads R 20 c — R 21 c - d and will join up at LESLOBES with the sections of No 113 I. F. A. marching via PARADIS and LESLOBES to form a mixed Field Ambulance under the command of O.C. 113 I.F.A

(2) Two motor ambulances will be despatched half an hour after your departure to join the mixed field ambulance at X 25 a

(3) Sections "C" & "D" No 7 B.F.A. will draw their rations from FEROZEPORE BDE.

L J Mitchell
Capt Lieut.
O.C. No 7 B.F.A

orders issued 5.40 pm.
28 - 9 - 1915

Copy no 1 to O.C. "C & D" Sections
  " " 2 War Diary

Serial No. 34

Confidential

121/7601

War Diary

with appendices

of

No. 1 British Field Ambulance, Lahore Division

FROM 1st October 1915. TO 31st October 1915.

F. 1915/30

Army Form C. 2118

No 7 B.F.A. LAHORE DIVISION
I.E.F.A.
VOL X Page 1.

WAR DIARY or INTELLIGENCE SUMMARY
(Erase heading not required.)

Instructions regarding War Diaries and Intelligence Summaries are contained in F. S. Regs., Part II. and the Staff Manual respectively. Title Pages will be prepared in manuscript.

Place	Date	Hour	Summary of Events and Information	Remarks and references to Appendices
L'EPINETTE	1-10-15		Field Ambulance to not receiving sick. Nothing to note. JJh.	
L'EPINETTE	2-10-15	6.30p 5p	C. & D. sections rejoined the unit. Capt. W. H. O'RIORDAN R.A.M.C. rejoined the unit. Weather cold bright. JJh.	
L'EPINETTE	3-10-15	7.30pm	Training of unit continues. Medical arrangements 1st Army Operations No 14 by D.M.S. 1st Army received. Weather bright frost. JJh.	
L'EPINETTE	4-10-15		Equipment of unit overhauled rechecked. Weather dull – cold frost. JJh.	
L'EPINETTE	5-10-15	11am	Medical Board. Candidate examined for physical fitness for commission in Regular Army. Weather cold frost. JJh.	
L'EPINETTE	6-10-15		Training of unit continues. Weather damp – dull frost. JJh.	
L'EPINETTE	7-10-15	1pm 5pm	D.D.M.S. Indian Corps visited the unit. Lieut E. MAPOTHER R.A.M.C. detailed under instructions from the A.D.M.S. to report to O.C. JULLUNDUR Bde for duty with 4th SUFFOLKS. Weather bright but cold. JJh.	

1875 Wt. W593/826 1,000,000 4/15 J.B.C. & A. A.D.S.S./Forms/C. 2118.

Army Form C. 2118

WAR DIARY
or
INTELLIGENCE SUMMARY
(Erase heading not required.)

No Y B.F.A
LAHORE DIVISION
I.E.F.A
VOL X Page 2.

Place	Date	Hour	Summary of Events and Information	Remarks and references to Appendices
L'EPINETTE	8-10-15		Capt. R.M ALLAN R.A.M.C. proceeded on leave - one fortnight to England. Training of unit continues. Weather dull & cold. 7ph	
L'EPINETTE	9-10-15	11 am	4th Class Assist Surg. H.G FUREY I.S.M.D detailed for duty with machine gun school	
		2-30 pm	D.A.D.M.S Sanitary LAHORE DIVISION inspected the water carts of the unit. Training of unit continues. weather dull & cold. 7ph	
L'EPINETTE	10-10-15			
L'EPINETTE	11-10-15			
L'EPINETTE	12-10-15			
L'EPINETTE	13-10-15	11-30 am	4th Cl Assist Surgeon J.E SWEENEY I.S.M.D. detailed by A.D.M.S for duty with 1st H.L.I. 7ph	
L'EPINETTE	14-10-15			
L'EPINETTE	15-10-15	11 am	Medical Board - Examining candidates for physical fitness for regular Commissions. 7ph	
L'EPINETTE	16-10-15	2-30 pm	Field Ambulance detailed to inoculate civil population & Labour Corps of La Gorgue against Enteric Fever. 5-90 inoculations carried out. 7ph	
L'EPINETTE	17-10-15	2-30 pm	608 Civil population of LA GORGUE inoculated against Enteric Fever. 7ph	

Army Form C. 2118

No 4 B.F.A LAHORE DIVISION I.F.F.A
VOL X Page 3

WAR DIARY
or
INTELLIGENCE SUMMARY
(Erase heading not required.)

Instructions regarding War Diaries and Intelligence Summaries are contained in F.S. Regs., Part II. and the Staff Manual respectively. Title Pages will be prepared in manuscript.

Place	Date	Hour	Summary of Events and Information	Remarks and references to Appendices
L'EPINETTE	18-10-15	5.40pm	Received orders from the A.D.M.S. to send an advanced party at 10 am on 19-10-15 to take over billets occupied by No 111 I.F.A at LA GORGUE	vide appendix 1 attached Appendix I attached
	"	"	Received orders to take over dressing station at GREEN BARN from No 8 B.F.A at 3 pm on 19-10-15. To clear the area cleared by No 8 B.F.A. vide appendix II attached. Weather bright. Hotel 7pm.	Appendix II attached
L'EPINETTE	19-10-15	7.45am	Inspected LABOUR CORPS after inoculation for Enteric Fever	
		10 am	Handed over present billets to No 8 B.F.A took over new billets from No 111 I.F.A	
		10.30am	Received orders from A.D.M.S. that No 4 B.F.A would march to new billets in LA GORGUE at 12 noon. vide appendix III attached	Appendix III attached
		12 noon	Unit marched from R 136.	
LA GORGUE		1 pm	Unit arrived at billets in LA GORGUE	
		3 pm	Dressing Station at GREEN BARN taken over from No 8 B.F.A by Capt H L PARSON R.A.M.C & Bearer party. And took bearers attached to each cart tool. Attached + 4 bearers attached to each cart tool.	Appendix IV attached
		5.30 pm	A.D.M.S. visited the unit.	
		7.30 pm	Inspected the Dressing Station. Weather bright. Hotel 7pm.	

Army Form C. 2118

WAR DIARY
or
INTELLIGENCE SUMMARY
(Erase heading not required.)

No 7 B F A LAHORE DIVISION I.E.F.A.
Vol X Page 4.

Place	Date	Hour	Summary of Events and Information	Remarks and references to Appendices
LA GORGUE	26.10.15	9.30am	Two recruits. One from No 5 RFA the other from No 113 I.F.A. joined the unit for temporary duty.	
		11am	A.D.M.S. visited the unit inspected two cases.	
		2.35pm	Received Orders from ADMS re the collecting of Sick & wounded from the new front to be held by the LAHORE DIVISION the formation of a combined Dressing Station by No 7 B F A & No 112 I.F.A	note appended V attached.
		6.pm	Received orders from ADMS re the change of billets of 1st MANCHESTER REGt & the 5.9th RIFLES the movements of the SIRHIND BRIGADE. Sick & wounded collected accordingly.	note appended VI attached.
			State of Sick & wounded BO 1 BRB 5 — nil nil 1	
			Weather bright & cold. J.M.	
LA GORGUE	21.10.15	10.30am	A.D.M.S. visited the unit nothing to note. Weather bright & cold.	
			State of Sick & wounded BO 12 ht BR13 13 3	
			Inoculated 340 Labour Corps against Enteric Fever. J.M.	
LA GORQUE	22.10.15	10.am	Inspected GREEN BARN Dressing Station with OC No 112 I.F.A. Arranged with him a combined Dressing Station.	
		11.45am	A.D.M.S. inspected the unit.	
		2.30pm	Lieut E. MAROTHER R.A.M.C. rejoined the unit.	

Army Form C. 2118

No 4 BFA
LAHORE DIVISION
I.E.F.A
Vol X Page 5

WAR DIARY
or
INTELLIGENCE SUMMARY
(Erase heading not required.)

Instructions regarding War Diaries and Intelligence Summaries are contained in F.S. Regs., Part II. and the Staff Manual respectively. Title Pages will be prepared in manuscript.

Place	Date	Hour	Summary of Events and Information	Remarks and references to Appendices
LA GORGUE	22-10-15	4 pm	29 of civil population inoculated against ENTERIC FEVER. LAHORE DIVISION line is from SUNKEN ROAD to CRESCENT TRENCH. It is held by FEROZEPORE BRIGADE plus two Regiments from the JULLUNDUR BRIGADE. Civil posts located trusted in spot not attacked vide appendix VII.	Appendix VII attached
			State of Sick + Wounded B.O. 1 nil O.R.B. 12 2	
			Weather bright + cold. JMc	
LA GORGUE	23-10-15	8.30 am	Capt. R.M.ALLAN R.A.M.C. rejoined from leave. State of Sick + Wounded B.O. Nil 2 O.R.B 25 Nil Weather dull + cold. WR	
LA GORGUE	24.10.15	10 AM 12 Noon 3 pm	CAPTAIN. T.J.Mitchell R.A.M.C proceeded to England on one week's leave. Bearer Division personnel changed at ADVANCED DRESSING STATION A.D.M.S visited hospital. 109 of civil population of LA GORGUE inoculated against Enteric Fever. State of Sick + wounded B.O. Nil Nil O.R.B 24 2 Weather dull + damp with rain in the afternoon	K/R Moreau Capt Rame
LA GORGUE	25.10.15	11.30	3rd Class Assistant Surgeon K P ELLOY I.S.M.D on one week's leave to ENGLAND. A.D.M.S visited hospital Weather dull + damp. State of Sick + Wounded B.O 15 Nil O.R 13 15 1 WR	

1875 Wt. W593/826 1,000,000 4/15 J.B.C. & A. A.D.S.S./Forms/C. 2118.

Army Form C. 2118

WAR DIARY
or
INTELLIGENCE SUMMARY
(Erase heading not required.)

No. 7. B.F.A
LAHORE DIVISION I.E.F.A
Vol X Page 6

Instructions regarding War Diaries and Intelligence Summaries are contained in F.S. Regs., Part II. and the Staff Manual respectively. Title Pages will be prepared in manuscript.

Place	Date	Hour	Summary of Events and Information	Remarks and references to Appendices
LA GORGUE	26.10.15	11 A.M.	D.D.M.S. INDIAN CORPS inspected hospital	
		11.15 AM	A.D.M.S. LAHORE Div visited hospital and selected two cases of defective vision for transfer to ARQUES.	
		11.15 AM	Two cases of wounds died in hospital. 6 of civilian population of LA GORGUE inoculated against Enteric fever	
			State of Sick + wounded	
			B.O. Nil 1.	
			O.R. B 25 3	W.R.
			Weather dull damp and rain	
LA GORGUE	27.10.15	7 A.M.	Two cases of defective vision transferred to ARQUES	
		10.30 AM	A.D.M.S visited hospital.	
		1.25 P.M	Orders received from A.D.M.S. JULLUNDUR Bde with assistance of two battalions SIRHIND Bde will relieve FEROZEPORE Bde in trenches tonight. vide appendix VIII. 10 of civilian population of LA GORGUE inoculated against Enteric fever.	Appendix VIII attached
		9.15.	Advanced Dressing station GREEN BARN shelled. One motor ambulance damaged.	
			State of Sick + wounded	
			B.O. 1 . Nil	
			O.R.B 32 . Nil	W.R.
			Weather bad. raining.	
LA GORGUE	28.10.15	10.30 AM	A.D.M.S visited hospital inspected three eyes and four Dental cases.	
		3 pm.	94 Civilian population of LA GORGUE inoculated against Enteric fever. Spot map of aid posts attached Appendix IX	Appendix IX attached
			State of Sick + wounded	
			B.O 1 . Nil	
			O.R.B 22 . Nil	W.R
			Weather very inclement	
LA GORGUE	29.10.15	10.30 AM	A.D.M.S visited hospital - Advanced Dressing station shelled - no material damage done.	
			State of Sick. + wounded.	
			B.O 3 Nil	
			O.R B 21 Nil	W.R
			Weather, dull + damp	

WAR DIARY
or
INTELLIGENCE SUMMARY

(Erase heading not required.)

No 4. B.F.A LAHORE DIV
Vol X page 4.

Army Form C. 2118

Place	Date	Hour	Summary of Events and Information	Remarks and references to Appendices
LA GORGUE	30.10.15	10.30 AM	A.D.M.S visited hospital and inspected one case of Palestine vover and three dental cases	
			State of sick and wounded	
			B.O 2 Nil	
			O.R.B. 22 1 wR	
			weather dull and damp	
LA GORGUE	31.10.15	10.15 AM	Bearer D unseen personnel at Advanced Dressing Station changed.	
		10.20AM	A.D.M.S visited hospital	
		3 P.M.	42 Civilian population of LA GORGUE inoculated against Enteric fever.	
			State of Sick + wounded.	
			B.O 2 Nil	
			O.R.B 20 4. 4 Nil	
			weather very inclement.	

L.J. Mitchell Capt.
R.aux.
OC No 4 B.F.A
LAHORE DIVISION
I.E.F.A.

Wt. W. 1786/-1402. 5/15. 36,000 Pads. L. S. & Co.

"B" Form   Army Form C. 2122.

MESSAGES AND SIGNALS.   No. of Message _____

Append 7

Prefix ___ Code ___ m.	Received	Sent	Office Stamp.
Office of Origin and Service Instructions. Words.	At ___ m. From ___ By ___	At ___ m. To ___ By ___	

TO { O.C. No 7 B.F.A.

Sender's Number	Day of Month	In reply to Number	AAA
535	18		

Please send an advanced party at 10 am tomorrow morning to take over the billets at present occupied by No III I.F.A. at LAGOROUE

T/L

From: Medical Lahor Dce
Place:
Time: 5.5 pm

Colonel
ADMS

5.45pm.

* This line should be erased if not required.

Wt. W. 1789-1402. 3/15. 36,000 Pads. L. S. & Co.

"B" Form Army Form C. 2122.

MESSAGES AND SIGNALS. No. of Message____

Prefix ____ Code ____ m.	Received	Sent	Office Stamp.
Office of Origin and Service Instructions. Words.	At ____ m.	At ____ m.	
	From ____	To ____	
	By ____	By ____	

TO { O.C. No 7 B.F.A.

Sender's Number	Day of Month	In reply to Number	AAA
530	18		

Please arrange to take over from No 8 B.F.A. dressing station at GREEN BARN 3 pm tomorrow afternoon and clear the area of the section at present cleared by No 8 B.F.A. aaa addressed No 7 B.F.A. repeated No 8 B.F.A.

From A.D.M.S.
Place
Time 5.5 pm

5.45 pm

Appendix III

"B" Form — Army Form C. 2122
MESSAGES AND SIGNALS.

TO: O.C. roy RFA

Sender's Number: 540
Day of Month: 18
AAA

Your Unit will march tomorrow 19th 12 noon via R.7.C R.8.B LESTREM to LACOUTURE and occupy the billets occupied by No.118 FA aaa Report on arrival to this office aaa all British sick and wounded of the Divn to your Unit.

From: ADMS 51st Div
Time: 10 pm

Recd 10.30pm

Appendix 4.

POSITION OF AID POSTS ON SPOT MAP.
19th October 1915.

No 1.   57th RIFLES.

No 2.   4th LONDON REGT.

No 3.   4th KING'S L'POOL.

No 4.   THE CONNAUGHT RANGERS.

No 5.   89th PUNJABIS.

L.J. Mitchell
Capt RAMC
O.C. No 7 B.F. Amb Ce.

"A" Form. Appendix 5 — Army Form C. 2121.

MESSAGES AND SIGNALS.

TO { O.C. No 7 B.F.A.
     O.C. No 112 I.F.A.

Sender's Number: *No 546
Day of Month: 20
AAA

The front of Lahore Divn is being changed aaa Lahore Divn will hold the trenches from CRESCENT Communication Trench inclusive to Sunken road aaa movement of troops will be completed on night 22/23rd aaa The troops of Dehra Dun Bde will take over from Cinder Track to Crescent Trench and will be cleared to STVAAST A.D. post by Bearer Divn of No 112 I.F.A. on night 21/22nd aaa On 22nd October at 10 a.m. OC No 112 I.F.A. will hand over STVAAST post to Meerut Divn removing equipment & kit of his Unit from the post aaa

3.35 P.M.

"A" Form.
MESSAGES AND SIGNALS.
Army Form C. 2121.

From 22nd October OC No 7 BFA and No 112 IFA will form a combined dressing station at the Greenbarn. aaa one motor ambulance to be kept at Greenbarn. aaa one Lieut Surgeon one Sub Asst Surgeon with necessary Est are to be on duty at the dressing station aaa arrangements for bearers motor ambulance and duties at the dressing station to be made by the OCs No 7 BFA & 112 IFA aaa British sick and wounded to No 7 BFA Indians to No 112 I.F.A.

From ADMS Lahore Divn

Appendix VI.

Wt. W. 1789-1402. 5/15. 36,000 Pads. L.S. & Co.

"B" Form — Army Form C. 2122.

MESSAGES AND SIGNALS.

No. of Message _____

Prefix	Code	m.	Received	Sent	Office Stamp.
Office of Origin and Service Instructions.	Words.	At _____ m.	At _____ m.	
		From	To	
		By	By ✓	

TO { O.C. 20 7 B.F.A.
      O.C. 20 112 2.F.A.

| Sender's Number | Day of Month | In reply to Number | AAA |
| 548 | 20/10 | | |

1st Manchesters and 59th Rifles will leave their present billets for RIEZ BAILLEUL area tomorrow to arrive in their new billets by 6 p.m. aaa Sirhind Bde less one battalion will come out of the trenches night 21/22nd and will proceed to LAGORGUE area aaa one battalion Sirhind Bde will come out of the trenches night 22/23rd and will rejoin the Bde in LAGORGUE area aaa arrange for collection of Ack accordingly.

From: ADMS Lahore Divn
Place:
Time: 6 p.m.

* This line should be erased if not required.

Appendix 7.

POSITION OF AID POSTS
                  ON SPOT MAP.

23rd October 1915.

No 1.   89th PUNJABIS.
No 2.   4th LONDON REGT.
No 3.   47th SIKHS.
No 4.   THE CONNAUGHT RANGERS.
No 5.   57th RIFLES.
No 6.   4th SUFFOLK REGT.

T.J. Mitchell
Capt Raine
OC No 7 B.F. AMBce

"A" Form.   Army Form C. 2121.
MESSAGES AND SIGNALS.

| Prefix ... Code ... m. | Words | Charge | This message is on a/c of | Recd. at ... m. |
| Office of Origin and Service Instructions. | Sent At ... m. To ... By | | ... Service. (Signature of "Franking Officer.") | Date ... From ... By |

TO { OC No 7 BFA
     OC No 112 I.F.A }   appendix VIII

Sender's Number: 550   Day of Month: 27   In reply to Number: AAA

Jullundur Bde with assistance of two battalions Sirhind Bde will relieve Ferozepore Bde in trenches tonight aaa 57th Rifles will be relieved by 1st Gurkhas as Bde reserve to the Bde holding the line during the 27th aaa Remaining two battalions Sirhind Bde will replace two battalions Jullundur Bde now in RIEZ BAILLEUL area aaa Ferozepore Bde on relief to billets in LAGORGUE area. aaa collect sick and wounded accordingly

From: ADM Lahore Div
Place:
Time: 1-10 pm

1·25 pm.

Appendix 9.

POSITION OF AID POSTS on SPOT MAP.

29th October 1915.

No1. 59th RIFLES
No2. 4th SUFFOLK REGT.
No3. 47th SIKHS
No4. 1st MANCHESTERS
No5. 27th PUNJABIS.

Mitchell
Capt R.A.M.C.
O.C. No 7 B.F. Amb.ce

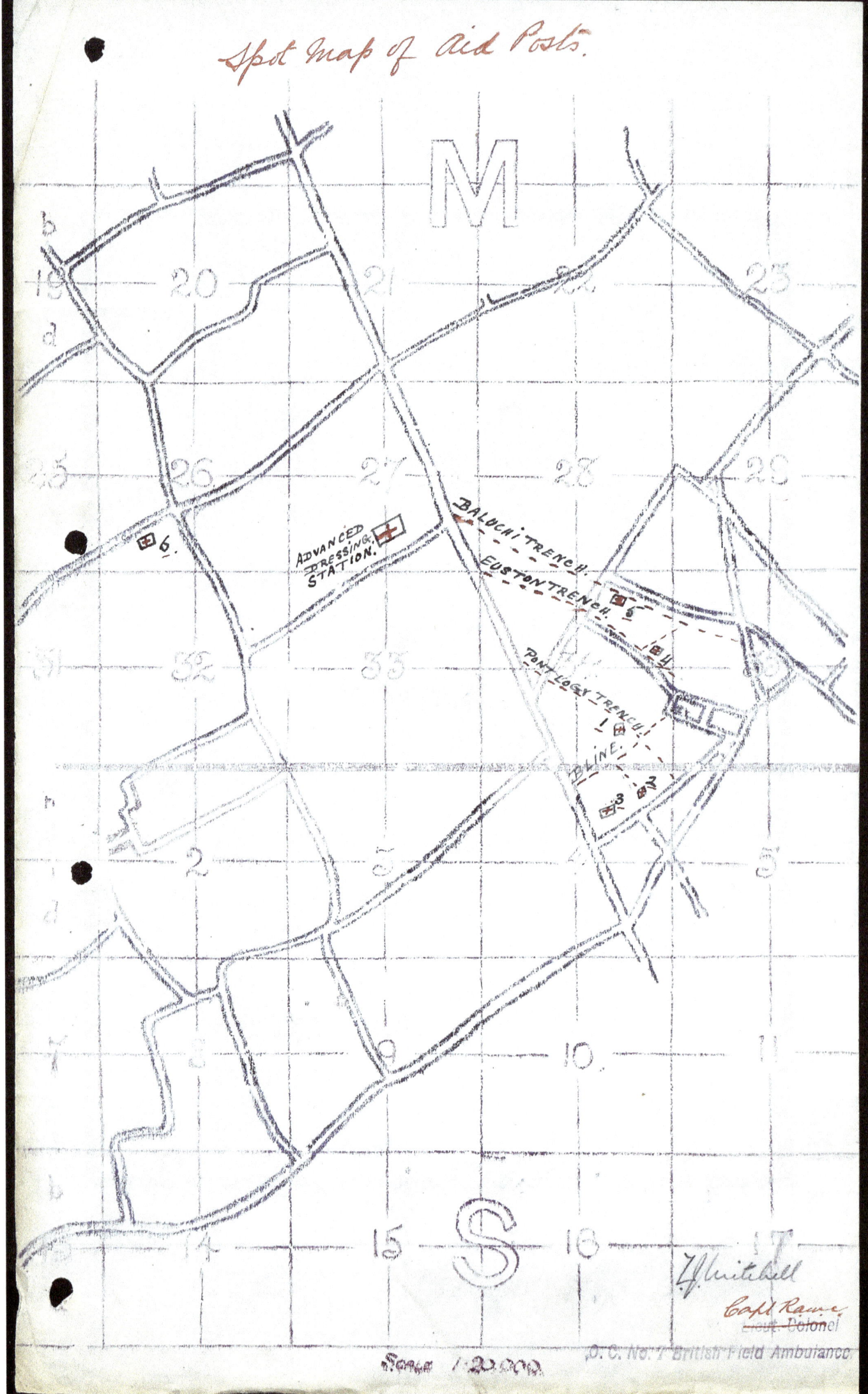

Serial No. 34.

Confidential

Army Diary

With Appendices.

of

No.1 British Field Ambulance.

FROM 1st November 1915 TO 30th November 1915

Army Form C. 2118

No 7 B F A
LAHORE DIVISION
I. E. F. A
Vol XI Page 1

WAR DIARY or INTELLIGENCE SUMMARY

(Erase heading not required.)

Place	Date	Hour	Summary of Events and Information	Remarks and references to Appendices
LA GORGUE	1-11-15	8am to 11am	Capt. T.J. MITCHELL R.A.M.C. returned from leave. Sick & wounded collected as usual. A.D.M.S. inspected B.X. cases from the JULLUNDUR BRIGADE	
		3pm	Civil Population of LESTREM inoculated against Enteric Fever. One suspicious anthrax case transferred to No 7 C.C.S.	
		3.30pm	2 M.A.C. cleared the unit. Sick & wounded	
			B.O. 2 nil ORB 38 nil	
			Weather cold very wet. JM	
LA GORGUE	2-11-15	11am	A.D.M.S. inspected B.X. cases from the SIRHIND BRIGADE.	
		3pm	165 Civil population of LESTREM inoculated against Enteric Fever. One assistant Surgeon rejoined the unit from M.G. School.	
		4pm	No 2. M.A.C. cleared the unit. Sick & wounded collected as usual State of Sick & wounded	
			B.O. 2 1 ORB 32* 1	
			Weather cold very wet. JM	
			* includes 2 climatic Feet cases.	

WAR DIARY
or
INTELLIGENCE SUMMARY
(Erase heading not required.)

Army Form C. 2118

No 7 B.F.A. LAHORE DIVISION
or I.E.F.A
VOL XI   Page 2

Place	Date	Hour	Summary of Events and Information	Remarks and references to Appendices
LA GORGUE	3-11-15	11 am	Capt W H O'RIORDAN R.A.M.C. on leave. A.D.M.S. visited the unit. Reinspected B× cases from the FEROZEPORE BRIGADE.	
		3 pm	One asst. Surgeon 4th Class H B BLAKER I.S.M.D. transferred to No 8 B.F.A.	
		4 pm	No 2 M.A.C. cleared the unit. State of Sick Evacuated. B.O. - 1 O.R.B. 18× 1 × One trench foot case. Weather dull with bright intervals. 7pm	
LA GORGUE	4-11-15	10 am	One Assistant Surgeon and one Hospital Cook transferred to the MEERUT DIVISION under orders from A.D.M.S. LAHORE DIVISION	
		10.15 am	Transfer of assistant Surgeon cancelled by order of D.D.M.S. INDIAN CORPS	
		3 pm	65 of civil population inoculated against Enteric Fever at LESTREM	
		1-10 pm	Received orders from A.D.M.S. re Relief of troops in the trenches. SIRHIND BDE + 1/4th SUFFOLKS ↓ 1/4th LONDONS take over the line on night of 4.11.15. FEROZEPORE BDE less 1/4th LONDONS ↓ one INDIAN BATT. move into RIEZ BAILLEUL AREA. JULLUNDUR BDE less 1/4th SUFFOLKS move on relief into LA GORGUE Vide appreciation 1 attached	Appendix 7 attached
			Sick Evacuated collected as usual 1 trench cleared by No 2. M.A.C. at 4pm. State of Sick Evacuated B.O. 1 - O.R.B. 32 2. Weather bright frost	

Army Form C. 2118

No 4 B F A
LAHORE DIVISION
I. E. F. A
VOL II   Page 3

WAR DIARY
or
INTELLIGENCE SUMMARY
(Erase heading not required.)

Instructions regarding War Diaries and Intelligence Summaries are contained in F.S. Regs., Part II. and the Staff Manual respectively. Title Pages will be prepared in manuscript.

Place	Date	Hour	Summary of Events and Information	Remarks and references to Appendices
LA GORGUE	5-11-15	11am	A.D.M.S. inspected B× cases. Smoke Helmets ordinary returned to ordnance. Equipment checked & exchanged with the view to a possible move. Sick & wounded collected as usual. No 2 M.A.C. cleared the unit. 186 cases inoculated against Enteric Fever at LESTREM.	
			State of Sick & wounded. B.O. — 1 — O.R.R. 16 — 1	
		4pm	Weather dull with bright intervals. Spot map of aid posts attached vide appendix 17 4/pm	appendix 17 attached
LA GORGUE	6-11-15	11am	A.D.M.S. inspected B× cases. Tube Smoke Helmets. Respirators, blankets & stretchers returned to ordnance depot. No 2 M.A.C. cleared the unit. Sick two wounded collected as usual from the aid posts.	
			State of Sick & wounded. B.O. 1 — O.R.R. 28 —	
		4pm	Weather dull with bright intervals 4/pm	

Army Form C. 2118

WAR DIARY
or
INTELLIGENCE SUMMARY
(Erase heading not required.)

No 7 BFA
LAHORE DIVISION
Vol XI Page 4

Place	Date	Hour	Summary of Events and Information	Remarks and references to Appendices
LA GORGUE	4.11.15	11.30 am	Lieut E. NIAPOTHE R.A.M.C on leave to ENGLAND. A.D.M.S inspected BX cases Received orders from A.D.M.S. to move to HAM ref. map FRANCE sheet 36A	Appendices III attached.
		0.27.C.3.5.	vide appendix III	
		1 pm	Detachment of unit marched out to Dressing Station to relieve bearer sub division. & collect evacuate British Casualties of the SIRHIND Bde.	
		4 pm	Unit cleared at 4 pm by No 2 M.A.C. Sick & wounded collected as usual from A.d. Posts. State of Sick & wounded. BO — 1 — ORB 33 5 — J.M. Weather bright.	
LA GORGUE	5.11.15	8 am	No 2 M.A.C cleared the unit. Hospital Hospital settings & surplus stores	
		10 am	Hospital closed & billets handed over to No 9 F.A GUARDS DIVISION	
		10.45 am	Unit marched out —	
HAM O 27.C.35. Ref 1:40000 FRANCE MAP Sheet 36 A		4-45	Arrived in new billets — Detachment still at Dressing Station State of Sick & wounded. BO — 1 — ORB 6 evacuated J.M. Weather dull with bright intervals	

Army Form C. 2118

WAR DIARY
or
INTELLIGENCE SUMMARY
(Erase heading not required.)

No 7.B.F.A.
LAHORE DIVISION
VOL XI. Page 5-

Place	Date	Hour	Summary of Events and Information	Remarks and references to Appendices
HAM	9-11-15		Unit in closed billets. Equipment overhauled. Weather dull rainy. JM.	
HAM	10-11-15	3pm	Capt W.H O'RIORDAN R.A.M.C returned from leave in ENGLAND. Capt H.L. GARSON R.A.M.C proceeded on leave to ENGLAND. Heavy draught horses replaced by mules. JM. Weather dull rainy	
HAM	11-11-15	12pm	Detachment of unit from Bearing Station reported the unit. Weather bright with dull rainy intervals JM.	
HAM	12-11-15	11am	Mules thrives equit- widened. Hollen teal:- Weather very damp. Transport equipment being completed. JM.	
HAM	13-11-15	11am	J.B BARDINET INTERPRETER on leave. Medical Board. Commissions in Territorial Force. Examination for Physical fitness for Rmr.	
HAM	14-11-15	11am	D.D.M.S. visited the unit. Rmr	
HAM	15-11-15		Lieut E. MAPOTHER R.A.M.C returned from leave to ENGLAND. Rmr.	
HAM	16-11-15	2pm	Capt. H.L.GARSON R.A.M.C returned from leave to ENGLAND. Orders received from A.D.M.S to hold unit in readiness, as the Division was expected to move into a new area at short notice. One N.C.O reported for duty as Punjabi Sergeant Rmr.	

Army Form C. 2118

WAR DIARY
or
INTELLIGENCE SUMMARY
(Erase heading not required.)

No. MY. B. F. A   LAHORE DIVISION

VOL XI   Page 6

Place	Date	Hour	Summary of Events and Information	Remarks and references to Appendices
H.A.M.	17.11.15		All nursing orderly & one officers Batmen granted seven days leave to ENGLAND	Appendix day 4 attached. Appendix v attached
		4:30pm	Orders received from A.D.M.S. that unit will march tomorrow forenoon under arrangements of O.C. FEROZEPORE BRIGADE to a new area W. of AIRE and there go into closed billets. Appendix 4.	
		8.45pm	FEROZEPORE BRIGADE operation order No 61 received – vide appendix v	
H.A.M.	18.11.15		Unit paraded at 10:15 am and marched at 10.30 am to starting point 4 Road Junction O.21.C reference MAP FRANCE sheet 36 A. 1:40.000.	
ENQUINEGATTE M.M.D		3:15 pm.	Arrived at NEW AREA and proceeded into closed billets. MULE NEW TRANSPORT very satisfactory. Weather wet & cold. RMN	
ENQUINEGATTE	19.11.15		6/4 Assistant Surgeons posted to unit. Temporarily on withdrawal from RFA BRIGADES. One Assistant Surgeon divisial to report to D.D.M.S. INDIAN CORPS for temporary duty. 2 officers Batmen proceeded to ENGLAND on seven days leave. RMN	
ENQUINEGATTE	20.11.15	11.30 AM	A.D.M.S. visited hospital.	
		3 p.m.	Hospital Personnel listen for route march. One Assistant Surgeon attached to unit temporarily. RMN	
ENQUINEGATTE	21.11.15		Three Assistant Surgeons temporarily attached to unit transferred to Corps units. 1. RAMC NCO transferred to 16 M.A.C. Weather cold & frosty. RMN	
ENQUINEGATTE	22.11.15		CAPT. R. M. ALLAN R.A.M.C. proceeded on five days leave to ENGLAND. One Assistant Surgeon attached to the unit temporarily. Training of Personnel continued. RMN	

Army Form C. 2118

WAR DIARY or INTELLIGENCE SUMMARY

(Erase heading not required.)

No 4 B.F.A. LAHORE DIVISION

Vol XI   Page 4

Instructions regarding War Diaries and Intelligence Summaries are contained in F. S. Regs., Part II. and the Staff Manual respectively. Title Pages will be prepared in manuscript.

Place	Date	Hour	Summary of Events and Information	Remarks and references to Appendices
ENGUINEGATTE	23.XI.15		2 A.S.C. drivers proceeded on 5 days leave to ENGLAND.	
		11.30AM	A.D.M.S. visited hospital. Training of unit continues. Weather dull, damp & foggy.	RMR
ENGUINEGATTE	24.XI.15		Captain T.J. MILLER, R.A.M.C. proceeded on seven days leave to ENGLAND. Lieut. E. MAPOTHER, R.A.M.C. temporarily detached for duty with LAHORE DIVISIONAL TRAIN. One Assistant Surgeon sent O.C.U. to No 8 B.F.A.	RMR
ENGUINEGATTE	25.XI.15	10.30AM	1 Officer 1 Assistant Surgeon. 1 A B C allowed parade of representatives of the INDIAN CORPS at the CHATEAU LILLETTE, to hear H.R.H. THE PRINCE OF WALES deliver HIS MAJESTY THE KING'S farewell message to the INDIAN CORPS on their departure from FRANCE.	RMR
		11.AM	A.D.M.S. visited hospital. Two Assistant Surgeons transferred to Corps units. Three Assistant Surgeons temporarily attached to unit on withdrawal from 15th Bde R.F.A.	RMR
ENGUINEGATTE	26.XI.15		FRENCH INTERPRETER returned from leave. Training of unit continues. Weather cold & foggy.	RMR
ENGUINEGATTE	27.XI.15	8.a.m.	2nd Class Asst Surgeon P. BELL to 3rd Class Asst Surgeon A.E. BROWN transferred to 2nd Indian Cavalry Div.	RMR
ENGUINEGATTE	28.XI.15	10.20pm	Orders received from A.D.M.S. Lahore Divn. that the unit would march under Brigade orders to a new area, vide appendix 6.	Appendix 6 attached
ENGUINEGATTE	29.XI.15	2.30am	Orders received from Ferozepore Brigade (Brigade Operation Order No 62) re move to new area, vide appendix 7. Captain W.H. O'RIORDAN, R.A.M.C. proceeded on 5 days leave to England. Three Assistant Surgeons (temporarily attached) proceeded to 32nd C.C.S. to vacant. 4th Class Asst Surgeon J.G. FUREY transferred to 1st H.L.I. for temporary duty.	Appendix 7 attached
		11.10am	Unit paraded & marched with Ferozepore Brigade for Matringham.	RMR

1875 Wt. W593/826 1,000,000 4/15 J.B.C. & A. A.D.S.S./Forms/C. 2118.

Army Form C. 2118

WAR DIARY
or
INTELLIGENCE SUMMARY

No 7 B.F.A.
LAHORE DIVISION.

(Erase heading not required.) VOL. XI. PAGE 8

Place	Date	Hour	Summary of Events and Information	Remarks and references to Appendices
MATRINGHEM	29/XI/15	2.40 p.m.	Unit arrived in MATRINGHEM and took over billets. Lieut E. MAPOTHER. R.A.M.C. rejoined the unit from Lahore Divisional Train. RWA	
MATRINGHEM	30.XI.15	10 a.m.	4th Class Amt Surgeon A.R. D'ABREU. I.S.M.D transferred to Lahore Divisional Signal Company. Capt. R.M. ALLAN. R.A.M.C. returned from leave. Capt. H.L. GARSON. R.A.M.C. proceeded to England on ten days leave. Received FEROZEPORE BRIGADE Operation Order N°63 re march to new area tomorrow. Weather wet & cold. RWA	

R.M. Allan
. Capt R.A.M.C.
for O.C. N° 7 B.F.A.

"A" Form. Army Form C. 2121.
MESSAGES AND SIGNALS.

Prefix	Code	m.	Words	Charge	This message is on a/c of:	Recd. at ___ m.
Office of Origin and Service Instructions					Service.	Date
		Sent At ___ m. To By			Appendix (Signature of "Franking Officer.")	From By

TO { OC 707 BFA
     OC No 112 SFA

| Sender's Number | Day of Month | In reply to Number | |
| * 555 | 4th | | A A A |

Surhuis Bde with 1/4th Londons and 1/4th Suffolks will take over the line on night 4/5th Novr aaa Ferozepore Brigade less 1/4th Londons and one Indian Batn will move into RIEZ BAILLEUL area aaa Jullundur Bde less 1/4th Suffolks will move on relief into LA GORGUE

[signature] Mulchell

From: A.D.M.S. Lahore Division
Place:
Time:

The above may be forwarded as now corrected. (Z)

Censor. Signature of Addressee or person authorised to telegraph in his name.
Lt. Colonel
for MNMS

Recd 1·10 P.M.

Appendix II

M

S

8-11-15		

Aid Posts.
1. Unoccupied
2. 4th Kings
3. 1st Gurkhas.
4. H.L.I.
5. 4th Londons.

SCALE 1:20,000

for O.C. No. 7 British Field Amb.

"A" Form.
MESSAGES AND SIGNALS.
Army Form C. 2121.

TO { OC No 1 /F.A.
OC No 112 /F.A.

Sender's Number: 60/57
Day of Month: 7
AAA

Your Unit will march tomorrow to HAM via L 28 D MERVILLE Canal Bank to ST VENANT GUARBECQ aaa No 112 F.A. will lead and will pass starting point Crossroads L28D at 11 a.m. in rear of Telegraphic Coy aaa all sick and wounded to be evacuated as far as possible before marching aaa O.S.M. contacts to march aaa Billeting officers to come to my office at 12-30 P.M. today to be instructed in position of new billets aaa Refilling point in new area with Emergence Res aaa Report arrival to this office

From: ADMS Kahae???
Place:
Time:

The above may be forwarded as now corrected. (Z)

H. Boam. Censor.

Appendix IV

URGENT.

Officer Commanding, No. 7 B.F.A.,
Officer Commanding, No. 112 I.F.A.

No. 60/196.

Your unit will march tomorrow forenoon under arrangements of O.C., Ferozepore Brigade to new area W. of AIRE and there go into closed billets.

The two scabies cases in 112 I.F.A. should march with the field ambulance.

Arrival and location of new billets to be reported to my office at ROQUETOIRE.

4.30pm

17th November, 1915.

Colonel,
A.D.M.S., Lahore Division.

Rec'd 8.45 pm

Appendix V

Copy No. 14

FEROZEPORE BRIGADE OPERATION ORDER No 61

17th November 1915.

1. Ferozepore Brigade will march to area West of AIRE tomorrow, 18th instant, as follows:

2. Starting Point is 4 Road Junction O.21.c. which Brigade H. Qrs will pass at 8-45 a.m.

Starting Point at	Order of March.	Route.
8-45 a.m.	Bde. Hd. Qrs.	On arrival on road junction O.20.A. units whose destinations are MARTHES or ENGUINE GATTE will take turning to left proceeding via MALINGHEM and BLESSY - The remainder will turn to right and proceed via LE HAMEL - H.33.b. - H.27.a.
8-50 a.m.	89th Punjabis	
9-5 a.m.	129th Baluchis	
9-20 a.m.	57th Rifles	
9-40 a.m.	20th Coy S & M.	
10-0 a.m.	21st Coy S & M.	
10-20 a.m.	Field Troop S & M.	
10-40 a.m.	Connaught Rangers	
11-0 a.m.	No 7 B.F.A.	
11-20 a.m.	No 112 I.F.A.	
11-40 a.m.	429 Coy L.D.T.	
11-50 a.m.	F.W.A.U.	

3. All baggage carts will march with their own units.

4. Units will report to Brigade Headquarters (G.35.a.9/8) their arrival in their new billets.

5. March Table and Situation of Billets attached hereto.

_____ Captain.
for Brigade Major Ferozepore Brigade.

Issued to Signals at 8-45 p.m.

1. Connaught Rangers   8. Lahore Division.
2. 89th Punjabis.   9. C.R.A.
3. 129th Baluchis.   10. C.R.E.
4. 57th Rifles.   11. 20th Coy S & M.
5. Bde Signals.   12. 21st Coy S & M.
6. 429th Coy L.D.T.   13. Field Troop S & M,
7. Bde Supply Officer.   14. No 7 B.F.A.
   15. No 112 I.F.A. 16 A.D.M.S. 17 Staff Captain.
   18-20 War Diary. 21. Office.

"A" Form. Army Form C. 2121.
MESSAGES AND SIGNALS. No. of Message _____

| Prefix _____ Code _____ m. | Words | Charge | This message is on a/c of: | Recd. at _____ m. |
| Office of Origin and Service Instructions. | Sent At _____ m. To _____ By _____ | | _____ Service. (Signature of "Franking Officer.") | Date _____ From _____ By _____ |

TO {
OC. NO 7 B.F.A.   OC No 112 I.F.A
OC NO 8 -"-   OC No 113 -"-
OC No 111 I.F.A   OC F.A. workshop Unit

| Sender's Number | Day of Month | In reply to Number | **AAA** |
| 60/246 | 28 | | |

The field ambulances and Field Amb workshop Unit will march tomorrow under Bde orders AAA No 8 B.F.A and No 111 I.F.A. will open for collection and evacuation of sick at Noeux AAA British sick to AIRE Indian to STVENANT AAA Two additional motors will be placed at the disposal of No 8 B.F.A and No 111 I.F.A. by OC No 112 I.F.A. (already with No 8 BFA) and No 7 BFA respectively to assist in evacuation aaa all other motor ambulances will rejoin their parent Units forthwith aaa Report arrival and position of new

From _____
Place _____
Time _____

"A" Form.
Army Form C. 2121.
MESSAGES AND SIGNALS.

Sender's Number	Day of Month	In reply to Number		AAA

Billets to my office at BOMY AAA copy of billeting area of all units hereafter to No 8 BFA and No 111 2FA

From
Place
Time

10.20 pm

Appendix 7

Copy No. 13.

FEROZEPORE BRIGADE OPERATION ORDER No. 23.

28 November

Reference HAZEBROUCK Map 1/10,000.

1. Lahore Division is moving to a new area South of THEROUANNE to-morrow.

2. Ferozepore Brigade will move in accordance with attached March Table, troops will be billeted as shown therein.

3. 2nd Line Transport will accompany Battalions.
   1st and 2nd Line Transport of Brigade Headquarters will follow immediately in rear of that of the Connaught Rangers.

4. Five motor lorries will be available for conveying the extra blankets, and will be at Brigade Headquarters at 9.0 am. to-morrow. They will be distributed one to each battalion and one for Brigade Headquarters.
   Battalions will each send a man to be at Brigade Headquarters at 8.54 am. to take over his lorry. They will accompany battalions' 2nd Line transport, and when unloaded at the new billets will be sent to Bde. Headquarters at MATRINGHEM.

5. Halts as in Divisional Standing Orders. There will be no long halt during the march.

6. Coal for all Refilling Groups will, on 29th inst, be issued at cross roads South-East of "Q" of DENNEBROEUCQ (2 miles N.N.W. of MATRINGHEM).

7. Units will report to Brigade Headquarters on arrival in their new billets.

8. Reports after 9 am. to MATRINGHEM.

Captain,
Brigade Major Ferozepore Brigade.

Issued to Signals at 12 midnight.

1. Connaught Rangers,
2. 89th Punjabis,
3. 129th Baluchis,
4. 57th Rifles,
5. Brigade Signals.
6. 429th Coy. A.S.C.
7. Bde. Supply Officer,
8. Lahore Division,
9. Sirhind Bde.
10. Jullundur Bde.
11. C.R.A.
12. A.D.M.S.
13. No. 7 B.F.A.
14. No. 112 I.F.A.
15. C.R.E.
16. 20th Coy. S.& M.
17. 21st Coy. S.& M.
18. Field Troop S.&.M.
19. Office.
20. Staff Captain,
21-23. War Diary.

MARCH TABLE.

Unit.	Starting Point.	Hour to pass Starting Point.	Route to Starting Point.	Route from Starting Point.	Billets.	Remarks.
Bde. Headquarters,		10.30 a.m.			MATRINGHEM	
Connaught Rangers,		10.40			-do-	
89th Punjabis		10.45	via		LUGY	
57th Rifles,		10.50	MAMETZ	PETIGNY - BOMY and thence direct to billets.	HEZECQUES	All Units to be West of the THERROANNE — ESTREE BLANCHE Road by 11.15 am.
129th Baluchis,		11.0	and		BEAUMETZ-LES-AIRE.	
20th Coy. S. & M.	Cross Roads at third "E" in ENGUINEGATTE		MARTHES		SENLIS	
21st Coy. S. & M.					SENLIS	
Field Troop S. & M.		11.10			MATRINGHEM	
No. 7 B.F.A.						
No. 112 I.F.A.					BEAUMETZ-LES-AIRE	
F.A.W.Unit						
429th Coy. A.S.C.		11.20			MATRINGHEM.	

CONFIDENTIAL

WAR DIARY

OF

No. 7. B. F. Ambulance

FROM 1st Dec. 1915 TO 31st Dec. 1915

(VOLUME)

WAR DIARY

December 1915

WAR DIARY
or
INTELLIGENCE SUMMARY

Army Form C. 2118

No 7. B.F.A. AMBULANCE E.
LAHORE DIVN

Vol. XII

Place	Date	Hour	Summary of Events and Information	Remarks and references to Appendices
MATRINGHAM	1/12/15	9 a.m.	Unit paraded and marched to new area in AMETTES, under arrangements of FEROZEPORE BRIGADE. Vide APPENDIX 1.	Appx. 1. attached
AMETTES		1 p.m.	Arrived in closed billets.	
AMETTES	2/12/15	10 a.m.	A.D.M.S. visited unit. Weather wet + mist.	Rwk.
AMETTES	3/12/15		Capt. T.J. MITCHELL RAMC returned from leave.	
AMETTES	4/12/15		Lieut. DEWEY I.S.M.D on leave. Assist. Surg. G.H. LAWRENCE I.S.M.D on leave. 7/h.	
AMETTES	5/12/15		Bre M.A. brain returned from leave. 7/h	
AMETTES	6/12/15		Lieut. E. MAPOTHER RAMC on leave. 7/h Medical Board - Candidates for examination for physical fitness in the Regular Army.	
AMETTES		11 a.m.	Recommendation re. Assist. Surg. G.H. LAWRENCE & Assist. Surg. G.H. BLAKER both I.S.M.D. sent in to A.D.M.S. LAHORE DIVISION. 7/h and Col. Sgt. HARE, R.WK Rg. and Col. Sgt. HARE R.WK Rg	
AMETTES	7/12/15		Capt. W.H. O'RIORDAN RAMC & Capt. H.L. GARSON RAMC returned from leave.	
AMETTES	8/12/15		Capt. H.L. GARSON RAMC detailed by A.D.M.S. to be at entraining station to meet with 1st H.L.I. at 10·21 a.m. 9/12/15 if Capt TAYLOR had not returned from leave. 7/h	
AMETTES	9/12/15	9·30 a.m.	Capt. H.L. GARSON RAMC left unit for entraining station of 1st H.L.I. 1/h	32-9 2-9
		10 a.m.	Medical board to assume one officer for physical fitness for a commission in the Regular army. Assist. Surg. G.H LAWRENCE rejoined from leave. Capt. TAYLOR RAMC joined from leave for temporary duty 7/h	

WAR DIARY or INTELLIGENCE SUMMARY

Army Form C. 2118

of No 4 B.F.A. LAHORE DIVISION
Vol XII Page 2. I.E.F.A

Place	Date	Hour	Summary of Events and Information	Remarks and references to Appendices
AMETTES	10-12-15		Received notification from A.D.M.S. that Interpreters are not to go to MARSEILLES but are to report at St. OMER. Received circular re BHAILAWA nut - used by Indians for producing blisters the use of Censor list through A.D.M.S. of Indians whose return into India has been prohibited.	
AMETTES	11-12-15		LIEUT MAPOTHER R.A.M.C. +heel DEWEY I.S.M.D. returned from leave. JRn. 6 BHUTIA bearers joined the unit for duty from No 113 IFA JRn	
AMETTES	12-12-15		A & D Books confidential documents reports - war diaries test of officers - NCOs + men who have served with the unit in FRANCE forwarded to A.G. BASE. A.D.M.S. notified. Nominal roll of A.S.C. personnel proceeding with the unit forwarded to O/C A.S.C. Section base 3rd Echelon G.H.Q. copy to A.D.M.S. Reported to A.D.M.S. that transport of the unit was complete. Billeting certificates original + duplicate of unit men to 31st March 1915 forwarded to B.R.O No 2 1st Army. Received Entrain ment orders. Weather dull + damp. JRn	

WAR DIARY
or
INTELLIGENCE SUMMARY
(Erase heading not required.)

Army Form C. 2118

No. Y.B.F.A.
LAHORE DIVISION
I.E.F.A.
Page 3. Vol XII

Place	Date	Hour	Summary of Events and Information	Remarks and references to Appendices
AMETTES	13-12-15	2.30 pm	Unit marched to Entraining Station at LILLERS and arrived at 4 pm. Unit entrained at 5-51 pm. One W.O. Mule - chargers & A.S.C personnel were left behind to entrain under orders from A.A. & Q.M.G. LAHORE DIVISION at a later date. Train due to start at 20-51. As train was moving out, Railway Clerk handed us the Railway Warrants & form for movement - acted as O.C. Train. 7pm.	
LILLERS to MARSEILLES	14-12-15		No arrangements had been made for Indian followers at halting place.	
	15-12-15		On 14-12-15 - Ground very cold & frosty.	
	16-12-15	9 am	Arrived MARSEILLES at 9 am. 7pm.	
		4pm	Arrived at LA VALENTINE CAMP. Billeting space cramped for Indian followers - weather very wet & dull. 7pm.	
LA VALENTINE CAMP.			Unit under canvas - weather wet - total 7pm.	
MARSEILLES	17-12-15			
	18-12-15	7-30pm	Received orders to embark on S.S. CHAKDINA with following personnel at 12 noon on 19th. Officers Six. , O.R.B. 52. , O.R.I. 84. - Animals 56. Whole 33 pairs.	

Army Form C. 2118

WAR DIARY
or
INTELLIGENCE SUMMARY
(Erase heading not required.)

of Y.B.F.A. LAHORE DIVISION. I.E.F.A

Page 4 Vol XII

Place	Date	Hour	Summary of Events and Information	Remarks and references to Appendices
	18.12.15		Received orders to detail M.O.s for S.S. MELVILLE & S.S. ANGLO-EGYPTIAN. Capt A.S. TAYLOR R.A.M.C & Lieut E. MAPOTHER R.A.M.C detailed to report to O.C's these ships by 12 noon on 19-12-15. Weather bright. JPh	
S.S. CHAKDINA	19.12.15	6.30am	Detachment from Unit for Embarkation left St. VALENTINE Camp at 8.20am	
		11-30	Arrived at Mole D. Unit Embarked has 10 officers - O.R.B 21. O.R.I 109 - Horses 10 - Mules 30 Wheels - 4 G.S Wagons 6 Ambulance wagons 2 water carts - the numbers left behind were allied frequently by the Embarkation Staff. All equipment was taken - Hot weather clothing was drawn from Ordnance Stores for the British Personnel 801 birds returned 143 new kits were drawn A stock of our Typhoid Vaccine & Vaccination lymph was obtained from Lahore Stationary Hospital. JPh The following was handed to the (1) Nominal Roll of Officers (4) List of Vehicles Embarkation Officer:- (2) " " of hops on board. (3) 3 Certificates:-(a) Indian Personnel Pay book were up S.S CHAKDINA sailed - (3) Embarkation state. (b) Hot weather clothing had been drawn (c) for O.R.R	23235 27
	20.12.15	12 noon		
		5 pm	Arrived at TOULON. Remained in harbour all night	O.R.R. was in possession of Blankets, Waterproof sheet & cooking tin -
	21.12.15	16am	S.S CHAKDINA left TOULON. JPh	

Army Form C. 2118

WAR DIARY
or
INTELLIGENCE SUMMARY
(Erase heading not required.)

4 B.F.A. LAHORE DIVISION I.E.F.A
Page 5 Vol XII

Place	Date	Hour	Summary of Events and Information	Remarks and references to Appendices
S.S. CHAKDINA	21-12-15		Personnel detailed for different boats - boat number is to be separated from the other boats.	
	22-12-15		Arranged for medical inspection of troops on Board - Also vaccination the inoculation 4pm. Personnel of 4 B.F.A. Vaccinated 58. 4pm Re inoculation 44. 4pm	
	23-12-15		Venereal inspection of troops. One man reported sick suffering from Gonorrhoea. 4pm	
	24-12-15	11 am	Arrived at St. PAULS BAY MALTA. 4pm	
	25-12-15	1 pm	Arrived in Grand Harbour MALTA. One case Gonorrhoea transferred to the FORREST HOSPITAL 4pm	
	26-12-15			
	27-12-15	1 pm	Sailed from MALTA. 4pm	
	28-12-15			
	29-12-15			
	30-12-15			
	31-12-15	10.30 am	Arrived at ALEXANDRIA.	

J. Mitchell Capt.
R.A.M.C.
O.C. No Y R.F.A. LAHORE DIVISION

> *Press*
> please omit
> this altogether

App. I.

Copy No. 13

FEROZEPORE BRIGADE OPERATION ORDER No. 63.

30th November 1914.

Reference – HAZEBROUCK Map 1/100,000.

1. Ferozepore Brigade Group will march to a new area to-morrow, in accordance with the attached March Table.

2. 2nd Line transport will accompany Units.

3. Orders for the carriage of extra blankets of Battalions will be issued later.

4. Halts as in Divisional Standing Orders, that is, from ten minutes before each clock hour, to the clock hour. These times are to be strictly kept by all Units.

5. No. 7 B.F.A. and No. 112 I.F.A. will detail for the march one horsed ambulance to the Connaught Rangers and each of the three Indian Battalions and the S.&.M. respectively. They are to be at Battalion Headquarters by 8.0 am.
All spare ambulances beyond the above should follow the tail of the column as far as FEBVIN-PALFART and then rejoin their Units.

6. Reports after 8.30 am. to WESTRELHEM.

P. C. Kensington
Captain,
Brigade Major, Ferozepore Brigade.

Issued to
Signals at 6 pm.

1. Connaught Rangers,
2. 89th Punjabis,
3. 129th Baluchis,
4. 57th Rifles,
5. Brigade Signals,
6. 429th Coy. A.S.C.
7. Bde. Supply Officer,
8. Lahore Division,
9. Sirhind Brigade,
10. Jullundur Bde.
11. C.R.A.
12. A.D.M.S.
13. No. 7 B.F.A.
14. No. 112 I.F.A.
15. C.R.E.
16. 20th Coy. S.& M.
17. 21st Coy. S.& M.
18. Field Troop S.& M.
19. Office,
20. Staff Captain,
21-23. War Diary.

*Press
please omit*

MARCH TABLE.

Unit.	Starting Point.	Hour to pass Starting Point.	Route.	New Billets.	Remarks.
129th Baluchis		Must clear Starting Point by 9.45 am.		AMETTES	
112 Indian F.A.		under orders of O.C. 129th Baluchis.		AMETTES	
F.A.W.Unit	Cross roads at South-Eastern end of BAUMETZ - LES - AIRE.		BAUMETZ – LES – AIRE – LAIRES – FEBVIN PALFART.	AMETTES	
No. 7 B.F.A.		9.50 am.		BELLERY (West of Cross Roads).	
Connaught Rangers		10.0 am.		NEDON	
Brigade Headquarters		10.10 am.		WESTREHEM	
57th Rifles		10.15 am.		WESTREHEM	
429th Coy. A.S.C.		10.25 am.		TALINELOUX	
89th Punjabis		10.35 am.		FEBVIN-PALFART	
Sappers & Miners		10.45 am.		LE PLOUY and HUNINGHEM	

www.ingramcontent.com/pod-product-compliance
Lightning Source LLC
Chambersburg PA
CBHW081435300426
44108CB00016BA/2372